Art,
Science,
Religion,
Spirituality

Art, Science, Religion, Spirituality

Seeking Wisdom and Harmony for a Fulfilling Life

David V. White

ISBN: 0989853802
ISBN 13: 9780989853804
Library of Congress Number: 2015904177
Meaningful Life Books, Sevierville, Tennessee

Meaningful Life Books
P. O. Box 1988
Knoxville, Tennessee 37901
Web Site: ameaningfullife.org

CHAPTERS

Introduction 1

1   The Way of Art.. 5

2   The Message in Art.. 21

3   In Good Company... 43

4   The Way of Science... 61

5   Science Versus Religion?.. 83

6   The Battle As Propaganda.. 101

7   A Brief History of Materialism 127

8   Science and Consciousness 153

9   Science and Spirit in Harmony..................................... 175

10 On the Wings of Assumptions...................................... 199

11 Is Your Faith Conscious or Unconscious? 219

12 No Escape—From an Act of Faith................................. 241

13 Faith and the Wisdom Traditions.................................. 257

14 The Golden Mean 283

15 Summing Up 297

Endnotes and References.. 317

Index... 333

Life is complex, and the current volume is one in a series concerning how to live a meaningful and fulfilled human life. Look for these other volumes by the same author:

On Being Human: An Operator's Manual
Consciousness, Identity, and Beyond
The Unseen Order

A note on endnotes:

When two or three citations from an author occur in close proximity to one another in this book, the source will only be listed once—with the last reference in the sequence.

Special Appreciation

I want to express my deep gratitude to Ralph Gonzalez, Ronda Redden Reitz, Marga Lacy, and Phillip Moffitt for their encouragement and invaluable assistance in turning early drafts into this finished manuscript.

I want to thank Sandra Sundari Smith for help with this book, as well as her help and support in many other areas of my life.

I also want to thank those intrepid souls who have volunteered their time, energy, ideas, and passion to the development of the Meaningful Life Center: Jerry Askew, Chris Austin, John Berry, David Bolt, Renda Burkhart, Sandy Cartwright, Laurie Curtis, Doug DeWitt, Bobby Gintz, Ralph Gonzalez, Steve Hancock, Birney Hand, Don and Glenda Henry, Marie Hofer, Judith Ideker, Shoray Kirk, Marga Lacy, Elizabeth Lewis, Ronda Redden Reitz, Sue Painter, Sandra Sundari Smith, Deb Sullivan, Valerie Taylor, Phyllis Leonard Turner, and Linda Weaver.

And I want to thank all those who have participated in workshops I have given through the years. Your insights and thoughtful questions have stimulated, guided, and inspired my own development.

My heartfelt thanks to all.

INTRODUCTION

We humans tend to create categories around which to organize our thoughts, but we don't live from those categories. Living happens from a moving center that includes every imaginable aspect of life: the psychological, political, emotional, rational, cultural, sexual, spiritual, religious, scientific, artistic, sociological, economic, and more. It can be valuable to study the separate parts, but the only way to a fulfilled life is to act and move from the point of intersection that contains them all.

Swirling around this center are many currents that arise from both the world outside and from within ourselves. Everyone has motivations and expectations involving food, shelter, sex, pleasure, adventure, power, wealth, fame, achievement, relationship, spiritual fulfillment, and on and on. It is not hard to *think* about these separately, but at the living edge, where life happens, these currents do not exist in individual boxes that can be examined one by one; rather, they constantly mix and mingle. Nor do these thought-boxes have actual boundaries, but only arbitrary and shifting shades of distinction.

It is no wonder, then, that the major fields of human knowledge began with an interrelated search for the good, the true, and the beautiful. A core motivation we humans have always had, beyond taking care of our basic needs, has been to find a meaningful and fulfilled life. From our beginnings, this has involved finding wisdom concerning what is good, knowledge about what is true, and a relationship to that which is harmonious and beautiful. For thousands of years, the world's wisdom traditions have said that there is more to life than the everyday things on which we spend much of our time, and many of the best and brightest have taken up the challenge and pursued wisdom. In ancient Greece, the quest for this wisdom was exemplified by the admonition of Socrates: "Know Thyself." Two thousand years later mathematician, physicist, and philosopher Blaise Pascal said, "It is an extraordinary blindness to live without investigating what we are." Continuing this theme in the 20th century, the humorist James Thurber advised, "All human beings should try to learn before they die what they are running from, and to, and why."

In this search, thinking in categories can be useful, but decisions do not spring from single categories (except perhaps in moments of desperation); most actions and decisions involve the input of many currents. Further, as we take in information and impressions, we do not file them in neat intellectual boxes; rather, they all exist in an interconnected web that we do not plan, control, or even understand. Impressions arise and flow from one to another with indistinct lines, and at the level of meaning and values, everything seems to be connected. This is what Ralph Waldo Emerson was trying to capture when he said there is one universal current out of which proceed all the virtues, such as love, justice, and goodness.[1] John Keats is reaching toward the same insight in the last lines of his poem, "Ode on a Grecian Urn" when he insists:

'Beauty is truth, truth beauty,'—that is all
Ye know on earth, and all ye need to know.

To find meaning and move toward a fulfilled life requires us to attend to the center where all the categories relate, interact, and even merge. For confirmation, simply examine yourself—your own awareness—and you will discover that when you think or have an experience, you do not separate your thoughts into boxes. When you hear something or see something, those impressions are intermixed with many other things. And when you think about your life, your mind constantly moves back and forth, around and through all that you know, mingling the categories, searching for the best response to whatever has attracted your attention.

If you simply examine your own experience you will see that answers to life's questions do not come from the separate categories. You can't separate things out in that manner even if you try, for memories, feelings, and ideas are not stored that way. When you focus on a problem, everything you know comes into play—all your ideas and experiences, even those you do not consciously remember. All the knowledge you possess in every area of your being informs and enriches every consideration, and living happens from it all—from all of what you know. Living happens from what you *are*.

One consequence of this is that if you become an expert in one of the categories (psychology, art, science, religion, and so forth), you can write papers and give talks about that area, but in living your own life, you will not be able to keep the various currents separate. Everything you know and have experienced in any area will enter into your decisions and actions. Furthermore, just because you become an expert in one area does not mean that life will offer the choice of avoiding the others. Each of us must come to terms with the full range of human questions, emotions, and possibilities; each of us must make decisions with regard to relationships, finances, health, spiritual matters, career, values, forms of entertainment, exercise, how and when we will help others, and many other things. There is yet another layer of complexity. All of the categories into which we try to divide life are constantly affecting each other; they continually overlap and intermingle.

To be human, therefore, means facing the daunting task of dealing with all the categories simultaneously. How, then, should we proceed? Where will we turn for guidance? Through the centuries, those who have gone before us have left trails through the wilderness. Four of the most important:

1. Creating and experiencing art
2. Engagement with science
3. Following a religious tradition
4. Undertaking a spiritual journey

Although there are differences between these four paths, there are many similarities as well: Their core motivations are surprisingly similar and even their major conclusions, although not exactly the same, are often quite harmonious. How can this be? Albert Einstein explained it succinctly: "All religions, arts and sciences are branches of the same tree."[2]

Let us explore, then, these four branches of the tree of life—art, science, religion, and spirituality, the commonalities between them and the guidance they each provide for a fulfilling and meaningful life.

Beginning with art.

CHAPTER 1

THE WAY OF ART

Through the years, New York has been a favorite destination, especially because of the museums. Opting out of tours, I meander about until a painting or piece of sculpture reaches out and touches me (figuratively, of course; don't know what I would do if it happened literally). Years ago I was walking though the Museum of Modern Art with no particular destination in mind when my attention was suddenly riveted on a painting. Moving closer, then stepping back, that painting became the center of my awareness. It was luminous—filled with light—and the light seemed to radiate out and fill the room. Feelings were stirred that I could not name. This particular painting was affecting me powerfully, in ways I did not understand.

Choosing not to analyze while immersed in the experience, I spent a long time appreciating, enjoying, being absorbed in an image that was vividly alive for me that day. It was only later that old questions began to return: How is it that art can communicate in such a powerful way? How can smears of color on a canvas touch one's heart, emotions, imagination—and lead to insights months or years after the experience? With this particular painting, a new question surfaced: How to explain such a strong feeling of communion with an artist I had never met and with whom I felt I had so little in common?

Whatever the explanation for the power of art, it has worked its magic on us for a very long time. Perhaps the reason is because art is one of the most important ways we humans have tried to understand our world and the meaning of our lives within it. For thousands of years we have immersed our senses, minds, and emotions in every imaginable form of artistic creation. We have continually sought to comprehend and express our visions about life through writing, sculpting, composing, painting, designing, performing, and decorating. Furthermore, when we have not been creating art ourselves, we have frequently turned our attention to the creations of others, wishing to experience and be touched by the currents that flow through inspired works of art.

Just think of the incredible amount of time, energy, and money that has been invested in the production and preservation of art through the centuries. For countless generations, in every corner of the planet, we have devoted untold resources to the creation of paintings, music, sculpture, literature, opera, theater, dance, movies, and magnificent buildings. Focusing just on the buildings dedicated to house and display art—museums, libraries, art galleries, symphony halls, opera houses, theaters, castles, and mansions (thousands of which have been built primarily to showcase art collections)—the commitment and expense devoted to providing a home for art is awe-inspiring.

And beyond the creating and preserving, there is also the time and effort we have spent simply taking it in: Think of the time we as a species have invested in reading, watching, and listening to art in all its forms. Given this, there can be no doubt that art is one of the central commitments of humankind and one of the ways we are most distinct from other species. (A few other species perhaps have artistic creations; for instance, whales seem to make music for the sheer pleasure of it, and some birds build elaborate dwellings that seem to have an artistic motivation. No other species, however, approaches the investment of time and attention we humans give to art. Perhaps we should have been called "homo artiens.")

Art and the Sacred

(At this point, let me introduce Skeptico, an old friend who asks challenging questions and sometimes disagrees with what I am saying.)

Skeptico: That was a pretty dramatic beginning. Why so many superlatives and so many lists?

Wisdom Seeker: To get your attention. Art is so much a part of our lives that we tend to take it for granted, so I want to encourage a fresh look at its role and importance.

Skeptico: Okay, I'm paying attention. Why do you think it is so important?

Wisdom Seeker: To understand the profound commitment we humans have made to art requires the recognition that it has seldom been separated from the quest to discover a whole and meaningful life. Throughout history, art has been intertwined with myth, ritual, religion, and things spiritual; it has been bound up with the attempt to understand how we should live and how to have a fulfilled life. In many cultures art has been considered sacred, the primary vehicle for connecting with and experiencing that which is larger than oneself. This is likely the reason that William Blake gave it such a central role in his understanding of human civilization. In his notes about the statue Laocoön, he proclaims that when art is degraded and imagination denied, war between nations is the result.[1] In another poem, Blake gives the most dramatic statement I know concerning the importance of art:

> Poetry fetter'd, Fetters the Human Race!
> Nations are Destroy'd, or Flourish, in proportion as
> Their Poetry Painting and Music, are Destroy'd or Flourish!
> The Primeval State of Man was Wisdom, Art, and Science.[2]

Blake's connection between art, science, and wisdom relates directly to the work of noted anthropologist Mircea Eliade, who reports in *The Sacred and The Profane* that every culture he studied (both ancient and modern) recognized two levels of reality, the sacred and the profane. The "profane" as he understood it is the world of everyday life: making a living, taking care of responsibilities, enjoying ourselves, fulfilling ambitions. The other dimension, the "sacred," involves a connection to something larger than the small ego self, something beyond the experience of normal time and space.

Using Eliade's definitions, most cultures through history have considered linking us to the realm of this "something larger" to be one of the primary functions of art, and for this reason, art has also been one of the preferred methods of dealing with the important issues of life. It is not surprising, then, that most artists through the ages have operated within established religious structures. In fact, much of the world's art was created for religious institutions—just bring to mind the great cathedrals of Europe, the Hindu and Buddhist temples of Asia, the mosques of the Islamic world, magnificent tribal art, religious music, sculpture, and paintings from every land, and so much more.

This does not mean, however, that artists have always been comfortable with the religious authorities with whom they had to deal. On the contrary, many have had uneasy relationships with the religious organizations around them—to the point that a significant number of artists have been seen as heretics. Most artists through the centuries, though—even the heretics—have considered their work to be coming from Eliade's sacred dimension; have felt they were inspired by something larger than the "small self" of their everyday lives. Efforts to define this "something greater" have always been problematic, for artists have understood it in many different ways, but almost all have felt there was a sacred dimension from which their inspirations arose and into which their art was a glimpse.

Although not obvious at first, this applies to a lot of modern art as well (not all, of course). While many modern artists do not take part in an organized religion, their work often involves issues of meaning and the spiritual dimension of life. Several books present this forcefully and clearly, such as, *The Spiritual in Art: Abstract*

Painting, 1890-1985 by Maurice Tuchman;[3] *Reclaiming the Spiritual in Art*, edited by Dawn Perlmutter and Debra Koppman;[4] and the lecture series by art historian Sarah O'Brien Twohig at the Tate Gallery in London, published as *The Spiritual in Twentieth Century Art.*[5]

This commonality of report—that inspiration comes from and speaks about sacred time and space—does not give a clear explanation of the source of artistic inspiration, but it does provide a clue about why art has always been such a central feature in human life.

Why Do We Do It?

Even though the urge to create art is powerful, being an artist is often a difficult and lonely profession. Think of the many stories of artists through the centuries who sacrificed everything to pursue their calling—writers, poets, sculptors, and musicians who lived in poverty and squalor so they could follow a creative dream. Many left their families and friends to pursue a vision, while others infuriated friends and family by following an inspiration that challenged the cultural values of their time and place.

To get a sense of the difficulty, simply read the stories of sacrifice of numerous famous artists or listen to their oft-told tales of woe. Yet these are the stories of the ones who eventually became well known. Beyond these accounts, think of countless other stories that have been lost—the unremembered stories of those who did not become famous. For every famous artist, many, many others almost certainly made the same sacrifice, gave the same effort, but did not achieve success. For every artist that history remembers as successful there must be a thousand, or ten thousand, who gave their lives to art—yet are not recognized or known today.

So think of the difficulty. Consider it for yourself. In most cases, to be an artist you must commit to years of practice and then more years of producing art before the world will decide whether to reward your efforts. You must do this even though you know that the majority of those who make such a commitment will not achieve worldly success.

Even if you are ultimately successful, recognition might not come for years; many of those considered great artists today received little or no recognition while they were alive. Yet aspiring artists keep offering themselves, living in obscurity, tasting the bitter fruit of rejection. They keep coming, making the effort, making the sacrifice—without knowing whether their work will ever be appreciated. The life of an artist can be very hard.

My favorite example of this is Vincent Van Gogh, who spent many years working without recognition. It is believed today that he did not sell a single painting in his lifetime! All those incredible works, worth billions of dollars today, stacked in his brother's garage, never seen by anyone. (Do you know an aspiring artist, perhaps your "Aunt Sue" or "Cousin Bill," whose art is unappreciated, stacked up somewhere like Van Gogh's? Is it possible their fate will someday be the same as his?)

It is very hard for me to imagine Van Gogh's paintings as they existed for years, piled up in a building that offered little protection from the weather and mice—paintings that would sell today for more than the combined works of any other artist. (An estimate, of course, but what other artist's combined works would be worth as much?) Yet while his art was being created, Van Gogh was a failure in the eyes of the world and was experiencing deep emotional pain—his letters to his brother Theo serve as a testament to that suffering.[6] But despite the failure and pain, Van Gogh kept painting, continuing to work day after day, year after year. It was clearly not easy. He wrote during this time, "I have a dirty and difficult trade—painting, and if I were not as I am, I should not paint."[7] Because of these difficulties, he died young, by his own hand, hoping to relieve the burden he felt he had become to the beloved brother who had faithfully supported him emotionally and financially.

Imagine, then, the wonder as the world began to discover and appreciate those paintings, sequestered in a dilapidated garage. It didn't happen overnight, of course, but today Van Gogh is considered one of the greatest artists of all time. So I have often thought about Van Gogh and the difficulties of his life, in contrast to the towering success he achieved after his death. And here is the thing: Although his example might be extreme, it is representative of the experience of many artists. This raises several questions, one of which is this:

> **Thought Experiment: Would You Choose Van Gogh's Life?**
>
> If you could have Van Gogh's life, with the pain and failure he had while alive but followed by great success after death, would you choose it?

Skeptico: That's not easy. I have always wanted to be famous.
Wisdom Seeker: It isn't an easy question, and people's goals and images for life are often quite different, but after a good bit of thought I have come to my own answer: I would not choose Van Gogh's life. But there is a second question that is even harder for me: If Vincent Van Gogh had been my friend and had asked for my advice about what he should do, what would I have said? More specifically, I have wondered what I would have advised if I thought he would have been happier becoming a blacksmith or a butcher. Would I have advised him to go the route of personal happiness, or would I have advised him to continue with his art—knowing that such a life would turn out to be incredibly difficult and painful?

There is, of course, no way to know if Van Gogh would have been happier if he had given up art, but many of us, at crucial moments, face similar questions: Do we choose a path that seems to offer greater passion and vitality, even if it appears risky and difficult? Do we choose what seems practical and "steady"—a hoped-for path to conventional happiness—or do we follow the way that seems to have greater meaning?

The Source of Creative Inspiration

One way to reach toward answers to these questions is to explore why Van Gogh made the choices he made, and more broadly, to examine why the creative process has so much power to call us to its service. Or more simply, to ask: Why have so many chosen the difficult path of becoming an artist?

In their book *Higher Creativity*, Willis Harman and Howard Rheingold provide one glimpse of an answer by pointing out a theme that runs through the reports of many artists—the source from which artistic inspirations arise. They document how the greatest artists (as well as scientists), frequently report that their inspirations came from a source beyond themselves, beyond what they normally thought of as "I." Summing up, they quote the poet Shelley: "One after another the greatest writers, poets, and artists confirm the fact that their work comes to them from beyond the threshold of consciousness."[8]

A dramatic example involves the composer Wolfgang Mozart, who said about the moment a major piece of music came into being: "Though it be long … the whole work stands almost complete and finished in my mind. … Nor do I hear in my imagination the parts successively, but I hear them, as it were, all at once."[9] Unbelievably, Mozart is telling us that he did not *think up* this work, but that it somehow *came to him complete and whole* from somewhere beyond his conscious awareness. How can that be? Even if I memorize a concerto written by someone else I cannot hold all the parts in my conscious mind at once. The mind doesn't work that way. Yet Mozart heard a whole piece of music "all at once," a work *that had not yet been written!* Where and how did it come to exist? By whom was it written?

As with Mozart, many artists have felt their inspirations as a gift. Beethoven insisted that some of his most valued works came from beyond what he thought of as his individual self. George Sand echoed this sentiment saying, "The Wind plays my old harp as it lists. ... It is the other who sings as he likes, well or ill."[10] Over and over this theme repeats itself as artists attempt to explain the source of their inspirations. The painter Paul Klee said: "Everything vanishes around me, and works are born as if out of the void. Ripe, graphic fruits fall off. My hand has become the obedient instrument of a remote will."[11] At another point Klee wrote that the artist "neither serves nor rules—he transmits. His position is humble. ... He is merely a channel."[12]

There are many other examples. The great German writer Johann Wolfgang von Goethe is reported to have said that he wrote his first novel, *Werther*, "almost unconsciously, like a somnambulist, and was amazed when I realized what I had done."[13] The composer Wagner said of the overture to Das Rheingold: "It has at last been revealed to me."[14] The poet Keats said a section of his poem *Hyperion* began to flow into his mind and "seemed to come by chance or magic—to be as it were something given."[15] He also wrote that sometimes, after he had written a poem, he was struck with "astonishment," for it seemed "the production of another person"[16] rather than his own. And the composer Tchaikovsky wrote, "Generally speaking, the germ of a future composition comes suddenly and unexpectedly."[17]

Higher Creativity gives many more examples of how "the muse can come, unbidden, and virtually dictate entire lines, passages, or works."[18] Two of those examples are Richard Strauss and William Blake. Strauss said, "While the ideas were flowing in upon me—the entire musical, measure for measure, it seemed to me that I was dictated to by two wholly different, Omnipotent Entities ... I was definitely conscious of being aided by more than an earthly Power." And Blake: "I have written this poem from immediate dictation, twelve or sometimes twenty lines at a time, without premeditation, and even against my will."[19]

Thought Experiment: Creating Against Your Own Will?

What might Blake have meant, that he wrote the poem against his own will? Have you ever had an experience that relates to his?

It is, of course, very difficult to use words to capture the mysterious source of inspiration, so some artists avoid naming it, while others use words from their religious tradition. This was the case with the composer Johannes Brahms, who said: "Straightaway the ideas flow in upon me, directly from God. ... Measure by measure, the finished product is revealed to me when I am in those rare, inspired moods." Giacomo Puccini joins him, saying, "The music of this opera was dictated to me by God; I was merely instrumental in putting it on paper and communicating it to the public."[20] But naming the source of inspiration "God" does not remove the mystery. What exactly did Brahms or Puccini mean by God? Did that word mean the same to both? Did it mean the same to them as it does to you? Thus, whatever the words, the question remains: From whence does inspiration arise?

Perhaps it is an unanswerable question. Still, thinking about it has much value; perhaps the goal is not a strict definition but to learn to open to the source of inspiration ourselves. Rudyard Kipling can help. Reflecting on his own experience, Kipling concluded that the key to finding deep inspiration was "not to think consciously" but to "drift."[21] An example of this "drifting" comes from Beethoven: One day, while riding in a carriage, he fell asleep and began dreaming of Jerusalem. Within the dream there arose a beautiful piece of music. On waking, however, no matter how hard he tried, he could not remember it. Being aware of the necessity to work with the unconscious, Beethoven arranged to take the same carriage ride the next day (and at the same time of day). As he rode along, he began to intentionally enter the mental state he had experienced the day before. Then, writing in his journal, he reports, "Lo and behold!" the music "flashed across me." But this time, because he was prepared, he "held it ... fast" and began to write it down.[22]

What is especially interesting is that Beethoven consciously decided to explore the terrain between sleeping and waking, and in doing so he discovered he could re-enter the dream world whilst still awake—a marvelous example of a creative genius intentionally opening the door to the world of inspiration and bringing its fruits back into human life.

Another story concerns the poet Coleridge, who went to sleep under the influence of laudanum (a mixture of opium and alcohol), and reported that he awoke three hours later with several hundred lines of the poem *Xanadu* in his mind. Coleridge said that in his dream the "images rose up before him as things, without any sensation or consciousness of effort." Then, upon waking, he had a "distinct recollection of the whole," and "instantly and eagerly wrote down the lines."[23] But who or what composed several hundred lines of a major poem while the poet, Coleridge, was asleep?

Skeptico: How am I supposed to make sense of these experiences?

Wisdom Seeker: Many try to dismiss them, and it would be easy to do so if the artistic creations involved were not so powerful and important. If there were only a few such examples, we could cry "Fantasy!" or "Delusion!" and ignore them. That however, would itself be the delusion, for there are thousands of such reports from every age and every land. The fact is that many great works by some of the greatest artists who have ever lived are reported to have come from these kinds of otherworldly inspirations.

Skeptico: Maybe these artists did not understand the source of their inspirations.

Wisdom Seeker: That's possible, but such a judgment seems a bit arrogant, especially when given by those who have not demonstrated the same level of inspiration as the artists themselves. Doesn't it seem wiser to listen to and learn from some of the greatest creative geniuses who ever lived concerning the source of their inspirations?

Skeptico: So how do you understand the source of artistic inspiration?

Wisdom Seeker: There is no easy answer, but the composer Brahms provided a clue I find helpful. He said: "I have to be in a semi-trance condition to get such results—a condition when the conscious mind is in temporary abeyance, and the subconscious mind is in control." He goes on, "In this exalted state I see clearly what is obscure in my ordinary moods."[24] For Brahms and many others, then, the source of inspiration is not the "ordinary mind," the mind I normally think of as "me." Rather, the source is directly related to Mircea Eliade's sacred time and sacred space, that "something" experienced as "greater" than the personal ego self. This is the direction in which artists have pointed through the ages—insisting we must look beyond our everyday selves for the source of creative inspiration.

Part of what arises as inspiration might have to do with things that one has known and then forgotten, but creative inspiration seems to go much further, bringing forth new ideas and images. (Such inspirations arise, of course, in all fields of human endeavor, from science to business to farming. Later chapters will explore this more fully.) You can say these images and ideas come from the "unconscious," but using that term in such a broad way makes it just as mysterious as the word "God," for no one has any idea how the "unconscious" could write a whole piece of music or provide a scientific breakthrough. Thus, in the face of the unknown, it is often worthwhile to let the poets speak, and one who considered this issue carefully was Shelley, who said that deep inspirations were "visitations of the divinity in man."[25]

Skeptico: But this doesn't really tell me about the source of inspirations; "divine" has a thousand different meanings.

Wisdom Seeker: You're right. Perhaps the only way to really understand is to develop, for yourself, a connection with the realm "beyond the threshold of consciousness."

Why Drift?

Skeptico: Why do you think Brahms said it was necessary to drift in order to experience these inspirations?

Wisdom Seeker: Writer Christine Cox gives a valuable suggestion: "In the lapsing of thought ... our awareness of our personal ego also lapses. It is this momentary loss of the noise of the ego that is the true cause of the bliss that accompanies the creative state." Here, then, is the deep connection between art and spirituality, for her words could equally apply to the experience of the mystics in every spiritual tradition. She continues: "This silencing of the ego allows us to hear not only the symphony of bliss, but also the many-stranded music of reality, and the voice of inspiration arising from it."[26] In other words, in order to get in touch with deep inspiration—to create inspired art, to experience spiritual opening, or to live a fulfilled life—we must get outside our self-centered point of view. Only this will allow a connection to the source of wisdom. Only this will bring us into contact with meaning, values, and that which is truly important. There is even a good possibility that it is only in this way that we will find the path to fulfillment and happiness.

And this is why Vincent Van Gogh's life has been valuable to me. Although his profession was difficult, he worked feverishly, sometimes ten to twelve hours a day, and was thus able to create two thousand works of art in just ten years. Why did he do it? In a letter to his sister he said, "At moments, when I am in a good mood, I think that what is alive in art, and eternally alive, is in the first place the painter."[27] In other words, when he was working, the ordinary, suffering Van Gogh was not present; rather, a different part of his being was present that he called "the painter." When he could step into this aspect of himself, into the painter, he did not feel bad. In fact, he went on to say, "Being as I am (a painter), I often work with pleasure."[28]

The key to Van Gogh's positive experience while painting seems to be that when he was immersed in painting he felt another part of himself to be present (I think a deeper part of himself, perhaps even his essence). When he reached this state of inspiration and creativity, he felt that his real self had come alive. In those moments he felt meaning, he felt fulfillment, he felt whole. Most of the rest of the time he was caught in his neuroses, his psychological problems, and his life was filled with suffering. But this was not the case when he could step out of his small self. In those moments he sometimes said things that resonate with the wisest of saints; in a letter to his brother he wrote: "Do you know what frees one from this captivity? ... Being friends, being brothers, love, that is what opens the prison by some supreme power, by some magic force."[29]

Perhaps, then, the reason Van Gogh remained a painter and worked such long hours—even though it was difficult—was to experience "the visitation of the divine," to enter "sacred time" as often as he as could. Especially since the rest of his life was such a mess.

Skeptico: Could he have been a great artist without the suffering?

Wisdom Seeker: There is no way to know, but, poignantly, he once said that he felt a deep connection between his pain and his creativity, and that he would not sacrifice the one if it meant the loss of the other. Echoing his words, the poet Rilke lamented that he was afraid if he lost his demons, he would lose his angels also. This is not necessarily true of all artists, but perhaps it was true for Van Gogh and Rilke.

Which leads back to my earlier question: If I had I been Van Gogh's friend, would I have suggested he give up painting for a more normal life? My answer, after much reflection, is: "No." Even though I have concluded that I would not have chosen Van Gogh's life for myself, the advice I would have given him is clear. Upon receipt of one of his letters asking such a question, I would have replied: "Vincent, only in those bursts of creativity, those moments when you lose yourself in painting do you find meaning and joy in your life. This, then, seems the best path to your fulfillment. Only in those moments have you found a way to be in touch with your higher self, your essence, your deepest spirit. So, dear Vincent, even if it is hard, go for it, continue your work—it seems to be your way to the fullest experience of life. It is your connection to whatever there is that is larger than your daily, worldly, suffering self."

For me, and seemingly for millions of others, to this very day Vincent Van Gogh is "alive" in his art. Something more is alive as well, alive through his creations and perhaps through his suffering. I know this for certain from my experience of the light that day in the Museum of Modern Art, lost in the mystery of "Starry Night."

I am not alone in this experience. Listen to these words from Don McLean's famous song, "Starry, Starry Night," the last lines sung as if to a living Vincent Van Gogh:

Starry, starry night.
Paint your palette blue and grey,
With eyes that know the darkness in my soul.
Flaming flowers that brightly blaze,
Weathered faces lined in pain,
Are soothed beneath the artist's loving hand.
Now I understand what you tried to say to me,
How you suffered for your sanity,
How you tried to set them free.
They would not listen, they did not know how.
Perhaps they'll listen now.

Vincent suffered much, but somehow, through his suffering, he was able to capture something that has touched millions. In many of his paintings the foreground is dark, the people and objects heavy and burdened, but somewhere in the painting there is a radiant light breaking through, sometimes faintly, sometimes dramatically. When he was in a deep contemplative state, Vincent must have experienced this light as pervading all existence, and in his paintings he was able to offer hope that each of us might experience this light too. This is what is alive in Van Gogh's art; this is what touches all those who are ready to "listen," who are ready to "see."

CHAPTER 2

THE MESSAGE IN ART

Sitting in a dark theater, tears streaming down my face, hoping no one will see, I realize it is just a play, but something at the core of my being knows that truth is being spoken here: truth about life, about living, and about me.

In the theater, answers are explored and consequences of actions made vivid. Sometimes a character brings to life a situation in a way that helps me avoid a ditch in my own road or inspires me to live less fearfully and more fully. In the theater, when a character wrestles with something I am trying to understand, it helps me in life. When a scene portrays an encounter with something as yet unknown to my conscious mind—something stirring in me that needs attention—the chances increase that I will recognize what is going on and deal with it more effectively.

Perhaps this is why Joseph Campbell declared: "This surely is the justification of art ... that beauty apprehended should have this power to illuminate the senses, still the mind, and enchant the heart." In so doing, it can "reestablish us in our own deep truth, which is at one with that of all being."[1]

In the act of creation, many artists speak of experiencing a connection to something greater than themselves. When the rest of us encounter art produced under the influence of this connection, it can have a powerful effect. When I read a book or encounter a painting produced under the influence of such inspiration, I can be transported to an inner world brought alive by the artist's creation. Other times, when joining with others in singing or making music together, watching a great play, or listening to an inspired performance, I can be taken out of myself into a shared experience of something greater, the effect magnified and enhanced by the sharing of that inspired and creative space with others.

We humans clearly value both the inner as well as the shared experience of art, as evidenced by the elaborate systems maintained worldwide to present and disseminate it. Whether taking us deep within or connecting us to others, artistic creations are a major commitment of the human species, occupying a staggering amount of our time and attention.

Thought Experiment: Why Art?

Why have we humans made such an incredible investment in art, in all of its many forms, for thousands of years?

Part of the reason art is central to human life surely involves entertainment, the momentary pleasures it can bring. Entertainment, however, is not sufficient to explain the vast commitment we have made. This leads to a second answer: Artists in touch with and inspired by images "beyond the threshold of the conscious mind" can carry us into their experience, providing the rest of us with a glimpse of that "something greater" for ourselves.

Philosophers and poets have recognized this for centuries: Goethe proclaimed, "Beauty is a manifestation of secret laws of Nature," and without their "revelation," they "would remain concealed from us for ever."[2] In the same vein the Scottish writer Thomas Carlyle observed, "In all true works of art, wilt thou discern eternity looking through time, the god-like rendered visible."[3] Even Freud recognized the ability of the artist to capture fundamental truths, saying: "Everywhere I go I find a poet has been there before me."[4] This understanding started a long time ago. Plato, one of the greatest minds the world has ever produced, asserted, "Beauty is the splendor of the true."[5] He also had this to say about educating children: "I would teach children music, physics, and philosophy; but most importantly music, for the patterns in music and all the arts are the keys to learning."

One way to understand Plato's point of view is to recognize that an encounter with an inspired work of art can change us for the better, and even give direction to our lives. Many a youth has been set off on a life adventure by a book or a story. How this happens is mysterious, but perhaps Plato was right in suggesting that at the highest level, beauty, truth, and the good are intimately connected. In his view, when we encounter beauty in any form it provides a reflection of True Beauty, bringing us into contact with the Highest Good. Thus, "the object of education is to teach us to love what is beautiful,"[6] with the implication that if we do so we will simultaneously know what is true and be committed to what is good. Twenty-three hundred years later the poet John Keats captured the same idea, saying simply, "Beauty is truth, truth beauty, that is all ye know on earth, and all ye need to know."[7]

Skeptico: But what did Plato mean by beauty? He seems to be taking a pretty broad view.

Wisdom Seeker: There is no question he had a very expansive understanding of beauty. For Plato, there existed a transcendent realm of pure Forms or pure Ideas, and anything that provided a glimpse into that realm was a manifestation of beauty.

Skeptico: That's pretty abstract. What is your personal experience of what he was getting at?

Wisdom Seeker: Artistic creations have definitely brought me closer to an understanding of my own meaning and fulfillment; many magical moments have occurred through encountering a great work of art when I could be open and receptive. At such times something reaches out from the work and touches me. Or perhaps it is the other way around; something in me reaches through a work of art and touches the source of the artist's inspiration. Maybe it is both; it is hard to tell the direction in which the effect runs—but it can be palpable.

Writer Christine Cox captures the experience: "True art is inspired by the divine, and the source of that inspiration may be discerned by the attentive and sensitive reader or viewer."[8] She is following the thought of her mentor, Paul Brunton, who observed, "The secret of art's highest mission is that ... it enables those who share in the experience ... to be brought into the absolute stillness for a moment."[9] In his *Notebooks*,[10] Brunton suggests that the inspired artist acts as a conduit, bringing the experience of something larger into life by manifesting the laws of the spirit here on Earth. Brunton was an early pioneer in bringing Eastern thought to the West, and what he is conveying reflects a convergence of Eastern and Western thought, for art has served this role on all sides of the planet.

Another keen observer of the power of art, Joseph Campbell, explores its importance in *Inner Reaches of Outer Space*. There he says, "There is another and further ... range of the revelation of art that is beyond beauty, namely, the sublime." To understand this *sublime*, Campbell follows the thought of James Joyce, who says it is "that which arouses sentiments of awe and reverence, and a sense of vastness and power outreaching human comprehension." The point both are making is that when we experience the sublime we are carried into a realm beyond ordinary experience, and there we encounter the broader framework within which ordinary life happens. Although the framework is larger than our usual experience, it is not in opposition to it; in fact, it is that which supports and sustains it. According to Campbell, "The sublime ... suggests magnitudes exceeding life; not refuting, but augmenting life."[11]

This is the realm of the sacred (returning to the thought of Mircea Eliade), and it is here that we must look for life's meaning. It is only when touching the sacred dimension that we finally have a chance to glimpse the whole picture, experience the whole gestalt of life and our place in it. As Campbell put it, "The way of art ... leads ... to the mountaintop that is ... beyond opposites." It leads to a "transcendental vision,"[12] one about which William Blake declares: "The doors of perception are cleansed and every thing appears to man as it is, infinite."[13]

Insofar as this is true, inspired art is a manifestation of the highest values toward which we humans can aspire and entering its domain brings the possibility of an experience of meaning for ourselves. Carried by art to this mountaintop, we glimpse a broader vision of life and our role in it. Shakespeare captures this possibility beautifully in A *Midsummer Night's Dream:*

> The poet's eye, in a fine frenzy rolling,
> Doth glance from heaven to earth, from earth to heaven;
> And as imagination bodies forth
> The form of things unknown, the poet's pen
> Turns them to shapes, and gives to airy nothing
> A local habitation and a name.[14]

Which I take to mean that an inspired artist can glance toward the mystery of existence and catch a glimpse of something that most of us are too busy or too self-absorbed to notice. (It's an "airy nothing" to most of us, most of the time, because our gaze is fixed upon the mundane.) But great artists find a way to bring what they have glimpsed "down to earth"; they find a way to manifest it here on this earthly plane in a form that the rest of us can understand and experience— and hopefully, claim for ourselves. Artists give the mystery a "local habitation and a name," give it an expression in a particular time and place so that those of us immersed in the daily grind can notice its existence and grasp its significance.

It was in recognition of these currents that Campbell came to believe that an artist was often a "seer and prophet," and a "justifier of life." For the same reasons the philosopher Friedrich Nietzsche declared that art was "the proper task of life."[15] These statements constitute high claims, but how else are we to understand the central role artistic expression has been given in human history?

Thought Experiment: Experiencing the Sublime

What has been your most powerful experience of a work of art: a play, painting, book, sculpture, music piece, movie, or dance? What happened for you in that experience?

Two Kinds of Art

To understand these claims being made for art, though, a distinction is necessary. Some artistic creations might be inspired by a connection to "something greater," but everything labeled "art" is not inspired in this way. Modernity has in fact exploded with "art" focused on selling goods, promoting a message, or titillating the senses. These functions are not new, but are much more prevalent today, and it would be a mistake to assume that everything referred to as "art" has a deeper meaning or can provide useful guidance.

Joseph Campbell takes up this issue in *Inner Reaches,* using James Joyce's distinction between "proper art" and "improper art." Joyce's view is that in proper art, "The mind is … raised above desire and loathing," and when experiencing such art, "One is not moved to physical action of any kind, but held in … contemplation and enjoyment."[16] Conversely, improper art is motivated by worldly energies and tends to arouse fear or desire. Such art moves us to action, either to get something we think will bring pleasure or to escape from something we don't like. (Neither Campbell nor Joyce is saying that worldly art should be banned or banished, only that it does not have the same effect, nor does it strive for the same end, as art that arises from deeper currents.)

In essence, improper (or profane) art is concerned with selling, entertainment, sensationalism, or propaganda, while sacred art connects us to something greater than ourselves. To better understand this distinction, Joyce turned to the thought of that great thirteenth-century medieval theologian, Thomas Aquinas, who wrote that there are three things necessary for higher art: *Integritas, Consonantia,* and *Claritas* (usually translated as Wholeness, Harmony, and Clarity). Joyce, following Aquinas, said, "The instant wherein that supreme quality of beauty ... is apprehended luminously by the mind which has been arrested by its wholeness and fascinated by its harmony is ... a spiritual state very like to that ... called the enchantment of the heart."[17]

In other words, proper (or sacred) art can bring clarity, offer a glimpse of wholeness, and help us experience the underlying harmony of existence. Crucially, it can bring these fruits even when we are surrounded by and immersed in the chaos of everyday life (which is what Joyce was trying to depict in his writings, while at the same time hoping to carry his readers into that experience themselves).

Skeptico: Then proper art doesn't include works that involve pain and suffering?

Wisdom Seeker: For works created to shock or elicit fear, that is the case. But if the pain and suffering are intended to arouse compassion or deep sympathy, such works can serve a higher end. Even a depiction that evokes terror can be "proper art" for Joyce if it "arrests the mind in the presence of whatsoever is grave and constant in human suffering and unites it with the secret cause."[18]

Joyce was certainly no puritan, and not even religious in the usual sense of that word. In fact, he was more focused on helping his readers break free from religious and cultural norms than upholding the prevailing ones (his books were banned in the United States for a decade for "obscene language"). But Joyce recognized the difference between what he experienced as the sacred versus what he thought was going on in organized religions (which he did not view with great favor). Because he could make this distinction, he was able to recognize and honor the sacred in works of art that were not considered religious by the culture of his time. In so doing, he could guide his readers toward an experience of art that allowed them to open to that which is "grave and constant," and finally to unite at the core of their being with the "secret cause"—the mystery at the heart of things.

Working through these ideas led Campbell to the exalted view of art quoted at the beginning of this chapter: "This is the justification of art ... that beauty apprehended should have the power to illuminate the senses, still the mind, and enchant the heart." Beauty is thus a pathway to the highest state of realization in life, and because proper art manifests that beauty, it can lead to one's "own deep truth," and ultimately to the understanding that our truth is "at one with that of all being." Thus proper art has the power to bring us to a recognition of the ultimate truth of our own lives. Simultaneously, it can carry us into full recognition of our connection with others and, finally, to an experience of Joyce's "secret cause," that mysterious *something greater* that so many artists have viewed as the source of their inspirations.

Skeptico: Wait a minute! I have seen my share of paintings and plays that didn't bring me into contact with the sacred or the sublime. I have wondered, though: Was it there in the work, but I didn't see it? Could the failure have been mine, rather than something lacking in the art?

Wisdom Seeker: Great questions! It would be a grave mistake to look for guidance in everything that falls under the rubric of "art." Some art is more likely to carry one toward the state T. S. Eliot labeled "distracted from distraction by distraction"[19] than toward the sublime. On the other hand, a work of art might affect one person in a profound way while having no effect on another, so drawing a firm line between proper and improper art is impossible.

Skeptico: You mentioned Plato's praise of art, but wasn't he critical of it as well?

Wisdom Seeker: Yes, he definitely was critical of some forms; he believed that art could be dangerous. Because art is powerful it can corrupt as well as inspire. Fire can cook and fire can burn, and so it is with art. It is therefore important to learn to use it wisely.

Skeptico: Didn't Plato even say that some art should be controlled, even banned? What do you think of that?

Wisdom Seeker: Basically, if I can be so bold, I disagree with Plato. The problem is, who is to decide which works are beneficial and which are not? The power to censure, once given, has historically been abused. Censors, even if they start with good motives, tend to slide away from high-mindedness toward selecting works that suit their personal preferences, or even their political agendas. For me, a key part of wisdom is developing the ability to choose the art that will be most valuable to me at each stage of life and then to immerse myself in those waters, unimpeded by outside authority.

Most of us in the modern world are fortunate in having the great freedom to enjoy art as it suits our tastes. Wisdom suggests, however, that we keep in mind that some artistic expressions will not have a beneficial effect; will not guide us toward meaning and purpose; will not help us to discover and live a fulfilled life. Although the lines are tenuous, there is an important distinction between the energies and motives associated with various works of art, which is the reason the opinions of people we respect are valuable in helping us select the art we will pay attention to and value. In the end, though, the only workable plan I can see is for adults to decide for themselves the art that is worthy of their time and attention. So I come down on the side of freedom, for this is the only long-range way to guard against tyranny. One hopes, however, that most of us will remember that art is a powerful force that can serve ill as well as good.[a]

The Promise and Peril of Metaphor

To bring us their gifts, playwrights and poets (in fact, artists of all stripes) often speak through metaphor and analogy. Those seeking

---

[a] The issue of managing the access of children to the various forms of art is different, and very complicated. To begin that discussion would require a chapter of its own—which will not be attempted here.

"hard" knowledge find this problematic, but these tools are an essential strength. In dealing with things that are not concrete (like emotions, visions for one's life, relationships, and consciousness itself), relying on hard data by itself leads away from wisdom, not toward it. Inescapably, almost every field of knowledge rides on the wings of metaphor and analogy.

There is no way to pin down or explain in a specific way how art affects us or what a particular work of art offers. This is not a problem, however, but rather an essential part of art's value. To experience art in a meaningful way we must set aside the desire for definitive explanations and simply open to the experience it stimulates. This setting aside of explanations is a process used in many fields, including science: Newton, for example, set aside trying to understand *how* gravity worked and simply focused on measuring its effects. Much of his contribution to science would not have been possible if he had not set aside the need to know how it worked.

Skeptico: Are you saying we should never analyze works of art?

Wisdom Seeker: Not at all. Analysis has its value and importance, but is not the only method to be used for understanding. If you wish for art to help in the movement toward meaning and fulfillment, analysis must not overpower intuition or emotion; it can work with them, but must not dominate. To gain the full benefit of art and what it has to offer, it is necessary to open to what Kant called the starting point for all knowledge: imagination. By making room for creative imagination, by diving into the world of creativity and inspiration, we will sometimes be *inspired* (filled with spirit), and thereby be able to connect with the deepest truths. By letting our hearts be enchanted we increase the possibility of discovering our path to fulfillment and meaning. After the enchantment, though, it is crucial to remember another piece of Kant's advice—to temper imagination with reason. This is the only way to follow the promptings of the heart wisely and well.

Skeptico: You keep talking about metaphors and analogies but I am not sure I understand either. How do you define them?

Wisdom Seeker: Analogies are pretty straightforward: You try to explain one thing by comparing it to another. When speaking with someone who understands baseball but knows little about cricket, you compare cricket to baseball. That's an analogy. The problem is, every analogy misleads as well as informs. This is unavoidable, for analogies compare two things that are different as well as similar. In addition, each person hearing the analogy will have a different image than the speaker's. This has to be true because everyone starts with a somewhat different understanding of whatever is being used for comparison; if it is baseball, each person will have a different focus concerning what is figural about baseball. This is why analogies often lead to further questions; just listen to the stream of questions asked by a child when something new is being explained through an analogy.

Skeptico: So why do we use them so much?

Wisdom Seeker: Because it is almost impossible to convey something new without the use of analogies: The learning process of each new human being is necessarily filled with them. Nor does the essential role of analogy end with conveying new things to the young. For instance, instruction in physics, no matter the age of the instructee, has always been replete with analogies, such as comparing the regular movements of the universe to a clock, comparing the way particles affect other particles to billiard balls colliding, comparing an atom to small balls circling around a larger ball, and comparing super-strings to a musical note. All these analogies were at one time widely accepted, and some still are—although they mislead as well as inform. Or consider neurology: One explanation for how the brain works is to compare it to a computer, though the two things are quite different. These and countless other analogies in science have been helpful but have also led to misconceptions about the nature of the physical world. (Newton, to whom the "clockwork universe" concept is attributed, saw the potential problem and warned against describing his conclusions that way.)

The misleading nature of analogy is magnified when moving to metaphors, for we are no longer comparing two things but speaking as if one thing *is* the other. For instance, if I say to my love, "You are the light of my life," I am not saying she is "like" the light of my life, but that she "is" that light. But what does this mean exactly? Speaking this way carries meaning and power and significance, conveying in a few words much more than could be conveyed by a long intellectual description, but what it means is open to interpretation. Thus, when Hamlet uses a metaphor for his life, "Tis a rank and unweeded garden that has gone to seed,"[20] he wonderfully conveys a feeling state, doing so much more vividly than if he had used a string of adjectives. Creating this unexpected relationship between two things that had previously seemed different is the effect that gives metaphor its force and power, but this also leads to confusion and misunderstanding.

Yet metaphors are crucially important. They make language rich and flexible, help to explain things that would be harder to explain otherwise, and are a primary tool through which language changes and grows. For instance, if I call the thing under my hand beside my computer a "mouse," I am using a word that started as a metaphor. Then, through repeated use, it became a concrete name for a new object. It is not an exaggeration to say that many of the words in every language began as metaphors.

Skeptico: Why is this important?

Wisdom Seeker: Because we cannot escape metaphors, no matter where we turn, so we need to learn to use them wisely.

Skeptico: You gave several examples of analogies in science, but surely metaphors aren't important there.

Wisdom Seeker: They are especially important in science. Scientists seek to arrive at concrete answers, but most every attempt to describe a new discovery requires metaphor and/or analogy. How could a scientist explain something new to anyone else without comparing it to something that was already known? This is not a problem, though. Problems only come when those using or hearing a metaphor or analogy take them literally.

In its mathematical underpinnings, science rests on solid logic, but in moving from the symbols of math to ideas and images that have to do with understanding and living in the world, metaphor and analogy are indispensible. When Einstein was attempting to explain what he had understood about gravity, he said it was "curved space-time." This is a metaphor, not a logical description. Key concepts in today's physics such as "string theory," "black holes," and the "big bang" are not literal explanations, but metaphors. When someone speaks of small particles moving as "waves" or of electricity as a "current," they are using metaphors borrowed from our knowledge about water. Calling time a "dimension" is a metaphor, as is speaking of the "wiring" of the brain (a metaphor based on electricity). Darwin's use of "selection" in "natural selection" was an analogy borrowed from humans who were breeding animals and selecting for certain traits. When biologists talk about cells "signaling" or "encountering" each other, they are using metaphors based on the human experience of communication. Thousands upon thousands of metaphors and analogies have been used in science, and they have been quite valuable, but they are not hard facts or precise knowledge.

Skeptico: I think I am beginning to get why metaphors and analogies are important, but I am not sure I really understand the difference between them.

Wisdom Seeker: That isn't important. Some people think of them as basically the same, and those who make distinctions do so in different ways. The only crucial thing is to realize that both metaphor and analogy are central in human communication, from religion to art to science, as well as economics, psychology, business, and language acquisition; in fact, in every field. We acquire much of our knowledge through comparing an unknown thing to something that is known—which leads back to the importance of art. Poets and artists have developed a sophisticated understanding of metaphor and analogy through the centuries; therefore, all of us, including scientists, would do well to take advantage of their wisdom as we use these tools in every area of our lives.

Following the Guidance

Skeptico: Okay, I feel more open to the value of art. How do I take advantage of it in my life?

Wisdom Seeker: There are two primary ways:

The first is to immerse yourself in the works of others. By experiencing inspired works of art, by encountering works that are filled with spirit (*inspired* means *filled with spirit* in its Latin root), you can catch sight of the truth, beauty, and harmony moving in and through them. By opening your heart and mind to the influence of great artists, you have the opportunity to share their glimpse into what constitutes an inspired life.

Van Gogh will once again serve as a fine example. His works are enormously popular today: Why is this so? I think it is because he was able to make visible the energy and presence of that mysterious "something greater." As I stood before "Starry Night," the lower portion of the painting portrayed a village that was cold, dreary, and dead. There was no light in the church in the valley. The numinous did not reside there for Van Gogh. But the sky! The sky was filled with light and energy and power.

Van Gogh was saying without words—is saying still through his paintings—that there is something that he senses, something we can each experience for ourselves if we will open to its presence. As I stood there, open to his message, years after his physical death, the vision portrayed there awoke in me an awareness of the numinous light. Without knowing anything about his intention, I felt what he was saying—had been saying continuously for a hundred years—to everyone who was ready to see.

Skeptico: Couldn't your experience have been a fantasy on your part?

Wisdom Seeker: It could have been. How do we ever know for sure what is in the heart and mind of another? But Van Gogh's letters, which I read only later, suggest that his intent was what I experienced. Further, the words other observers have used to describe "Starry Night" resonate with mine, and such resonance is the only means we have of arriving at shared truth. Only when one person's words or images feel like they resonate as true with the experience of another is it possible to know if anything is shared: We cannot take images out of each other's brains and compare them. Thus, those of us who are moved by the image gather in front of "Starry Night" to feel the presence of the numinous energy Van Gogh captured, the mysterious "something greater" still living there.

Skeptico: You think everybody comes for that reason?

Wisdom Seeker: No, many simply look at it because the painting is famous, and they move on without feeling a trace of my experience. But "Starry Night" became famous for a reason, and I believe it has to do with the depth and meaning I experienced there. (It brings a smile to my heart to imagine what Van Gogh might have felt if he had known his painting would be viewed by millions and considered one of the most important and valuable paintings of all time.)

The second way to experience moments of inspiration is to engage in the process of creativity yourself. Find your own capacity to "drift," to touch the source of imagination and inspiration which all the great artists found. All of us, to one degree or another, are constructed with a special gear into which we can shift, a gear called "creativity." This gear is not used fully by most of us, however, perhaps because engaging with it requires much effort, and its sustained use requires a great deal of practice. But if approached in the right way, this capacity will appear and operate actively in each and every life.

Of course, some folks open to and feel compelled to express their creativity from an early age, but for many of us, it is necessary to make a conscious choice to undertake the creative process. This can be scary, though, and we resist taking the risk, bombarded by thoughts such as: "I am not good enough!" "What if others make fun of my work?" "What if no one cares, or even notices?" All rewards, however, are reserved for those who push through such fears and make the effort.

When visiting Bali, I was struck by the importance to the whole community of valuing the creative side of each person's nature. Traditional culture is intact in parts of Bali, and it is a culture that many travelers through the centuries have considered a paradise. In Bali, the people in many villages seem especially fulfilled and happy, and this is almost certainly related to the fact that each child is trained to be, and treated as, an artist. From early in life everyone is encouraged to take up an artistic form and to continue its practice. (They can switch forms, but each person is strongly encouraged to have some form of artistic expression throughout life.) The motivation for this, however, is not to encourage every child to be an artist in the sense of earning a living from art; rather, it seems to spring from a deep understanding that all humans need a means of artistic expression in order to move toward the experience of beauty and into alignment with the larger harmonies of life.

There is also an intuitive sense that encouraging the artistic side of each person benefits not only the individual but the community as well. In traveling around Bali, one sees beautiful flower decorations each morning at the entrance to many homes, which uplifts the collective spirit. There are hand-carved sculptures, large and small, all along the roads and paths. Rice fields are laid out in patterns that seem to be works of art themselves. (Have you ever seen a picture of a beautiful hillside of rice fields? There is a good chance it was made in Bali.)

The natural landscape in Bali is beautiful, but it has been enhanced by the sculpting of the land through harmonious human additions. Everyone seems to live within a framework of intentional beauty: The furniture is made not just for functionality but to add to the beauty of the space it occupies; there is everywhere a profusion of lovely paintings, textiles, and jewelry, most of which has been made locally. At the communal level, village performances of music and dance and elaborate ceremonies and festivals bring the people together frequently to share in an experience of beauty and harmony. Many places in the world have natural beauty, but in most the human effect has been to mar rather than enhance. Not so in Bali.

Listen to the Music

No discussion of art and creativity would be complete without special attention being paid to music—the most accessible and broadly shared artistic undertaking. Singing has been with us since time out of mind, often carrying performers and audiences alike into transformative and even transcendent experiences. Songs, prayers, and chants have been passed down in every culture through the centuries, through the millenniums, and some of the oldest written documents that have survived consist of these songs and chants, such as the Vedas of India.

Who knows when songs were first sung? All over the world, starting long before historic time, people have used song and chant for many purposes, including to carry them into deep experiences. Paul Newham makes the point vividly in his book *The Singing Cure:* "Throughout the world the fundamental right to vocal expression has existed for centuries in the form of communal singing. At the lakeside, in the cotton fields, in battle and in love—in the funeral procession and at the wedding feast, in the mountains of Argentina and the great gospel halls of New Orleans, singing has been the most arousing and enlivening communal activity since the earliest of times."[21]

Through the centuries, there are many ways music has been used to create powerful experiences and alter awareness. One of those is group chanting, which has been practiced for eons in Christian, Hindu, Buddhist, and many other cultures. The effect at times has been profound. French physician Alfred Tomatis described in *The Conscious Ear: My Life of Transformation through Listening* how the monks in a monastery had been dramatically impacted in a negative way when an abbot reduced the amount of time given to Gregorian chant. After the commitment to chant was reinstituted, the health and well-being of the monks returned, and the community once again began to function harmoniously.

Chanting has been extremely important in many cultures. In India, Mahatma Gandhi said of chanting a mantra, "For each repetition has a new meaning, carrying you nearer and nearer to God."[22] The modern Sufi teacher Hazrat Inayat Khan echoed Gandhi with a statement that points to the connection between chant and the "something greater" of which artists speak: "Become yourself a pure vibration beyond space. If the sound generated by the vocal chords into the vibratory network of the universe has the faculty of tuning us, it is because it links us with the cosmic symphony. The repetition of a physical sound sets off a sound current, a vibrational tidal wave. You become pure vibration—and pass on through it to the other side."[23]

Skeptico: This discussion is getting a little too mystical for me. Can you bring it back to earth?

Wisdom Seeker: Well, that last quotation suggests a fascinating connection between music and modern physics. The most prominent attempt today to explain what exists at the fundamental level involves the idea of superstrings, or M-theory, which says that the basic material of the universe is made up vibrations, not tiny objects. I have developed a fondness for string theory since reading a description by Michio Kaku (best-selling author and Professor of Physics at the City University of New York). He describes string theory as saying that tiny vibrating strings, so small that instruments cannot detect them, create matter, thus "all the particles, atoms, molecules, etc. in the universe are nothing but musical notes on vibrating strings." These tiny vibrating strings create different forms of matter by vibrating at different frequencies, like a violin string creates different notes. In this model, "physics represents the beautiful harmonies of nature … chemistry represents the melodies played on these strings … and the universe is a symphony of strings ... cosmic music resonating through eleven-dimensional hyperspace."[24] I like that.

If even that is too mystical for you, look at what is happening all over the world today in cultures where music and singing are not defined as spiritual or even as transformative tools. In such places, many are still finding ways to use music to encourage powerful experiences and to stimulate deeper states of awareness. They join choirs, form small singing groups or bands, and sing along with recordings until consciousness begins to shift (if only just a little). I sometimes wonder how many people go to rock and country music concerts to be carried "outside themselves" by the music and the dancing. Perhaps part of the popularity of concerts and bands in the modern era is because they partially fill the void left by the absence of communal music and ceremonial practices. (Concerts only partially and incompletely fill the void because ancient gatherings were guided by elders who knew the terrain being explored. Today's concerts might bring about deep states, but there are seldom guides with much wisdom available, so concertgoers are opened into an experience, then left with no guidance about how to use that experience to go deeper or to grow from it.)

It would be difficult to overstate the importance of music in human history, in the past or in the present. British composer and performing artist Brian Eno (founding member of Roxy Music and producer for U2 and the Talking Heads) understands this, and attempts in an article to give singing its full due: "I believe in singing. I believe in singing together." Citing a study in Scandinavia that found singing to be one of three activities that was likely to lead to a "healthy and happy later life," he declares (with a bit of exaggeration but also as a real truth): "I believe that singing is the key to long life, a stable temperament, increased intelligence, new friends, super self-confidence, a good figure, heightened sexual attractiveness, and a better sense of humor." Not only that, but Eno says singing with others creates a sense of community, teaching us to let go of self-centeredness for a moment and become one with other people. The result? "Empathy, the great social virtue."[25]

Creating Yourself

Skeptico: You have spent all of this time on art and creativity, but what about people like me who feel they have no artistic talent, for singing or anything else?

Wisdom Seeker: Everyone can sing! Through the eons, almost everyone in almost every culture sang, at a minimum in the ceremonies and rituals of their communities. In the modern era, with the emergence of recording stars, we tend to compare ourselves to trained singers and conclude we "can't sing." But music and song are not about such comparisons; rather, they are about opening our hearts and minds to the full experience of life.

Carl Jung spoke directly to all those who do not think of themselves as artists in his foreword to D. T. Suzuki's *Introduction to Zen Buddhism*, giving a vivid image regarding how to engage one's creative energies, artist or not. His pithy advice: "If you have nothing to 'create,' perhaps you create yourself."[26] This is something each one of us can do, artist or not. Each of us can search for the deepest inspirations we can find and bring to bear the full force and power of the creativity discovered there upon the living of our lives. Perhaps the ultimate role of art—both the creating and the experiencing—is to teach us to "drift" into states that offer guidance that will help us fulfill our lives.

Henry David Thoreau declared, "To affect the quality of the day, that is the highest of arts."[27] If he is right, no matter the level of your ability with artistic forms, you can practice "art" by cultivating inspired moments each and every day. Even if such moments are short, you can make the effort to bring those experiences into the living of your life. In so doing, your deep inspirations will move beyond the creation of physical forms and become openings to the fullest experience of life. Then, "something greater" will begin to penetrate and inform your everyday life, and simultaneously the everyday will provide inspiration for the experience of the greater harmony in which we exist. Separation will begin to fade and unity will begin to emerge. You will then be able to affect the quality of your days, as well as the quality of the lives of all those you meet.

Skeptico: You have gotten pretty far away from what I normally think of as art. Where are you headed?

Wisdom Seeker: Perhaps I haven't make it as clear as I had hoped: I am after much bigger game than simply discussing separately the importance of art, science, religion, and the spiritual in human life. The real goal is to examine how all four are interconnected pillars that support the edifice of human existence. Art, science, religion, and spirituality have had a long and rich engagement with each other. A good example of their interaction in a single life is Leonardo Da Vinci, a great artist, pioneering scientist, and dedicated spiritual seeker. Leonardo's dazzling creativity in each of these areas enhanced his ability in the others—demonstrating with special force that all these sides of a person can interact continuously and productively. Perhaps, in the end, they are not as separate as they sometimes appear. Goethe, not only a famous writer but also a fine philosopher and outstanding scientist, said, "He who possesses science and art, possesses religion as well."[28]

Finding the right relationship to each of these pillars of existence in your life is one of the central tasks of the life journey. Another is to consider carefully the company you will keep as your journey unfolds. To that, let us turn.

CHAPTER 3

IN GOOD COMPANY

Traveling has been a great blessing, providing many magical moments, as well as fresh and unexpected glimpses of the world—and of myself.

When planning a trip, the guidance of travelers who have gone before is invaluable. I study what they have had to say and search for lessons on what to see, what to avoid, and how to traverse the territory in a safe but fulfilling way. Without the accumulated wisdom of those who journeyed before me, planning a trip to a foreign land would be next to impossible.

Having absorbed their lessons (as much as possible), though, I have discovered I must then make my own way, have my own experiences. Lessons are not laws; guidance is not edict.

When young, we tend to accept the guidance of the group with which we have been encouraged to identify, absorbing and incorporating their values and meanings. At first, living within the framework of this birth culture, we feel we know what is important, how to act, the goals worthy of pursuit. Some of us stay within these guidelines all our lives; others, upon reaching the "age of rebellion," challenge some or all of the lessons we were taught. There can be value in this, for it is the first movement toward more conscious decision-making, but as teenagers we do not have sufficient wisdom to formulate a new worldview for ourselves.

For this reason, teenagers do not undertake rebellions alone; rather, they form or join groups, absorbing and adopting the group's common point of view. They are, therefore, not as independent as they like to believe, for they are once again following the ideas and opinions of others. (Notice how teenagers dress almost identically with those in the group with which they have come to identify.) Nevertheless, this is the first step toward independence, even consciousness, for leaving an old group takes courage, and developing courage is essential if one is ever to find one's own way.

Perhaps seeking one's own way is a natural part of maturation, for many cultures have steps built in to facilitate this movement—rites of passage, like vision quests, that encourage those of a certain age to confront their fears and re-imagine their futures. This incorporation of self-exploration into the developmental process, when done well, strengthens both communal connections and individuality.

However much (or little) a person has rebelled, or explored, another common point in the developmental process involves a feeling of unease about adopting anyone else's framework concerning meanings and purposes. At this point, there is a growing urge for the energy, clarity, and vitality that we sense might come from a personal and direct experience of meaning and purpose within ourselves. As Henry David Thoreau put it:

I went to the woods because I wished to live deliberately, to front only the essential facts of life, and see if I could not learn what it had to teach, and not, when I came to die, discover that I had not lived. I did not wish to live what was not life, living is so dear; nor did I wish to practise resignation, unless it was quite necessary. I wanted to live deep and suck out all the marrow of life, to live so sturdily and Spartan-like as to put to rout all that was not life, to cut a broad swath and shave close, to drive life into a corner, and reduce it to its lowest terms, and, if it proved to be mean, why then to get the whole and genuine meanness of it, and publish its meanness to the world; or if it were sublime, to know it by experience.[1]

At this juncture, though, it is not uncommon to find oneself cut off, alone—alienated from both birth culture and new groups we have joined. Then, attempts to share questions and struggles often find friends and family uninterested or even hostile to our newly emerging thoughts and feelings. No wonder it is difficult to enter upon such a journey! If one persists, however, an awakening consciousness soon discovers bountiful resources that are available for assistance: The wisdom traditions of the world, if approached in the right way, are rich in resources for undertaking just this kind of quest. In addition, poetry, literature, philosophy, and psychology from all over the world are filled with ideas and images left by those who have sought greater meaning and fulfillment for themselves.

Those who dare the deeper questions, therefore, will often experience a moment of exhilarating confirmation, a recognition of being in very good company—the discovery that many of the best and brightest through history have travelled this way before. As one finds examples of past travelers to provide inspiration and sees how their journeys were similar to one's own, another confirmation comes: the discovery that many of these exemplars had periods of alienation, loneliness, and despair, yet were able to find their way through to a meaningful and fulfilled life. Many did so in times that were at least as difficult as our own. For myself, in recognizing these things, the feeling of isolation and aloneness is dramatically lessened.

Studying and learning from past travelers is essential. Still, at some point—if we are to experience the clear air and encompassing vistas available at the summit of the mountain we humans always seem to be trying to climb—each of us must undertake the venture for ourselves, must find our own way over and through the barriers that others have faced and surmounted.

The Quest for Meaning

Skeptico: You keep talking about finding meaning and fulfillment and I assume the "clear air" and "vistas" at the top of the mountain are metaphors for that. But I am a practical person: What exactly do you mean by "meaning"?

Wisdom Seeker: At the basic level, meaning has to do with giving value or significance to some things as opposed to others. We make decisions and organize our lives by giving value to some people (our family and friends), our ideas (and opinions), and objects (our car or house versus those down the street). We respond differently to the people we feel to be significant from the way we respond to others. Consider how much weight you give to the words of one person versus another. To make decisions about how to spend your time and resources it is essential to allocate meaning—the only question is *how* you will do it, not *if*. There is no escape from giving meaning to some ideas, people, and things.

Perhaps your question goes back to the attack in the last century on the word "meaning" by existentialists such as Sartre, Camus, and Samuel Beckett. It is time, however, to recover the word, for it is quite useful. In their defense, these existentialists felt that many of those who talked about "ultimate meanings" were just promoting interests and beliefs they liked, and there was truth in this. But these attacks simply put the existentialists' values and meanings ahead of those they opposed. In the end, these attacks did not reduce the importance of meaning but merely redefined what was to be considered meaningful.

Sartre, for instance, said that being authentic was important, which is just another way of saying that authenticity has meaning. (Some existentialists went to a lot of trouble to find words to substitute for "meaning," but these word games did not do away with meaning.) In fact, Sartre's own life is a clear example of a person giving meaning to some things rather than others—such as valuing writing and the sharing of ideas, engaging with the social and political causes he cared about, and choosing to spend time with certain people rather than others. The issue for each of us is never whether some ideas, people, and things will be given meaning, but simply where and how meaning will be assigned.

Skeptico: How do I decide what is meaningful?

Wisdom Seeker: There are three basic ways: Follow the meanings given to you when growing up, join a group and follow their guidance, or set off in search of a personal experience of what is meaningful.

Skeptico: Which should I choose?

Wisdom Seeker: There are advantages to each. If you choose either of the first two options you will receive a great deal of reinforcement from the group that holds the worldview you have chosen. If you decide to undertake the third option—a personal quest—you will also find much reinforcement, but it will be of a different sort, dispensed through the writings of wisdom figures through history, as well as the many stories about them. Make no mistake, though, there is much guidance to be found for this path. Since the earliest times, illustrious souls have attempted to discover for themselves what it means to find oneself alive, here, on this planet. Many of the greatest minds and hearts in history have questioned, sought answers, tried to comprehend what the meaning and purpose of life might be. In fact, this endeavor has been at the center of the human experience.

Peering into the mists before recorded history, it is fascinating to discover how long this quest has been going on. Every culture from the earliest we know has used stories and myths to deal with profound questions about life and living. The Vedas of India; the stories of Greek gods, goddesses, heroes, and heroines; Hebrew stories of the world's beginnings; Chinese stories of the ancestors; stories from the world's early tribes—all deal with these same questions.

What is more, although most early cultures emphasized the importance of community, each carved out a way for the restless individual to leave the confines of the group to go out into the larger world—in search of a personal experience of the goal and meaning of life. (Part of the reason was likely an intuitive understanding that the individual journey is the way communities can be renewed: If everyone endlessly follows the old ways, stagnation is likely to set in and growth and change will never occur.)

Some of the earliest versions of the journey to discover the meaning of life involve exploring the farthest reaches of the inner world, as is often the case in the Shamanic traditions. One of the earliest stories of an outer journey, though, concerns Gilgamesh (from an era as long as 4500 years ago). Gilgamesh, we are told, went to the edge of the world to discover the secret of the gods, and of immortality, venturing into the unknown to discover for himself what was truly important.

Long before Gilgamesh, however, we find clear signs of this same quest, some of the earliest coming from the Paleolithic caves of Europe (as well as similarly decorated rock outcroppings in southern Africa). In both locations, paintings and drawings beginning at least 50,000 years ago suggest a questioning beyond the basic necessities of life. In order to create these beautiful and haunting drawings the creators had to go to a great deal of trouble. They had to find a dependable source of light to work in the darkness of the caves, had to built scaffolding to access spots beyond normal reach, had to create painting instruments and paints (paints that have lasted for tens of thousands of years, a remarkable achievement in itself). Whoever these people were (and we know little about them), they devoted a great deal of time and effort to the creation of this artwork.

Why did they do it? We will probably never know for sure, but I suspect it had to do with attempts to make sense of life. It is not a significant stretch to imagine that these cave artists were dealing with the questions we are dealing with still. We know for sure that our ancestors were wrestling with these questions in a very sophisticated way several thousand years ago. As mentioned before, just look at the songs of the Vedas, the stories of Homer, the teachings of the Hebrew prophets, or the writings available to us from Pythagoras, Socrates, Plato, Buddha, Confucius, and Lao Tzu. Moreover, it is clear that some of these folks, and the traditions to which they gave rise, had great wisdom. It is therefore not far-fetched to suppose that these traditions, from which we have records, form a natural continuity back through the ages, back to even earlier peoples. Those mysterious folks who drew on cave walls as long as 50,000 years ago were, after all, our ancestors. Seen in this light, it is likely that at least some of these ancestors, going back a very long time, were motivated in the same ways we are motivated today; they with trying to understand the purpose and meaning of life.

Skeptico: So what's your point?

Wisdom Seeker: That it is likely that much of human history has been about the search for meaning, has been an attempt to understand how we should live, what is truly important, and what we should value. All the world's wisdom traditions started just this way. Jesus was dealing with these issues, and the early Christians went to the desert to contemplate these same questions for themselves. The Buddha left his wife and young son to search for answers to these questions. For thousands of years wandering sadhus left their homes in India (and are doing so still) for the same reason. To grapple with the issues of meaning, values, and the purpose of life Hebrew scholars developed the tradition of studying the Torah and rabbis practiced prayer and sometimes song. For these same reasons, Mohammed began meditating in his cave, Confucius devoted his life to seeking wisdom, and native peoples everywhere developed and told their creation myths.

Other motivations (creating community, self-protection, exercising power) have sometimes played a role in the organizations spawned by the wisdom traditions, but the founders of all the traditions—and many of the best and brightest within each—have undertaken a personal quest for meaning, and their experiences have been handed down to us as the heart of each tradition.

Philosophy, Science, Art, Religion, Psychology, and More

Engagement with meaning is clearly unavoidable in religion, but it is also unavoidable in art, science, philosophy, and psychology. The decision to focus on a particular project in science, create a particular work of art, or deal with one idea rather than another in philosophy or psychology hinges on a determination of what is meaningful for a particular person at a particular time. Any decision concerning what seems worth doing involves giving meaning to one thing versus another, either consciously or unconsciously.

To make these decisions unconsciously is to respond to an impulse or to operate out of old programming. On the other hand, to make them consciously requires grappling with the core questions of human life for oneself: How should I live? What are my deepest goals? What will I organize my time around? As detailed in the previous chapters, these issues have frequently been central to art, so much so that scholar of religions Huston Smith suggests that art is "spiritual technology." He goes on to say that when we encounter great art, it has the capacity to bring us "to a different state of consciousness," at which point the world will look very different. Then, if we can let ourselves go into the largest perspective for a moment, art will have given us a glimpse of "the way things truly are," and perhaps even have transformed us into "what we might truly be."[2]

But let me not stray too far from the theme to which all the currents under discussion are ultimately related. One scientist who clearly understood that art and science are both valuable and important was Albert Einstein. Einstein played the violin all his life and conveyed frequently that music was deeply important to him, saying at one point, "If I were not a physicist, I would probably be a musician. I often think in music. I live my daydreams in music. I see my life in terms of music. I get the most joy in life out of music."[3]

Thought Experiment: Thinking As Music

What might the "greatest scientist of all time," as Einstein has been voted, have meant by saying, "I often think in music"? Could the "Special Theory of Relativity" or the "General Theory," in their birthing moments, have been conceived as music? If so, what on earth does that mean?

We will never know exactly what Einstein meant by these words, of course, but there is no doubt he felt science and music were connected and that both were central to his life. One way they are connected is through the imagination, which he considered central to both science and art: "I am enough of an artist to draw freely upon my imagination [in my scientific work]. Imagination is more important than knowledge. Knowledge is limited. Imagination encircles the world."[4] For Einstein, then, both music and science come forth in some mysterious way from the deep reservoir of the imagination, and at that level they are deeply entwined.

Moving to philosophy, the same core questions are central there as well; an overwhelming number of the greatest philosophers (Socrates, Plato, Plotinus, Hypatia of Alexandria, Augustine, Hildegard of Bingen, Aquinas, Descartes, Kant, Spinoza, Hegel, Kierkegaard, Emerson, Thoreau, Avicenna, Confucius, Shankara, Hannah Arendt and many thousands of others in every culture and every age) have asked the core questions thoughtfully and repeatedly. What is more, many of the great philosophers were scientists too, so the core questions of philosophy spilled over into science.

In fact, the core questions are at the heart of science. The search for knowledge has always and ever had as a primary motivation the urge to understand the mysteries of life—how we came to be and what life is about. As Einstein captured it, "I assert that the cosmic religious experience is the strongest and noblest driving force behind scientific research." To make his point even more vivid, Einstein went on to assert the necessity of a healthy relationship between science and religion: "Science without religion is lame, religion without science is blind ... a legitimate conflict between science and religion cannot exist."[5]

In contrast to Einstein's view, some modern materialists such as Daniel Dennett and Richard Dawkins argue that science can answer all the important questions. But this has not been the belief of most scientists through history, and it is not the view of most scientists today. Einstein is representative in recognizing the importance of grappling with the core questions in the effort to discover what a fulfilling life might be:

> The most beautiful emotion we can experience is the mystical. It is the power of all true art and science. He to whom this emotion is a stranger, who can no longer wonder and stand rapt in awe, is as good as dead.[6]

Einstein even went so far as to say that the ultimate goal of the human journey is to arrive at a point where we "know that what is impenetrable to us really exists, manifesting itself as the highest wisdom and the most radiant beauty."[7] He said it is for this reason that:

> Humanity has every reason to place the proclaimers of high moral standards and values above the discoverers of objective truth. What humanity owes to personalities like Buddha, Moses, and Jesus ranks for me higher than all the achievements of the enquiring and constructive mind.[8]

Skeptico: What about psychology? You haven't said much about it.

Wisdom Seeker: I guess that's because it seems obvious that understanding how to live a fulfilled life is central there as well. In modern times, of course, much of psychiatry and psychology has been focused on managing mental illness and altering dysfunctional behavior, but neither of these is possible until a society has established an understanding about how people should live, how they should behave, and what constitutes mental illness. All these issues go right back to the core questions.

Skeptico: Are you saying modern psychology doesn't really understand what mental illness and dysfunctional behavior are?

Wisdom Seeker: That which is considered dysfunctional varies greatly from place to place and different cultures handle such things in very different ways. Some tribal peoples look at things we call dysfunctional as signs that a person is going to become a shaman. In

India, mental illness is understood very differently and can be a sign that a person is moving toward a holy life. In several cultures, those we consider mentally ill are welcomed by the community and seen as able to enrich the community as a whole.

In her book, *Mind, Modernity, Madness: The Impact of Culture on Human Experience,* professor Liah Greenfeld of Boston University argues that the major forms of mental illness in the modern world were much less common or even unknown in most earlier cultures, and therefore are, to a great extent, a product of our culture. Specifically, the modern world makes it difficult for individuals to develop meaning in their lives and to create strong and healthy identities, the consequence of which is more—and more severe—mental illness.

Skeptico: How does this relate to the core questions you were talking about?

Wisdom Seeker: I'm just trying to show that answers to the core questions lie at the heart of the practice of psychology and psychiatry, even the medical and behavioral forms. It is only on the basis of a belief about how people should live and how they should behave that a psychologist or a psychiatrist can practice in those professions. Working answers must be in place before a psychologist or psychiatrist can function. Of course, the answers might have been arrived at through enculturation, or even indoctrination into the field, but they must be in place. When the answers have been acquired through enculturation or indoctrination, though, the practitioner will not understand how arbitrary they are, nor the positive potentials that staying within one's inherited model hides from view.

Skeptico: Are you suggesting that dealing with mental illness is the same as searching for a fulfilled life?

Wisdom Seeker: It can be, although dealing with dysfunctional behavior precipitated by physical causes is not the same as a quest for meaning. But in societies too quick to label human questioning as "mental illness," deeper issues and healthy possibilities can be overlooked or overridden. Sometimes those who are struggling, asking questions, trying to break out of dysfunctional worldviews are labeled as "mentally ill" by unhealthy cultures. Extreme cases include Stalin's Soviet Union and Mao's China, but less extreme examples can be found in current cultures, where those who are struggling to find their own way, those who are questioning the views of the people around them, are ostracized or even given drugs to force them to fit in. If Liah Greenfield's analysis is correct, the extensive use of drugs to treat mental illness will not succeed and we will never find the "magic" drugs some keep predicting will cure most mental illnesses. At times drugs can be a blessing, but for many mental health issues we must look to culture, identity, and meaning if we are to turn back the rising tide of mental illness in the world.

Of course, many psychologists and psychiatrists understand that mental well-being is dependent on coming into a healthy relationship with the core questions, and much of psychology goes beyond the disease model, often far beyond. Studies show that a high percentage of those who consult psychologists in the modern world do so in an attempt to discover how to live a more fulfilled life; they are trying to decide how to spend their time and where to focus their attention—issues in the domain of meaning, purpose, and values.

Behaviorists and their offspring tend to take a fairly narrow view of these things, and some psychiatrists are primarily focused on the use of drugs, but many branches of psychology and psychiatry take a broader view. These include, according to Ken Wilber, all the branches of depth psychology, such as "psychoanalysis, Jungian, Gestalt, phenomenological, existential, and humanistic—not to mention the vast number of contemplative and meditative psychologies, East and West alike."[9] In other words, much of what we think of as psychology is concerned with an attempt to answer the important questions, the very questions that have always been at the heart of the quest for meaning.

Carl Jung is a good example of a psychiatrist who took a broad approach. In his later years, after a lifetime of working with thousands of individuals, he came to a startling conclusion: "A psychoneurosis must be understood, ultimately, as the suffering of a soul which has not discovered its meaning."[10] If Jung is right, the implication for psychology is profound, for he is suggesting that behaviors and thoughts that mess up our lives often constitute a call to search for greater meaning. If so, then psychology's great task is to help us overcome our suffering through the discovery of what is truly important; to help each of us find what we are called to do with the time and energy of our lives. In this light, neurotic suffering should not be seen as something to be feared but rather as a motivation to find how we can escape from our stuckness; how our life energies can be better applied. When seen in this way, difficult issues become allies that can help us discover what is truly worthy of our time and attention.

Skeptico: Given my difficulties, accepting my suffering as valuable is a little hard to do. Mostly I just want to run away from it.

Wisdom Seeker: Most of us feel that way a lot of the time, and I am certainly not suggesting that you create difficulties or suffering for yourself. But one only has to observe the lives of others for a short time to see that it is impossible to avoid all difficulties and suffering. Therefore, when it comes, we might as well try to find a way to use it for a positive end.

Skeptico: How do I do that?

Wisdom Seeker: Acknowledge as honestly and fully as possible what is actually going on. As you do this, you will find yourself increasingly able to let go of neurotic suffering—the unnecessary suffering created by resistance and denial. Difficulties will still come, and you will still have pain, but you will not be adding unnecessary, neurotic suffering on top of the pain.

The next step is to ask: What can I learn here? If you do this sincerely and commit to working to change what can be changed within yourself, you will gradually be able to grow in response to the difficulties.

Skeptico: That sounds great, but very abstract. Can you give me a practical way to do it?

Wisdom Seeker: Examine your stories about yourself and the world and notice which ones are negative. Most of those negative stories are not true. We have a strong tendency to create negative images about what might happen when things aren't going the way we had hoped, yet most of our negative images don't materialize. I have awakened in the night many times with a minor ailment and in that groggy state had dramatic images of what was wrong with me and how badly it might turn out. Most of us do the same thing in waking life, in all kinds of situations. If, however, you can recognize your negative stories and gradually release them, you will find yourself able to respond more fully to whatever is actually going on, and you will be able to use the situation to grow and develop.

This is precisely the hero's quest as described by Joseph Campbell in *The Hero With a Thousand Faces*; it is the heroine's journey as told by Maureen Murdock in her book, *The Heroine's Journey*. If you can muster courage and determination and release the negative stories your mind has created, you will be able to move forward on your journey, guided by the lessons of the heroes and heroines of all time.

Thought Experiment: Playing With the Questions

Think back to a time when the core questions were alive for you and invite them back into your awareness, perhaps during a hike, or sitting by the ocean, or while on a leisurely drive. Just be with them, treat them as old friends you have not visited for a while. Catch up with them; see where you are in relation to them at this point in your life.

The Necessity of Others

Taking the core questions seriously will sometimes involve going one's own way, looking at things differently from the masses (in Thoreau's words, listening to a different drummer rather than marching in lockstep with the crowd). In short, it means entering upon an individual journey. There is a paradox involved, though, for such a journey also involves others. Anyone who sets off on an individual path must have, at least at the beginning, others who encourage and inspire, people who recognize there is a journey to take and who can point in the direction of the trailhead. Later, when lost, others are needed for help in resetting the direction and avoiding new pitfalls. Everyone gets lost at times; those who already know the way have become guides. (Sorry Skeptico—I don't think anyone can avoid all the pitfalls.)

In this journey, there are stretches of going it alone but there are also times of sharing—as all the fairy tales and the lives of actual heroes and heroines make clear. Everyone needs someone at times. Moreover, no journey begins in a vacuum; rather, each begins in a cultural milieu, within a context that gives that particular journey definition and meaning. Most figural journeys of human history began when questioning was in the air and when there was a broadly shared sense that something new was needed, or emerging. The Buddha set off at a time when thousands of others were asking the same question with which he wrestled: How does one get off the unsatisfactory wheel of rebirth? Jesus began in a time of great ferment, with people like John the Baptist challenging the prevailing views of the time. Socrates was asking questions and forging ideas in the wake of the societal disruption caused by the Peloponnesian War.[b] The stories of Confucius, Mohammed, and many other famous men and women are similar.

In recent centuries, many examples can be found in which individuals came together to consider, debate, and grapple with the boiling issues of their time and place. Groups of people gathered in cafes and drawing rooms in Europe during the seventeenth, eighteenth, and nineteenth centuries—debating and discussing art, literature, science, and the meaning of life, setting in motion new ideas and great change. In Russia in the eighteenth and nineteenth centuries, salons sprang up where men and women gathered to discuss the great issues and to attempt to understand the crucial questions of life and living. In New England in the eighteenth and nineteenth centuries,

---

[b] The war between Athens and her allies versus Sparta and its allies between 431–404 BC, which resulted in the defeat of Athens. The Greek historian Thucydides considered this the most momentous war in Western history up to that time.

Transcendentalists such as Emerson and Thoreau sparked discussions in public forums and private parlors about how best to live. From these kinds of discussions grew the Chautauqua movement, in which people gathered in town halls and town squares all over America to hear speakers and discuss important questions.

Individuals played important roles in all of this, but equally crucial was the general tumult and synergy of the interactions. For individual growth to take place, others are necessary for stimulus and guidance, and sometimes to point out where the individual has taken a wrong turn. This is likely the reason Jewish scholars for millennium have used discussion with each other to explore how best to live and rabbis have served as guides for those embarking on the journey. Christianity is filled with stories of debate as well as with the creation of various methods for guidance such as spiritual direction. In medieval Japan, Buddhist monks made journeys to other monasteries to discuss and debate the most essential questions—to sharpen their own understanding and to learn from others (a practice that continues to this day). Wandering Sufis have done the same for centuries across the Middle East. This impulse to share and to be inspired by others is a major part of every wisdom tradition and is a crucial part of every quest for meaning.

Skeptico: You make it sound like everybody is on this quest.

Wisdom Seeker: In a sense, everyone is, but there is a significant distinction to be made—some have undertaken it consciously while others are less aware of how it is playing out in their lives. Those who are following the answers given by their culture, definitely seek meaning—but they might think they have already found it. Perhaps they have. Many cultures apply a good deal of pressure on members to do this: pressure to go along with the accepted values and meanings, to avoid making waves, to live without questioning what is given by family, community, tribe, or religion.

This is not all bad, for everyone must learn to live within a culture of some kind; we are, after all, social creatures. Further, for humanity to continue to exist in a form recognizable to us, cultures are essential. Even more, the ability of a culture to function depends upon the effectiveness with which it can persuade (or force) members to "stay on the bus," to stay at least somewhat on the path that most everyone else is following.

Skeptico: Well, should they stay on it?

Wisdom Seeker: There is no one answer. Anyone who feels deep down that life is rich and meaningful, that the path they are on is leading to a fulfilling and complete life should probably keep doing what they are doing. Those, however, for whom a gnawing question begins to peek around the corners of their lives, who begin to wonder—"Is this all there is?" or "Is what I was taught really true?"—those who feel the movement of these questions should probably begin a more conscious search. And certainly, anyone who is beset by the modern diseases of depression, despair, and alienation would be very wise to undertake a quest for meaning.

Doing so, however, is seldom easy. Those who begin questioning within a culture must find a way to deal with the sometimes intense pressure to accept what has been given as right and true. They must also find others, either within the culture or outside, who can provide guidance and support for new directions. On the other end of the spectrum, those who are alienated from traditional answer systems often find it hard to undertake a quest for meaning because of the relentless attack in some intellectual circles on the possibility of finding meaningful answers to life's questions. The postmodern vogue is skepticism and irony, which leads to self-absorption and/or nihilism. Instead of valuing the quest for meaning, modern culture often suggests everyone settle for immediate gratification. For those who do not feel this is enough, the frequent reply is: Get even more wealth, power, or fame and you will be happy.

Skeptico: I am pretty attracted to wealth, power, and fame. What are you trying to tell me?

Wisdom Seeker: Just that if you ever feel an urge to find your own way, to grapple with deeper questions rather than settling for easy answers or immediate gratification, you are in very good company. If you ever feel inclined to begin a quest for meaning rather than just seeking more of the same old things—take heart, for the heroes and heroines of all time have made this same journey before you.

Skeptico: Do you ever have any doubts about this journey?

Wisdom Seeker: Having discovered so many people through the centuries who have trod this path before, I no longer question its value and importance. Rather than doubting my interest, I am more likely to wonder: "How can it be that so many are comfortable giving little time and attention to issues of such central importance to the human experience?"

Skeptico: If I decide to begin, what is the best way?

Wisdom Seeker: As far as I can tell there is no "best way." This quest has been conducted in many ways through the centuries, including through a life in art, a life in science, through adherence to a religious tradition, and through the formulation of an individual spiritual journey. Each has value, so follow the path that seems right for you, while at the same time remaining open to lessons from those who followed each of the other paths with sincerity and determination.

Skeptico: Okay, but I especially want to know how science fits in with this journey you are talking about.

Wisdom Seeker: All right, let us turn to the lessons of science.

CHAPTER 4

THE WAY OF SCIENCE

I remember the day the Soviets launched Sputnik. That man-made shooting star changed the world. As it happened, I was headed toward a science class when the news came, and the teacher immediately began shifting our life-dreams and ambitions toward science and engineering. This was an instantaneous, spontaneous happening all over the United States, as if a memo went out to science teachers across the land to encourage students to study science—a collective shift of major proportions. Large numbers of us began to take up the challenge.

It is hard to imagine today, but science and engineering were not very popular careers in the United States before Sputnik. Thereafter, many of the best and brightest headed toward lives not envisioned a short time before and university departments, fueled by government grants, mobilized for the growing influx of students.

Who could have guessed the results of that one small rocket and the tiny payload it carried? (Small by today's standards, that is.) I wonder how many discoveries and inventions of the last fifty years came as a result of the commitment to science and engineering that arose from the feeling that "we" had fallen behind "them." (This is a marvelous example of unintended consequences; spurring a powerful commitment to science in the United States was not the outcome the Soviets intended.)

Alternative histories are tricky: They are easy to create, but likely to conform to the prejudices of the person doing the creating. I do wonder, though, how the world would be different without the response in the United States to that small rocket and satellite, and what they came to symbolize.

Science, of course, existed for thousands of years before Sputnik. In fact, there were many periods of intense scientific development before the modern era. Aristotle initiated one such wave over twenty-three hundred years ago and that wave has crested at various times on many different shores.

Even before Aristotle, however, humans in every age and every land were hearing some version of the following story, the story of how our questioning minds have led to much of what we think of as civilization:

Once upon a time a child wondered: "What makes the stars shine?" Another saw a problem and said: "Someday I will find a solution to that problem and life will be better for my people." And when that young boy grew to be a man, when that young girl grew to be a woman, solve problems they did. A new vaccine was created and a disease was eradicated; a new kind of bridge was developed and travel time between destinations was significantly shortened; a better type of food crop was propagated and fewer people went hungry; an advanced machine was designed and a back-breaking job became easier; a new theory was proposed and a better understanding of the workings of the world spread among all those who wished to know. From all these efforts came new modes of transportation, new ways of communication, improvements in agriculture, and new ways of treating disease.

The world of today is built on scientific and engineering advancements in design and construction of buildings, bridges, cars, and airplanes; on new communication systems; on the continuing improvement of tools, gadgets, and devices; on increasing knowledge about cells, organisms, and the human body; on the penetration of the secrets of the atom; and on the discovery of new ways to use materials (and even how to create new ones). The list, of course, could go on and on.

Is there any area of human endeavor that has filled practitioners with more dedication, solved more problems, inspired greater creativity, or called forth more effort than science and its close companions: engineering, mathematics, and technological innovation? These ways of engaging with life, propelled by the drive to know and discover, have affected humankind profoundly since our beginnings. No wonder some observers have suggested that what it means to be human involves our ability to create and use tools more extensively than any other species.

The Beginning of Science

The roots of the tree of science go very deep and the motivations for science, art, and religion are closely entwined, as suggested by Einstein's words (as quoted earlier): "All religions, arts and sciences are branches of the same tree."[1] Equally close are science and philosophy; in fact, they lived in the same house until modern times. (Until less than two hundred years ago scientists were called natural philosophers.) Science and philosophy spent all those years together because they grew from the same soil—human questioning and the search for wisdom. This search is at the heart of being human and encompasses all branches of inquiry, and it goes back in history as far as one cares to look. For example, thousands of years ago the Hebrew Bible proclaimed wisdom as "better than rubies," saying that "all the things that may be desired are not to be compared to it." In the Book of Proverbs, Wisdom (Sophia) is a person who says that she was with the creator from the beginning, "I was by him, as one brought up with him: and I was daily his delight, rejoicing always before him."[2]

Wisdom has always had an exalted place in Judaism, so it is not surprising that for a very long time study has had a central place in that tradition. Starting with study of the Torah and the Talmud, a commitment to learning branched out to embrace study in many fields, including science. In this way, the spiritual quest of Judaism became a major building block of science. No wonder the proportion of scientists of Jewish descent far exceeds their percentage in the overall population today. One of the greatest gifts of Judaism to humankind has been its delight in knowledge and its unending search for wisdom.

This urge for wisdom moved from Judaism into Christianity, with countless Christian scholars trying to understand the world and our relationship to it. As in Judaism, there was study of the sacred texts as a spiritual practice—*Lectio Divina*—growing out of the same insight and longing as Torah study. Spilling out from this practice, though, came the desire for wisdom in many areas. Consequently, many of those who created the scientific revolution were monks, priests, and scholars working within and for Christian institutions.

In Every Land

The longing for wisdom has burst into bloom at many times and in many different places. When tribal cultures overran Rome and destroyed a great deal of its civilization, much of the knowledge of antiquity was saved and enhanced by the Christian empire centered in Constantinople (and by its scholars in Alexandria). When this empire eventually fell, so much would have been lost had not the scholars of Islam been committed to maintaining and advancing knowledge and wisdom. Centers of scholarship in the Islamic world continued the task of collecting and cataloging the works of Greece and Rome, maintaining magnificent study centers and libraries to house these works, along with their own. Eventually, hundreds of years later, as this wisdom began to find its way back into Europe, one of history's greatest explosions of creativity, discovery, and learning occurred: the Renaissance.

Do not think for a moment, however, that this influx of knowledge from the Islamic world was a rote transfer from classical times. On the contrary, many new and expanded ideas developed during hundreds of years of Islamic research and study, especially in math and science—ideas that form the bedrock of modern mathematics. The modern world owes a great debt to Islamic cultures for the development of the decimal system, the concept and use of "zero" (Roman numerals were letters), and the Arabic numbering system (1, 2, 3, and so on, instead of Roman letters as numbers, such as XXVIII for 28). Crucially, the Roman system basically maxed out at 3999, so in order to write 1,000,000, one had to put a line over M (one thousand—the line meaning multiply M by M). The use of that line meant you basically had to do the calculation in your head. To grasp the difficulty, try to multiply 3983 by 2787 in your head or try to write 897,563 in Roman numerals. If we were still using Roman numerals today, science and commerce as we know it would be impossible.

Another fascinating feature of good ideas is how, for thousands of years, they have found a way to spread around the globe. It is easy to see how this happens with the communications of today, but this sharing has been with us for a long time. As an example, the three important mathematical concepts discussed above first appeared in India, but were then blended with Greek and Roman ideas and developed into a coherent system by Islamic mathematicians. Islamic scholars, by borrowing and creating, made numerous other important contributions to scientific knowledge. Al-Khwarizmi laid the groundwork for algebra and found methods to deal with difficult mathematical problems such as complex fractions and the square root. Ibn al-Haytham wrote the first modern treatise on optics, collecting and expanding knowledge from ancient sources. His work played a major role in the development of telescopes, the magnifying lens, and eyeglasses. Other discoveries in chemistry and medicine poured into Europe from the Islamic world, providing valuable fuel for the scientific revolution.

Of special importance, this outpouring of scientific knowledge in Islamic cultures arose mostly in harmony and cooperation with religious and spiritual currents. In Islam, as in Judaism and Christianity, study of the world frequently went hand in hand with spiritual scholarship, for both types of study were often motivated by the same urge:

to find the deepest truths. And in all three traditions, scientific and spiritual scholarship was frequently carried forward by the same people, those driven by a desire to know the world but also wishing to discover the meaning of life within it.

It has been the same for thousands of years all over the globe. In China, Confucius taught that practical knowledge, cultural values, and spiritual understanding exist as an intertwined whole and his ideas gave rise to a system of scholarship that led to many scientific insights. Science in China, though, began long before Confucius: He was merely continuing an ancient tradition. In fact, science began there long before anything resembling science appeared in Europe or America. I remember walking through an exhibit entitled *China: 7000 Years of Discovery*, and thinking over and over, "I didn't know that was discovered in China" (a few "trivial" things like the compass, paper, printing, gunpowder, rockets, and many astronomical devices). In another category, under the influence of Taoism, China developed methods for preventing disease and promoting health that rival the work of modern medicine—and this wisdom is increasingly being incorporated into the medical practices of the West today.

Then there is India. There is now evidence that large and complex cities existed in India as long as 5000 years ago,[3] and I remember reading that the number of books published through the centuries in India is as numerous as all those produced in Europe and America combined. I don't know if this is literally true, but what is certain is that India has a vast number of books in almost every field, rivaling that of the West, with many containing scientific knowledge. There is, in fact, a special title reserved within Hinduism for the dedicated seeker of wisdom, *pandit*, and for a very long time Indian pandits have been seen as carriers of both scientific and spiritual knowledge.

Or consider *jnana yoga*. Although many in the West think of yoga as primarily dealing with the body, jnana yoga concerns the development of wisdom and is considered by many to be the noblest yogic path. This ties in with the idea of the seven *chakras*, a central Hindu system of thought and spiritual development. The highest chakras involve wisdom that arises in the practitioner through a direct connection with the Source, and many believe one cannot reach the Divine fully and completely without opening to the influx of that wisdom. Needless to say, then, for thousands of years in India the relation between science and spiritual knowledge has been mostly cooperative rather than conflictual.

One special strength of India (and Asia in general) in the search for wisdom has been a centuries-long focus on the workings of the human mind. Many individuals, especially within the traditions of Hinduism and Buddhism, have focused vast amounts of time and attention on the inner world and the nature of consciousness. Therefore, as East and West have increasingly met,[c] one of the most valuable lessons for the West has been a greater understanding of the mind through studying the insights accumulated through the ages by the "inner astronauts" of the East. A good example is Siddhartha Gautama, who came to be known as the Awakened One, the Buddha, precisely because he felt he had awakened to a deep understanding of how the mind works and how it creates our perceptions of the world. Furthermore, he arrived at this understanding because he had committed his life to the effort to find for himself the greatest wisdom available to a human being.

Continuing since the Buddha's time, thus for 2500 years, Buddhism has focused on inner wisdom: wisdom about the mind, how to work with emotions, and the nature of consciousness itself. It is not surprising, then, that as physicists have increasingly concluded that consciousness is a core component of reality, Buddhist concepts have become increasingly useful in understanding these inner realms. The rich world of Buddhist psychological insight is today helping researchers gain a better understanding of the human mind.

Another corner of the globe that pursued wisdom for a very long time is what we in the United States think of as Latin America. It is fascinating to discover that, long before the "Latin" conquerors, the

---

[c] Sorry Kipling, I have to disagree with your thought that "East is East, and West is West, and never the twain shall meet."

Incas of Peru developed numerous varieties of crops that we still use today, and created buildings of a grace and beauty equal to anything the world has ever known. Visiting the marvelous remains of this highly advanced civilization, I was deeply struck by the combination of harmony, precision, and grandeur of Machu Picchu and Sacsayhuaman—to this day we cannot figure out how they built these magnificent buildings. And returning to a central theme of this book, the achievements of the Incas came about in a society in which science, art, religion, and spirituality were intertwined and harmonious.

This review could go on and on, of course, to include Egypt, with its vast and intricate pyramids built thousands of years ago; Persia; Mesopotamia, and so many more places. But the crucial point is simply that in all these cultures, scientific developments were not separate from the search for wisdom, nor separate from religious and spiritual currents. As in Judaism, Christianity, and Islam, the urge to know was, in all these cultures, part and parcel of an intertwined spiritual and scientific search, with each supporting and sustaining the other in countless ways.

This inevitably means that to understand science we must recognize that it developed and flourished hand-in-hand with spiritual and religious currents in countless cultures over thousands of years. This pattern is universal because the deep urge that fuels the spiritual search fuels science as well: a desire for wisdom. This urge is at the very heart of being human and has continued to call many of us to its service to this day. Einstein once again captures the idea beautifully: "I maintain that the cosmic religious feeling is the strongest and noblest motive for scientific research."[4] Looking at the world of his time and the difficulties that many religious movements had fallen upon, he even concluded: "In this materialistic age of ours the serious scientific workers are the only profoundly religious people."[5]

A more recent spokesperson for this unifying vision is Peter Russell, who studied mathematics, theoretical physics, experimental psychology, and computer science before turning to philosophical pursuits. Writing about how his quest for wisdom began, he said:

I have always been a scientist at heart. As a teenager, I delighted in learning how the world works—how sound travels through the air, why metals expand when heated ... how plants know when to bloom ... how spinning tops keep their balance ... and why the sky is blue. I had a passion for knowing, an insatiable curiosity about the laws and principles that govern the world.[6]

This urge led Russell to study science, then to explore philosophical and spiritual questions, and finally to his attempts to reconcile all these currents in a harmonious way.

Science and Art

Skeptico: You got my attention a little while ago when you said that no field has inspired greater creativity than science, especially since you had just been extolling creativity in art. So which is it: Does art or science inspire greater creativity?

Wisdom Seeker: Good question, worthy of a thought experiment.

> ### Thought Experiment: Which Has Inspired Greater Creativity?
>
> Think of the countless creations of art and then of the countless discoveries of science through the centuries. Which would you say has spawned the greatest creativity, art or science?

Skeptico: Sounds like a trick question; tell me what you think.

Wisdom Seeker: True, it was kind of a trick question, for the creativity of each has been so vast that there is no way, and no need, to decide between them. In the same way that there is no need to decide which is more beautiful, violin or piano music, no decision is necessary concerning the degree of creativity inspired by art versus science. Although they are sometimes seen as opposites, and even as being at odds, nothing could be further from the truth. Both science and art have inspired the best in human creativity and we have benefitted enormously from both. On the surface they may seem different, but underneath they have much in common: Both are driven by a desire to discover, to create, and to communicate what has become known; both ride on metaphor and analogy; both advance, to a great extent, on intuition.

No surprise, then, that genius in both fields has often resided in the same person; to return to an earlier example, Leonardo Da Vinci was creative in art, science, and engineering. The various sides of his creativity interacted continuously, cross-pollinating each other. Just one example: He experimented throughout his life with scientific ways to improve the materials and paints used in his artistic endeavors. During the Renaissance, many others did the same, to the point that art was a driving force in the advancement of science during that time. Significant resources were directed toward improving paints, colors, and surfaces on which to paint, which served as a major motivation and source of funding for the development of chemistry and the science of materials.

Besides the effect of technical advances (new paints, canvases, colors, cameras, computers), science has impacted art through inspiration—just walk through any museum of art today and notice the number of images inspired by science and technology. Further, there have also been significant shifts in ways of understanding the world, ways that originated in science but eventually took up residence in art.

The effect of science on art has been great, but the influence also runs the other way, from art to science. Art historian Eliane Strosberg makes the point that for thousands of years artists have been central figures in various areas of science and for an equal length of time science has influenced art through its discoveries. In the modern age, Strosberg says, the influence of science on art has been especially strong, so much so that abstract art owes its origins to science.[7] And in *Art & Physics: Parallel Visions in Space, Time, and Light*, Leonard Shlain presents many examples that show how art seems to have foretold, and sometimes influenced, scientific breakthroughs.[8]

In these and many other ways science and art have forcefully impacted each other for eons, probably all the way back to Paleolithic times with the cave and rock art of that era. Examples fill books, such as *Exploring the Invisible: Art, Science, and the Spiritual*, which records many instances in which art and science dramatically impacted each other.[9] In *Einstein, Picasso: Space, Time, and the Beauty That Causes Havoc*, Arthur I. Miller traces the influence of aesthetic theory on the development of Einstein's ideas. Miller also highlights a fascinating synchronicity: Both Einstein and Picasso were working simultaneously at understanding time and space in a new way, suggesting that the unfolding of both art and science in any age are mutually influenced by the broader currents of that age.[10]

Art and science share another distinct similarity: They both frequently and continuously use metaphor and analogy. To communicate something new, the one wishing to communicate is forced to compare the new thing to something the listener already understands. This has dramatic consequences. In *Making Truth: Metaphor In Science*, Theodore L. Brown demonstrates how science became dependent upon metaphor a very long time ago, building its very structure of understanding upon that foundation.[11] This happened because scientists had to use images to visualize for themselves the concepts they were exploring and they also had to use images to convey those concepts to others. The images they chose, however, influenced their thinking. The way a scientist—or anyone—visualizes a question or problem has a tremendous impact on the solution that will be conceived. As physicist Alan Lightman explains: "In doing science, even though words and equations are used with the intention of having precise meaning, it is almost impossible not to reason by physical analogy, not to form mental pictures, not to imagine balls bouncing and pendulums swinging."[12]

In other words, metaphors and analogies do not simply explain but are formative in the scientific process—once chosen, the images affect the process, the images chosen affect the ideas that can be conceived as solutions. For instance, comparing the universe to a clock brings up quite different solutions than comparing it to a field of energy; comparing the brain to a computer brings up a different set of ideas than comparing it to a hologram, or an orchestra, or a television set receiving signals; choosing an image related to war creates a different scientific outcome than selecting an image related to romance. Note, however, that the images chosen by scientists to think about their work are not scientific, rational, or logical; nonetheless, these images greatly influence the solutions that arise to the problem being considered.

Getting at this in another way, physicist David Bohm points out that science works with theories, and the word *theory* in Greek has the same root as *theater*. A theory takes a "view," presents one interpretation about what is going on, helping scientists to organize information in a manageable way. But in order to provide a coherent view, some things must be left out. Because of this, one of the greatest philosophers of science in the twentieth century, Karl Popper, went so far as to assert that every scientific theory is a myth, a story about how things fit together. All this has led some researchers to suggest that one function of the mind in developing scientific theories is to serve as a reducing valve, to filter out enough of the available information so that a theory can present a coherent picture, a picture simple enough to provide a degree of clarity in understanding the world. (This is true of all theories in every field.) The result, however, is that significant information is left out of every theory, and the information that has been left leads to anomalies—inconsistencies that cannot be explained by the theory.

Skeptico: Given all the problems with metaphors, maybe scientists should stop using them.

Wisdom Seeker: On the contrary, they are essential. The only way scientists can think and talk about their concepts is through images that they and their audience can grasp—in other words, metaphors and analogies. Because they are essential to communication, these tools cannot be dispensed with, but this means that the descriptions can never be precise or firmly fixed. Metaphors and analogies, however, can always be made *better*, which leads us back to art. Artists (including poets and writers) have been working with metaphors and analogies, perfecting their usefulness for thousands of years, so art is the human enterprise that has the most accumulated wisdom in working with images, metaphors, and analogies. Science, therefore, can learn much by studying the methods of art in this area.

Art and science, therefore, have much in common and much to learn from each other. Perhaps at the quantum level they are closer than we have yet conceived. One of the greatest physicists of all time, Niels Bohr, put it dramatically: "We must be clear that when it comes to atoms, language can only be used as poetry. The poet, too [like the physicist], is not nearly so concerned with describing facts as with creating images."[13]

Science and Philosophy

To emphasize again a key point: In most cultures, art, philosophy, things spiritual, and science were not divided into isolated boxes. Rather, science and art were frequently good friends, philosophy and the spiritual domain mostly lived together, and science and philosophy were the closest of all—were in the same immediate family. For thousands of years, science was part of philosophy. Gradually, though, as the philosophic stream became more distinct from the spiritual, the two moved into separate houses, and science had a choice to make. It chose philosophy, and in Western culture became a member of philosophy's house until modern times.

The only way to understand science today, therefore, is to keep these close connections in mind, especially that science arose from philosophy and became a separate field only recently. When the scientific revolution began its modern journey in the sixteenth and seventeenth centuries, all the central figures were philosophers *as well as* scientists (and all had a deep interest in spiritual questions too). Even as the separation began to occur, the motivation to do science overlapped intimately with philosophical and spiritual issues: How did this world come to be? What are the rules by which it operates?

Where did those rules come from? How do we know what we know and how do we determine whether what we think we know is right?

In one form or another, these questions still provide the core motivations for science as well as philosophy. Noted economist and best-selling author E. F. Schumacher called the search for answers to these questions "science for wisdom." He observed, however, that in early modern times a much narrower view of science began to take shape: investigating the material world in order to use it for human pleasure, comfort, and convenience. Schumacher called this "science for manipulation."[14]

Skeptico: What's wrong with wanting to make our lives more pleasurable and comfortable?

Wisdom Seeker: There is nothing wrong with science for manipulation—as long as those who use it keep firmly in mind that it cannot answer the broader questions of life or make good decisions about its own actions.

Skeptico: What does that mean?

Wisdom Seeker: There is nothing within science for manipulation to guide it in using its discoveries. For instance, it built the weapons with which Hitler conquered Europe and carried out the Holocaust. It has delivered chemical and biological weapons to many bloodthirsty rulers. It has created enough bombs to destroy the planet several times over and it has spawned so many polluting devices that the planet might someday be unable to sustain human life.

Science for manipulation is simply not capable of making value judgments about what is good or bad, for it is willing to serve terrorists and tyrants as fully as it is willing to serve what Lincoln called the "better angels of our nature." It therefore cannot be left to its own devices in deciding how its discoveries will be used. A science organized around manipulating the material world for human ease and pleasure does not have the capacity to make good decisions about whose pleasure will be served, or how, so decisions will tend to be made by those who have the most power. If science for manipulation becomes the organizing point in a society, everyone starts to look out for "Number One," or for his or her own tribe at the expense of everyone else.

This is where science for wisdom comes in, with its roots in philosophic and spiritual soil. It is only science for wisdom, in connection with its past relations, that is capable of providing healthy guidance with regard to issues like how scientific discoveries will be used, the values that will guide scientists, and the priorities for science that will be chosen. For example, will the present generation use its scientific abilities to preserve or deplete the Earth's resources? Will we use the Earth's bounty for fun, pleasure, and comfort today, even if it is at the expense of all those who will come after? In response to such questions, science for manipulation stands mute. In fact, decoupled from philosophic and spiritual guidance, science for manipulation creates as much harm as it does good. Perhaps more.

Skeptico: So how do I draw a line between these two sciences?

Wisdom Seeker: Drawing a clean line between them is not easy, for they overlap. Yet there is a crucial distinction to be made: Science for wisdom takes into account values and meanings, the ultimate goals of life. It takes into account the ancient motivation of science, which was to discover answers to the deepest questions of life and living. By staying in touch with this pole star, science for wisdom can play a full and beneficial role in the human drama. Science for manipulation, on the other hand, has nothing within itself to keep it from being used to crush those with whom a person in power disagrees, and it can easily be used in the acquisition of wealth in a way that is harmful to other people and to the environment. Unrestrained by ethics or compassion, it can easily be used for torture, criminal activities, and the suppression of everyone's rights except those of the most powerful.

In spite of this, some materialists, physicalists, and naturalists have advanced the notion that a materialistic science should be the sole arbiter of truth; they have asserted that all questions of value and meaning must come under their sway. This usually takes the form of an assertion that all the important questions must be answered by science because nothing except physical stuff exists. They go on to argue that because science has been so successful at solving some problems, all problems must be placed under its patronage. This, however, is like asking a fine hockey player to perform heart surgery—there is a confusion of categories. Having skill in one area does not indicate ability in another.

The irony is that science set off on its course with the clear goal of focusing only on the physical world, leaving other issues like values, meanings, and beauty to others, others to whom scientists accorded great respect. As science succeeded, however, materialists saw an opportunity and asserted that anything that could not be found and studied by science did not exist. This is the heart of the split between science for wisdom and science for manipulation. No matter their assertions, however, the materialists really had no answer for the fact that the tools and methods of science, developed to focus on the material world only, were not suited for dealing with what is good, the experience of beauty, or what is meaningful. The tools of science are simply not suited for choosing beneficial goals and purposes of human life because they were not developed for that function.

Therefore, in the areas of values, meaning, and aesthetics, when materialism and science for manipulation alone are tasked to provide answers, unintended consequences proliferate, and no answers come. In the absence of a broader perspective, irreplaceable rain forests are destroyed, weapons of destruction proliferate, traffic jams clog cities, oceans are poisoned, the air becomes ever more toxic, deserts overtake and consume habitable land, and human life becomes increasingly meaningless and empty. This is what many artists have been trying to tell us with the dark images they have thrown at us in science fiction novels, comic books, computer games, and movies—making clear that the ascendency of science for manipulation is not bringing forth a better world, but a dark shadow of that world. (Huston Smith's *Forbidden Truth* and Schumacher's *Guide for the Perplexed* forcefully present the problems of a materialistic science attempting to do things it cannot.)

The Limits of Science Alone

Skeptico: What alternative do you suggest?

Wisdom Seeker: That philosophy, "science for wisdom," and the world's spiritual traditions work together in dealing with societal issues having to do with values and meanings. The answers provided through the centuries by these three close relatives have not been perfect, but in cooperation they have provided the best approach we have found for discovering how to live in a fulfilling way. Most scientists know this, for as Ken Wilber has pointed out, all the physicists who developed relativity and quantum theory—"the crown jewels of twentieth century science"—came to an essentially mystical view of reality. "Individuals such as Albert Einstein, Werner Heisenberg, Erwin Schrödinger, Louis de Broglie, Max Planck, Wolfgang Pauli, Sir Arthur Eddington—the vast majority of them were idealists or transcendentalists of one variety or another."[15]

These physicists and many great scientists before them adopted a transcendental view because they understood that scientific discoveries by themselves could never answer the ultimate questions about life. They recognized that the nature of the universe is such that more is required than what scientific experiments and mathematical formulas can provide. The great British astrophysicist Arthur Eddington put it this way: "We have learnt that the exploration of the external world by the methods of physical science leads not to a concrete reality but to a shadow world of symbols, beneath which those methods [the methods of physics] are unadapted for penetrating."[16]

Skeptico: So you don't think that physicists will be able to answer our broader questions about life as they understand the quantum world better?

Wisdom Seeker: Not likely. In the early twentieth century there arose the hope that physics, with its incredible sweep of success in explaining many things, would eventually explain everything. But that has not been the case. Rather, the tables have been turned—the deeper physics has gone in exploring the material world the more it has found that some things, such as consciousness, escape its grasp. This, in turn, has led a number of physicists to the conclusion that consciousness is itself the source of the material world. For instance, Nobel Laureate Eugene Wigner observed: "It is not possible to formulate the laws of quantum mechanics in a fully consistent way without reference to consciousness."[17] The point he is making is that quantum theory says that for a physical object to exist as an object, there has to be a subject, a consciousness separate from the object that is observing it. Otherwise, the wave function has not collapsed and the potential object does not yet have a physical reality—only a potential existence. Therefore, consciousness is necessary for an object to take on actual existence, and this consciousness cannot be located in the material realm.[18]

Skeptico: So you don't think the answer to the puzzle of consciousness will come from the quantum level?

Wisdom Seeker: There is no way to know for sure, but the signs are not positive. Nobel physicist Niels Bohr, one of the founders of quantum mechanics, dismissed the possibility, saying: "We can … find nothing in physics or chemistry that has even a remote bearing on consciousness."[19] Another of the greatest minds in quantum mechanics, Werner Heisenberg, went further: "There can be no doubt that consciousness does not occur in physics or chemistry, and I cannot see how it could possibly result from quantum mechanics."[20] Thus for Bohr and Heisenberg, physics will never account for consciousness, although perhaps both would agree with Wigner on the reverse point: that consciousness is necessary to account for physics.

Given these emerging limitations of science with regard to significant questions, it is somewhat ironic that a number of religious leaders in the modern world are trying to recruit science to their cause, are trying to use science to prove their religious views. But science can never prove the validity of any worldview or belief system, for it does not encompass the whole picture; it was designed to study matter and not whatever lies beyond the realm of matter. Science alone cannot provide answers to the broad questions of life and living. In *Quantum Questions,* Ken Wilber quotes several leading scientists regarding the problem of using science to resolve these issues. Their answers are similar. Albert Einstein: "The present fashion of applying the axioms of physical science to human life is . . . entirely a mistake."[21] Sir James Jeans: "Speaking as a scientist, I find the alleged proofs [about philosophical questions] totally unconvincing."[22]

Nobel Prize-winning physicist Max Planck was another great physicist who thought long and hard about these issues, and came to a rather startling conclusion about why science cannot solve fundamental questions by itself:

> As a man who has devoted his whole life to the most clear headed science, to the study of matter, I can tell you as a result of my research about atoms this much: There is no matter as such. All matter originates and exists only by virtue of a force which brings the particle of an atom to vibration and holds this most minute solar system of the atom together. We must assume behind this force the existence of a conscious and intelligent mind. This mind is the matrix of all matter.[23]

His view corresponds, of course, to many ancient wisdom traditions and the understanding that consciousness gives rise to—lies behind— the world we know. Arthur Eddington agrees completely in *Science And The Unseen World,* noting that many physicists of his time were beginning to look for answers in the only place "where more might become known," the starting point for the whole process of understanding itself, "human consciousness." This, he says, is the only place to look for deeper answers—the reason being that "the stuff of the world is mind stuff." In other words, the place to look for ultimate answers, "which science is ... unable to give" is consciousness. It is only in consciousness that "we find other stirrings, other revelations ... than those conditioned by the world of symbols."[24] (Math and physics always work with symbols, so his point is that neither can penetrate behind their symbols, for that would no longer be science.) Joining in this conclusion is mathematical physicist Roger Penrose, who states his position emphatically:

> I am arguing for some kind of active role for consciousness [in physics], and indeed for a powerful one. Consciousness, for me, seems to be such an important phenomenon ... it is the phenomenon whereby the universe's very existence is made known.[25]

And in an interview, Max Planck summarized the clear conclusion from this train of thought:

> I regard consciousness as fundamental. I regard matter as derivative from consciousness. We cannot get behind consciousness. Everything that we talk about, everything that we regard as existing, postulates consciousness.[26]

If this is true, it makes vivid why science must work with the other members of its family tree—philosophy, art, religion, and spirituality—if it is to successfully approach the most important questions about life and living. The reason is crystal clear: These branches of human understanding have focused for millennia on exploring the nature of consciousness. The contributions science can make to the broader questions of life are dependent upon its embracing once again its broader role as science for wisdom, which involves reintegration with the other members of its family tree.[d]

Skeptico: Okay, I like being in the company of Einstein, Planck, Eddington, Jeans, Wilber, Huston Smith, and E. F. Schumacher, so I'll stop looking toward a narrow science for answers to my meaning and

---

[d] There will be more on the relationship between science and consciousness in Chapter Eight, but to explore science's relationship to other fields for yourself, look at Ken Wilber's *Quantum Questions*, John Hedley Brooke's *Science and Religion: Some Historical Perspectives*, and Mario Livio's *Is God a Mathematician?*

value questions. But a lot of recent books say there is an unbridgeable gap between these fields that you are calling close relatives.

Wisdom Seeker: Some do argue that these family members have become irreconcilably estranged, but this need not be the case. I believe they can—they must—live in harmony and cooperation if any one of them is to reach its full potential. The recent view of an irreconcilable conflict has been so prevalent, however, it might be helpful to explore more fully the history of that conflict. For that, turn to the next chapter.

CHAPTER 5

Science Versus Religion?

Outside the large bay window in my dining room, a bird feeder silently and patiently calls together a community of birds to attend it—perhaps as a grove of trees, a spring, or a rich meadow called together a community of my ancestors. Once, as I sat writing, a shimmering-red cardinal attacked the glass in the window. It was pecking madly, as if engaged in the fight of its life. Perhaps it was.

Carl Jung described how each of us spends enormous amounts of energy fighting the projections of our own minds. Like a movie projector, our minds constantly throw images onto the people and situations we encounter. Our inner film superimposes on the world images of *our* wounds, *our* fears, *our* unmet needs. No wonder we encounter the same problems over and over as we move through our days; often what we are fighting is an image projected onto those we meet by our own minds—like the cardinal at the window, attacking its reflection, engaged in the fight of its life.

Although much ink has been poured into describing the conflict between science and religion, there remains great confusion about the nature of this "battle." Much of the confusion comes from a failure to distinguish between four concepts that are related (that are sometimes used interchangeably), but which have significantly different meanings. To better understand these concepts and the relationship between them, here are my working definitions. (Definitions are never "definitive," of course, because they vary between persons and in different times and places, but the following are the most useful ways I have found to think about these four concepts.)

1. **The Spiritual Dimension:** Having to do with ultimate concerns. To engage in exploring the deepest questions about existence: What is truly important? How can I experience that which is most important? Does my life have a meaning? What is the underlying nature of reality? What is the best way to spend the moments of my days? All the world's wisdom traditions have grappled with these questions and all offer suggested answers. Their answers vary, but all have these conclusions in common: (a) life has a meaning beyond personal desires and whims; (b) some values are grounded in an "unseen order" that lies beyond personal preferences; (c) there is a higher good beyond self-centeredness; and (d) true fulfillment comes from living in harmony with that higher good. Because all religious traditions share these broad conclusions about the nature of the world, these agreements provide a foundation for understanding what "spiritual" means, and anyone who seeks answers to these questions is being spiritual.

2. **Religions:** Religions provide specific answers to the spiritual questions as well as guidelines for how one should live in attempting to be in harmony with those answers. In other words, a religion is a set of answers about the nature of ultimate reality and the best way to live in relation to that reality. Religions can be comprehensive or narrow, rigid or loose, but each religion provides answers about the basic questions of life and living. In this broad sense, communism, an authoritarian political movement, or materialism can become one's religion—forming the core organizing belief system for a person or a group. (It is usually more useful to limit the definition of religion to only those systems that speak of a transcendent reality, however.) Finally, some people consciously choose the religion they will follow, while others simply follow the one they were taught or the one the powerful people around them assert to be true.

3. **An Established Religion:** An organization created to teach, promote, and enforce a set of answers, including beliefs, practices, rules, and prohibitions. As a religion becomes an Established Religion, rules and procedures come into being beyond the spiritual questions, having to do with the functioning of the organization, including how it will maintain and perpetuate itself. Thus many rules and procedures that do not speak to spiritual questions, but deal with how an organization will function in the world, build up over time within Established Religions.

4. **A Dominant Established Religion:** This is an Established Religion that has become dominant in a culture and taken on the role of justifying and enforcing some of the culture's rules and beliefs. A Dominant Established Religion will always have many rules that strengthen its position in the culture and help it perpetuate itself and its power. Significantly, some of these rules, involving its worldly role, will be quite different from the original message the founder or founders of the religion articulated.

> **Thought Experiment: Discerning the Difference**
>
> Identify examples of each of the four in your own culture, and then in another culture you are familiar with somewhere else in the world.

Centuries of Cooperation

In light of these definitions, the concept of a "battle" between science and religion can be considered in a fresh and valuable way. In the modern West, the battle story is usually seen as beginning with the scientific discoveries of the sixteenth century, discoveries that called into question the Earth's place in relation to the Sun. The scientists who made these discoveries, however, were not "battling religion"; they were deeply religious men who did not disavow their religious beliefs because of the new discoveries. On the contrary, they sought knowledge of the universe as a means of knowing the Divine plan more fully and completely. For instance, Copernicus (often credited with beginning the scientific revolution with the publication of *On the Revolutions of the Celestial Sphere* in 1543) was a canon in the Church and dedicated his book to the Pope. Johannes Kepler, who made the calculations demonstrating how the planets revolved around the Sun, was a deeply committed Christian. His writings reveal that his chief aim as a scientist was to discover how the Divine was reflected in the harmony of the universe.

Then there is the story of Galileo Galilei, the "father of modern science," and his fight to publish his ideas. His struggle, quite rightly, has been held up as an example of a Dominant Established Religion opposing the advancement of scientific knowledge. But in using Galileo as the premier example of a battle between science and religion, it is often overlooked that he did not question the existence of a spiritual dimension nor did he question the truth of his own religion. He did not even question the religious beliefs of the Established Religion of his time. Rather, he questioned a specific view about the *material world,* and it is fascinating to note that many of those who opposed him were the scientists of his day.

Galileo was a religious man, a friend of Pope Urban VIII, and in no way did he intend his ideas to challenge "religion" or "the spiritual" in some broad way. What he wished to do was to persuade his scientific colleagues—whose theories had been incorporated into the cosmology of the Church—to abandon the Ptolemaic/Aristotelian view that the Sun revolved around the Earth. The Roman Catholic Church, however, had become the Dominant Established Religion in his part of the world and had acquired the power to resolve political and scientific disputes. For this reason, Galileo made numerous efforts to persuade the Pope and the Pope's advisors that his research indicated a new and more accurate picture of the universe. Simultaneously, scientists holding the old view tried to persuade Church authorities and the Pope to condemn Galileo's ideas.

Galileo was also an ambitious man, and he had a fierce desire to be recognized for his accomplishments. (As a scientist, he also wanted to bring the scientific and theological understanding of his time into harmony with the facts he was discovering.) The interesting thing is that, although he was challenging a *scientific* idea, he turned to the Dominant Established Religion of his time to resolve the issue because it was the arbiter of truth in his society. But scientists who opposed him did the same, making clear that this was not a battle between science and religion. Rather, this was a very human affair involving individual failings, and Galileo was one of the main culprits. So too was the Pope. Thus the story of Galileo is not primarily an example of a battle between science and religion but rather a cautionary tale about the dangers of a Dominant Established Religion extending its reach too far. And it is an example of the problems created by arrogance—in this case Galileo's. It is also a cautionary tale about how inaccurate myths can come to dominate perceptions and, in the process, produce a distorted image—in this case suggesting that Galileo's science was at odds with "religion."

The all-too-human part of the story starts with the fact that Galileo was a brilliant but also grandiose man who made enemies quickly and frequently. Interestingly enough, for many years one of his key supporters was the man who finally agreed to put him on trial, Pope Urban VIII. Also illuminating, the book that eventually led to his condemnation, *Dialogue Concerning the Two Chief World Systems*, was published with papal permission and with formal authorization from the Inquisition. That permission, however, was based on Galileo's agreement that he would present Copernicus's view—that the Earth moved in perfect circles around the Sun—as one among several options for understanding the movement of the heavens. This was, in fact, what the most advanced scientific evidence of the day supported, for the Copernican theory could not be proven when Galileo published his book. (At that time, no one had been able to measure the stellar parallax involved, and without that information, several different theories could have been correct. Furthermore, there was no way for anyone to know in a scientific way which was correct.)

Another factor that is often ignored in the modern tale about Galileo: Pope Urban VIII had a fairly sophisticated understanding of astronomy, and he specifically gave Galileo his approval to present the Copernican theory (that the Earth moved around the Sun) as the most accurate way known at that time to measure the movement of the heavens. The one condition he insisted upon, however, was that Galileo not present this theory as final and proven "Truth." And, since the Pope's position was supported by the best science of the time, his actions were not those of a person engaged in a religious battle with science but, rather, those of someone in authority trying to balance several points of view while maintaining his own power. Confirmation of this comes from the fact that many within the Church hierarchy were sympathetic to Galileo and his position. The Jesuits had begun presenting Copernicus's heliocentric view as one alternative for calculating the movement of the heavens, and some key cardinals were open-minded about this issue. The powerful Cardinal Roberto Bellarmino wrote that if the Copernican/Galilean view was proven, then the Church's interpretation of the Bible would have to be changed to accord with that proof.[1] And another Cardinal, a friend of Galileo, was steering the Church toward Galileo's position. This cardinal, Cesare Baronio, was in fact arguing that science should have the last word in such matters, and is reported to have said to Galileo: "The Bible teaches us how to go to heaven, not how the heavens go," a phrase that Galileo later used to justify his position.[2]

All this indicates that the true story is very complex, with Galileo asserting something beyond the facts available to him and beyond what he could prove (as seems to have been his tendency). Scholars examining his records have discovered that at times he would come to a view of how he thought things worked and then treat his insights as if they had been demonstrated by actual experiments—when they hadn't. Insofar as his theory of how the planets and Earth moved in relation to the Sun is concerned, it turned out to be wrong in at least two important respects.

First, he thought that the orbits of the planets were circular and uniform. But they are not circular (they are elliptical), and Johannes Kepler had written to Galileo providing strong evidence for elliptical movement long before Galileo took his stand. Galileo, however, refused to listen. He liked circular orbits, not because of scientific evidence, but because (it seems from his notes), he liked the idea of symmetry in the heavens. He thought this was how God would do things; he thought he knew how God would act, so he ignored Kepler's evidence.

The second way in which Galileo was mistaken is that he believed that the ocean tides were caused by the Earth's rotation around the Sun. This was, in fact, in his view the strongest proof that the Earth rotated around the Sun. But this idea was not correct (the tides are caused by the moon), so Galileo's strongest "proof" for his view was false. All in all, then, he did not know, or have proof, about how the solar system worked.[3]

One more example of Galileo's bull-headedness concerns the fact that he completely ignored the ideas of another great astronomer of his time, Tycho Brahe. Brahe had a theory to explain the movement of the heavens that several key astronomers had accepted. Galileo, though, liked his own theory better, but had no evidence to refute Brahe's view. Rather than dealing with this honestly in his book, he simply acted as if Brahe's theory did not exist, asserting that there were only two possible ways to understand the movement of heavenly bodies—the old Ptolemaic/Aristotelian view and the Copernican/Galilean one.[4]

None of this is meant to take anything away from Galileo's brilliance or to diminish his substantial role in developing a new and more accurate view of the heavens. It is meant, however, to show that Galileo's ideas were not the main reason for his troubles, and to make clear that his story does not primarily concern a battle between science and religion. Rather, Galileo was the victim of his own personality and the way it became entangled in the power struggles of his day.

Vivid confirmation of this comes from the fact that during this same time frame, Kepler published extensive mathematical proofs showing that the planets moved around the Sun (with elliptical, not circular, orbits), and he was not condemned or tried.

The political component of this story involves the terrible and bloody Thirty Years War that was raging throughout Europe between Protestant and Catholic countries (and factions within countries) during this time. The Catholic Church, as a Dominant Established Religion, was deeply involved in the war, and it was taking an increasing amount of the Pope's time and energy. Although he respected Galileo's brilliance and had defended him numerous times, the Pope increasingly felt there were more important issues going on in the world, and he became increasingly frustrated with the distraction Galileo was causing. Thus, as leading figures of the scientific community and one branch of the Church hierarchy pressed an attack on Galileo, the Pope finally relented and ordered him to stand trial.

Skeptico: Wait a minute! I thought the scientific community supported Galileo in his fight against the Church.

Wisdom Seeker: Not at all. During this period only a small group of thinkers and scholars had adopted the Copernican view that the Earth revolved around the Sun. Galileo was part of a distinct minority, and they were opposed by the majority of the scientific community as well as most of those who taught in the universities. Radicals like Galileo were roundly criticized, dismissed, or ignored (not unlike the way anyone who advocates a departure from the conventional view is treated today). Thomas Kuhn, in his book *The Structure of Scientific Revolutions,* documents how those with new ideas are often treated badly by the scientific establishment, and in *The Copernican Revolution* he makes clear that this was a significant factor in Galileo's fate. Kuhn captures the mainstream scientific view of Galileo's time (that the Earth could not possibly move around the Sun), by quoting a leading intellectual of the time, Jean Bodin, who said, following Aristotle, that when things find a place "suitable to their natures," they "remain there." In this regard, Bodin said:

No one in his senses or imbued with the slightest knowledge of physics, will ever think that the Earth, heavy and unwieldy from its own weight and mass, staggers up and down around ... the Sun.[5]

It is hard for us to grasp today that the mainstream view of that age was that the Earth was fixed and that the Sun moved. Come to think of it, though, doesn't the direct empirical evidence, the evidence given by our senses, tell us that the Earth is fixed and that it is the Sun that moves around us? Look up at the sky: What do your senses suggest to you about which is moving? Furthermore, every normal person's direct empirical evidence was then, and is now, just the same. (So much for direct empirical evidence in this matter!) What this means is that it is only a theory supported by obscure evidence (into which we have been enculturated, into which everyone has been enculturated) that keeps us from believing that this massive Earth, which stretches to the horizon in every direction, is moving around that bright, but not very big, ball in the sky.)

Skeptico: Are you saying you don't believe the Earth circles the Sun?

Wisdom Seeker: I believe that it does, but not because I have any personal experience that indicates that to be the case. In this, I trust my enculturation, not the experience of my senses. If I relied on my senses, I would have to side with Jean Bodin. But don't distract me from Galileo: When his book was published he had managed to insult and alienate almost everyone, and understanding this is necessary to explain what happened next. When the book came out, it was discovered that Galileo had put the views of his friend and protector, the Pope, into the mouth of a character portrayed as a fool.[6] This was the final straw for Pope Urban VIII. With this affront (and I suspect feeling a bit overwhelmed by all the conflicts going on about him), he finally acceded to the demand that Galileo be tried. This was a mistake, but a mistake by a person feeling betrayed by a difficult genius that he had supported and tried to defend. Thus, in the midst of a long, drawn-out war, probably feeling vulnerable, the Pope gave in to political pressure and brought Galileo to trial.

After the trial, the story again plays out somewhat differently from the modern myth, with images of imprisonment and deprivation lingering about. When the trial ended Galileo was 69, and his "imprisonment" was to stay as a guest with his friend, the Archbishop of Siena, for a few months. After those months, he returned to his own villa to live out the remainder of his years under "house arrest." But this was not "arrest" in the way we understand it today. He was cared for by his daughter in his villa, received many friends as guests, and continued his work. Importantly, he created a major book during this time, *Discourses and Mathematical Demonstrations Relating to Two New Sciences*. This became one of his most important contributions to science, receiving high praise from many, including Albert Einstein. This book, in fact, written while he was under "arrest," is one of the primary reasons Galileo is frequently called the "father of modern physics."

Skeptico: So are you saying that the Church was blameless?

Wisdom Seeker: No—just that this was not so much a battle between science and religion as a battle over scientific ideas in which a Dominant Established Religion had unwisely taken upon itself the role of resolving scientific conflicts. For a Dominant Established Religion to have a position of authority with regard to scientific ideas is a lousy idea that causes harm both to science and to the Dominant Established Religion. From the scientific side, such an approach adds a layer of bureaucratic authority that hinders the quest for truth. In terms of the interests of religious organizations, having this kind of worldly power is spiritually corrupting. Furthermore, constructing religious beliefs on scientific ideas is a precarious platform upon which to build, for scientific ideas are always changing. As Sir James Frazer, author of *The Golden Bough* said a century ago, the theories of science are always being replaced by new theories, and there is little doubt that "brighter stars will rise on some voyager of the future … than shine on us."[7] Not a very good base on which to build a religion.

The story of Galileo is thus a cautionary tale for all religions, suggesting that they should avoid assuming power in the scientific arena, and avoid trying to make scientific decisions, a role for which they are ill equipped. It is also a powerful lesson in the dangers of tying religious beliefs to specific scientific findings, for science does not speak to questions of meanings and morals. Science is not the kind of ground upon which to construct answers to spiritual and religious questions, for the views of science are constantly changing; this is to build your religious house on sand.

The Lessons for Science

The story of Galileo is also a cautionary tale for anyone involved in enforcing the "orthodox" view of science at any time and place, for science advances on changing views and sometimes-controversial ideas.

Skeptico: So who is supposed to uphold the "right" answers in science?

Wisdom Seeker: Very good question. For science to function, there has to be a broadly shared understanding of the "best answers we have right now." This necessity, however, creates a tendency for those in authority to become rigid in upholding the current answers—which can stifle new ideas. Consider the conflicts that are going on today within various research establishments and university departments. Those in authority often feel they must maintain the orthodox view when mavericks challenge established ideas. In this sense, Pope Urban VIII is like a department head or project leader who is trying to reconcile opposing sides. This situation exists all over the world right now, and it is not uncommon for mavericks to lose scholarships, grants, jobs, and even reputations when they challenge the prevailing views. (The stories are legion of those who have been dismissed or ridiculed, but later proven right, in every academic discipline, including science.) Therefore, rather than use the story of Galileo as an example of science overcoming small-minded religion, it would be much more useful if the defenders and admirers of Galileo would use his example as an inspiration to discover and overcome attachment to the orthodoxies within their own ranks, orthodoxies that are stifling creativity and holding up new discoveries in science today.

To facilitate this open-mindedness, a better understanding among those in authority concerning how science advances would go a long way toward helping everyone take advantage of the lessons of Galileo's experience. The scientific method is important—it is helpful in verifying insights and determining which new theories are best. In *The Scientific Adventure*, however, Herbert Dingle (who was president of the Royal Astronomical Society in Britain) takes issue with the idea that this is the way new discoveries are made. Instead, he suggests that the belief that science advances through the scientific method was created by "logicians unacquainted with the practice of science," and that, when the scientific method is actually compared to how scientific discoveries are made, there is "scarcely a single instance in which there is the slightest resemblance."[8] In other words, the organized methods of science consist mainly of principles by which the existing mainstream ideas are continually reconfirmed "by those who already know them." His book then presents compelling evidence that the scientific method has little to do with how new breakthroughs occur. During his long career, Michael Polanyi, who did important work in physical chemistry, economics, and especially the philosophy of science, came to a similar conclusion.

According to Dingle and Polanyi, then, scientific breakthroughs are explained after the fact in ways that are quite different from the way they first arise (when non-linear, non-systematic intuitions are often the key factor). Galileo is a perfect example of this: His frequent use of thought experiments rather than actual experiments led to intuitions that revolutionized science, and his fierce determination to support his intuitions against the prevailing orthodoxy was an important factor in his ultimate success. He was sometimes wrong in his intuitions (even the intuitions of geniuses are sometimes wrong), but he was right often enough to accomplish much and to affect the course of scientific history.

It would therefore seem that the main lesson his story suggests for those in authority in science today is the importance of making room for the mavericks—even finding ways to encourage them in exploring their radical intuitions—while still upholding the conventional views as long as they are useful. Mavericks sometimes, of course, are supported, but all too often, mainstream views become sacred totems, scientific theories become rigid, and taboos are enforced against new ideas, taboos that can only be breached at great cost to a maverick's career (at least in the short term).

Then Came Newton

A wonderful example of how scientific breakthroughs actually occur involves Sir Isaac Newton and his theory of gravity. Newton did not go through an organized series of steps or build his theory on the basis of accumulating facts. Rather, he had a flash of insight into a problem and then postulated a series of axioms (assumptions) that gave him a way to explain his insights. The prevailing view of the time was that an object had to physically touch another object in order to have an effect on it. When Newton suggested otherwise, another great mathematician and philosopher, Gottfried Wilhelm von Leibniz, quickly challenged him, asking, in essence, "How can one body affect another at a distance?" To this question, Newton had no answer; his theory could not explain the "how" of gravity, and because of this he was ridiculed, even mocked for the preposterous notion of a mysterious "action at a distance." In the face of this challenge, he was never able to explain in a logical way how he had arrived at his theories or why they worked. The only response he could make to his challengers was that his theory worked; that he could make accurate calculations with it—calculations that predicted how objects would actually behave.

The challenges to Newton persisted for a while, but as others began to make calculations using his theories, everyone began to discover that in fact the theories worked, so his ideas were accepted.

He was forced, however, to abandon his explanations for *how* gravity worked (which troubled him until the end of his life). To this day, no one has been able to explain *how* gravity works. And Newton's axioms did not rest on proof, but on intuitions. Furthermore, paradigms change; today quantum theory has called much of Newtonian physics into question.

A modern attempt to explain gravity involves Einstein's "curved spacetime." But "curved spacetime" is a metaphor, not a logical explanation. Further, this metaphor does not correspond with Newton's ideas about gravity, instead positing a different understanding from the one Newton envisioned. We are thus left in the strange position of continuing to use Newton's theory without understanding how it works, while at the same time accepting as true a more modern notion that challenges key concepts in the Newtonian theory we are using. Is this rational?

There are many, many other examples of how scientific breakthroughs have proceeded along a path inconsistent with the linear scientific method; instead, a deeper sense of intuitive knowing is almost always involved. The modern scientific revolution was launched partly by a dream (which led Descartes to his life work and therefore to his contributions to the creation of modern science). Not only did Newton's great insight about gravity come as an intuitive flash, but Einstein's first glimpse of relativity was based on an intuitive insight as well. Einstein, in fact, is widely quoted as saying: "I believe in intuition and inspiration. Imagination is more important than knowledge."[9] This is not new, of course; Aristotle helped launch Western science with the belief that intuition was the source of all new knowledge.

A few more examples: August Kekule von Stradonitz's idea for a new theory of molecular structure was, according to one expert, "the most brilliant piece of prediction in the whole history of science."[10] How did he do it? He turned his chair toward the fire and dozed, and in the ensuing dream the idea came to him.[11] Nikola Tesla, in a vision central to the creation of the modern world, said the idea for an electric motor came to him in a flash as he walked across a city park. French mathematician Jules Henri Poincare reported that on two occasions major breakthroughs came to him "from thin air." And Niels Bohr joins this parade with his report that his model for the structure of the atom, for which he won the Nobel Prize, came to him in a dream. (Numerous other examples can be found in Herbert Dingle's *The Scientific Adventure*, Willis Harman's *Higher Creativity*, and Arthur Koestler's *The Act of Creation*.)

Even Darwin's core idea did not develop over time; rather, on a day he was relaxed and away from his workplace, riding in a carriage, he reports: "I can remember the very spot in the road ... when to my joy the solution occurred to me."[12] And in *Quantum Questions: Mystical Writings of the World's Great Physicists*, Ken Wilber documents how all the founders of modern physics, as they explored and were changed by the mysteries of the quantum world, developed intuitionist and even transcendental views about the nature of reality.

The crucial point of this review is that discoveries in science, as with those in art and the spiritual realm, arise primarily from flashes of insight, which means that these three fields are not as separate as they are sometimes portrayed. Science is at times logical, linear, and empirical—it often uses what we think of as the scientific method— but at its creative edge it does not proceed in this way. Arthur Deikman puts the point succinctly: "The scientific method is employed for verification rather than for discovery."[13] No one knows how insights or intuitive flashes happen or where they come from, which makes some people uncomfortable, but this does not change the fact that this is how creativity in science actually occurs. As Isaac Newton put it, "Truth is the offspring of silence and unbroken meditation."[14]

To emphasize again, the scientific method is important—in verifying insights and sorting out the best ideas from the less valuable and the less accurate. But even this does not separate science from spirituality, for there are sophisticated methods to verify spiritual insights as well. These methods are, in fact, absolutely essential in overcoming fantasy and delusion in the spiritual domain: All the wisdom traditions have developed ways for elders—those who have integrated a tradition's wisdom, such as Zen masters, Christian spiritual directors, Rabbis, Hindu and Sufi teachers—to confirm or reject the insights of those practicing within the tradition. Confirmation can also come from a "felt sense of rightness" that people experience in the presence of someone who has had a deep spiritual understanding, someone who has been able to incorporate that understanding into how he or she lives.

These verification processes in the spiritual realm are not perfect, but neither are those in the scientific arena. As Thomas Kuhn made vividly clear in his works, inaccurate ideas can be "verified" by the scientific establishment for decades, even for centuries: Like the belief in parts of Europe for several centuries that the earth was flat, in spite of earlier knowledge to the contrary; the belief that persisted for decades that germs did not cause disease, even though Louis Pasteur had made a strong case that they did (he was actually greeted with a firestorm of derision when he proposed his theory); the view that continued for generations that giant meteors had not struck the earth (in spite of dramatic evidence that they had); or the ridicule directed toward a young, obscure Australian physician who, only twenty-five years ago, suggested that bacteria were a primary cause of ulcers (which is now accepted as true, but not without a fierce fight). That inaccurate theories can be "verified" for long periods of time becomes easier to understand through an insight of William James: In considering what actually goes on when someone claims that something has been objectively shown to be true, James realized that the "conviction that the evidence" that has been accepted "is of the real objective brand," is not itself objectively verifiable, but is simply "one more subjective opinion."[15] In other words, there is no objective evidence to indicate when the evidence one has accepted actually proves something; whether the evidence is sufficient is strictly a subjective opinion.

A similar phenomenon is at work in art as well. New insights and creations are confirmed or rejected over time by the "felt sense" of those who respond or do not respond. As in science, the learned opinion of the day can be quite different from that which develops over the longer run—the works of countless artists have been panned when first produced, only to rise, years later, to great pinnacles of acceptance. Thus another similarity: In art, science, and spirituality, deep insights are frequently unrecognized by the broader community within which they first arise, and often have to wait years for acceptance.

Skeptico: What is this "felt sense" you keep mentioning?

Wisdom Seeker: It is a deep experience of "this feels like the right answer to me," or "this feels like the solution to the problem." What I am trying to describe is quite different from what we normally think of as feelings. A "felt sense" goes much deeper than normal feelings; it is more like a strong intuition. A felt sense is not just a thought, nor is it just a bodily sensation. It is a strong sense of "Yes, this is right," or "No, this is not right." This kind of felt sense does not eliminate thought or sensation but includes a deep experience of giving value that goes beyond thought and sensation. Importantly, this deep experiential sense is active in every area of life: A scientist has a gut feeling that she is on the right track, a businessman has an instinct about how best to guide his company, a physician has a quick insight into what is wrong with a patient, a mystic has a profound spiritual awakening, and an artist creates a work of art from a vision. All involve this deep sense of knowing.

Thought Experiment: A Time You "Just Knew" Something

Think of a time that you felt like you just knew the answer to a problem, or something you should do—or should not do.

Discussing these kinds of insights in relation to science makes materialists nervous, because they would like to think that science is always fact-based and objective. But a full understanding of science must include this aspect of its nature as well as its long-term relationship to philosophy, art, and the wisdom traditions of the world.

Skeptico: If these fields are as connected as you claim, why do I still hear so much about the conflict between science and religion?

Wisdom Seeker: In the next chapter, I will recite some of the history of how that strange story became popular.

CHAPTER 6

THE BATTLE AS PROPAGANDA

Waking in the night, a vague dream fades into the shadows of memory. There was confusion, uncertainty, not knowing how to live or what to do. The unsettled feeling carries over into my waking consciousness. I lie in bed, wrestling with the same issues I felt in the dream: What is the right way to live? What kind of person will I try to be?

A part of me longs for certainty. I want to know what is true and right and good. I need to know. When difficulties and confusion press in, the absence of certainty makes the difficulties seem almost too much to bear. Without established answers, a fear creeps in that I might wake one morning and discover that the foundation upon which I have built my life has collapsed in the night.

Most of us have a need to believe we are right. We are not strong enough to continually question everything. Doing so can lead to neurosis, inaction, and wild swings in behavior. This is one role of culture: to reassure us with regard to what we believe. Cultures give children a framework for living and provide adults with guidance about the best way to interact with others. And, child or adult, when we follow the guidance of our culture we receive re-enforcement for our actions.

The Foundation of Modern Science

Science seeks certainty. Religions do the same. This is a noble motivation, as long as helpful truths are not presented as "the only truth." To come to that conclusion closes the door on growth; slams the door in the face of all those who do not agree with you. Galileo slammed a few doors in people's faces, but throughout his struggles he did not abandon his belief in the existence of a spiritual dimension. On the contrary, his scientific breakthroughs were predicated on the assumption that the world was divinely given and governed by intelligible laws. One of his core motivations, in fact, was the desire to understand those laws.

This was also true of Copernicus, Kepler, Newton, and most of the other great names of the scientific revolution. They wished to understand the mysterious "order" that seemed to govern the universe, and they believed that order was grounded in the spiritual or religious domain. The crucial point is that the founders of modern science were not at odds with spirituality, nor were they at odds with religion (although some of them were at odds with the worldly authority exercised by the Dominant Established Religion in their culture). It is probably not a stretch to say that most of the founders of modern science viewed their scientific work as a way to complete their spiritual and/or religious understanding, which is one of the reasons religious organizations and religiously governed universities funded much of their work.[1]

All of this means that during the seventeenth, eighteenth, and even most of the nineteenth century, there was no "battle" between science and religion. Nor were the Dominant Established Religions of Europe during that time attacking science or scientific thought in some organized way. Rather, what was occurring was that the strongest Dominant Established Religion in Europe, the Catholic Church, was being challenged on a number of fronts, and as various Protestant churches became powerful, their authority over worldly matters was being challenged as well.

A few of these attacks came from scientists, but most did not, for the primary battle was over who would exercise authority in the political domain, as well as what values and ideas would be supported by the culture—and neither of these battles was focused on scientists or science. The most central and influential figure in this broad attack on all Dominant Established Religions during this time was probably Voltaire, who for over fifty years wrote thousands of books, articles, and letters condemning religions that, in his view, exercised too much worldly influence (and against political leaders whom he believed failed to support tolerance and freedom). Voltaire, however, was a writer, not a scientist, and freedom of scientific thought was only one aspect of his crusade.

The revolt against established authority, both religious and political, continued into the late nineteenth and early twentieth centuries, with many battles and many shifts in cultural and political power. Simultaneously, scientific insights continued to multiply. But the underlying motivation for science did not change; it continued to spring from the desire to understand fully and completely the divinely given universe. This is clear from the writings of many of the leading figures in science during this time—most of whom believed in a personal God or held either a Neoplatonic or a Deistic view of ultimate reality. In other words, they believed that order arose from a divine source, which was the reason laws existed that could be discovered. The great task of science, then, was to understand this order.

No less an authority than the brilliant mathematician and world-renowned philosopher Alfred North Whitehead emphasized this motivation of scientists, and also noted that medieval theologians laid the groundwork for the scientific revolution. They did so by establishing the belief that every occurrence in the universe could—

> be correlated with its antecedents in a perfectly definite manner, exemplifying general principles. Without this belief the incredible labours of scientists would be without hope. It is this ... conviction ... which is the motive power of research—that there is a secret, a secret which can be unveiled.[2]

In other words, at the heart of modern science is the belief, formulated and articulated by the medieval church, that there is a divinely given order that can be studied and understood by human beings. And science is still operating from this imbedded assumption today.

Some components of this assumption are that the laws of nature are constant, that they are the same throughout the universe, and that they have not changed one whit through billions of years of history. Modern scientific theories and calculations about the universe are based on these ideas, yet there is no logical or rational basis for them, and there is certainly no proof. But to this day, no one has found any other basis upon which to assume fixed and unchanging laws in nature. Thus the irony: Even those scientists who believe that science and religion are in opposition continue using core assumptions that were formulated by the medieval church and arise out of the belief that the laws of nature have a divine source.

All ideas have a history, of course, and the ideas of the medieval church were influenced by ancient Greeks who believed there was a divinely given universal order. The core assumptions of science, therefore, are not dependent on any specific definition of the divine, only on the assumption that a universal order has been given in some way that we do not understand. This shared view—that there is a divinely given universal order—provides the basis for science in all cultures: Chinese, Indian, Islamic, Jewish, Shamanic, and many, many more.

Incredible Diversity

Another crucial factor that challenges the idea of a broad battle between science and religion is the incredible diversity of religious belief in the world today.

Thought Experiment: Who Speaks for Religion?

To grasp the current diversity of religions in the world, simply ask yourself, "Who speaks for religion in the world today?"

Considering this question makes vivid the incredible range of religious beliefs all over the world. There are nineteen major world religions, but these are made up of 270 often-competing denominations. Yet this is only the beginning: According to the *World Christian Encyclopedia* there are 34,000 separate Christian sects, half of which are not associated with a major denomination.[3] Further, in all the religions of the world, there is constant movement and change—new religions are continually being created while others are dying. One study found that hundreds of "new religions" are born every year; not many survive, yet each year a few new ones grow and prosper.

Looking at the flux in just the United States, the Pew Forum found that one-fourth of all adults have left the faith in which they were raised (and if movement between Protestant groups is included, 44 percent of adults have switched religions or dropped religious affiliation altogether). Moreover, when an individual changes religious orientation, that person's views about the nature of the world, the nature of reality, and the relation between science and religion change as well. I have personally known hundreds of people who have changed denominations, changed religions, dropped in, dropped out—all triggering changes in their thoughts about the role and importance of religion as well as changes in how to understand and incorporate the information that science provides. I have changed several times myself, which makes it comforting to reflect on Emerson's thought: "A foolish consistency is the hobgoblin of little minds."[4] And I especially like John Maynard Keynes' widely quoted response to someone who accused him of changing his view: "When the facts change, I change my mind. What do you do, sir?"[5]

As with religion, there is great diversity within science as well. During the last few centuries scientific knowledge has increased exponentially, making it impossible for any individual to stay abreast of everything, so science has splintered into smaller and smaller areas of specialization. Today there are hundreds of specialties, each with detailed knowledge of a small area. This specialization is necessary for exploring the details of the material world, but leads to specialists who are not trained to deal with broad questions, even broad scientific questions. Where is the science that integrates all the specialties into a coherent whole? Where would I turn for a "scientific view" of cultural, political, or value questions? Who is it within the specialties that can be asked to state the point of view of "science" in general? There are many who claim to speak for science, of course, but their credentials are self-proclaimed and questionable.

Not only that, but scientists frequently disagree—even those who specialize in the same field. Brilliant scientists, as well as brilliant scholars of all sorts, are notorious for their fights. For instance, two of the greatest physicists of all time, Albert Einstein and Niels Bohr, were friends until a difference of opinion about how to understand the new theories in physics drove them apart. They tried for a long time to convince each other, but finally gave up, basically ceasing to communicate even as friends, as each held fast to his own view. Nor was this merely a personal squabble, for it involved a core understanding in physics about which they could not agree. Thus, if even the best scientists cannot agree concerning questions about which they know the most, how can they possibly be expected to agree on questions about politics, education, values, religion, or life—areas in which they have no more expertise than the rest of us? How, then, can anyone speak for "science" in any of these areas?

The "Battle" as Propaganda

Skeptico: If what you are saying is true, why has the idea of a "battle" between science and religion been so much discussed in recent years?
Wisdom Seeker: Maybe the history of that idea will provide the understanding you are looking for. The view that there was a battle between science and religion first began taking hold in the modern mind in 1874, when John William Draper wrote a book entitled *A History of the Conflict Between Science and Religion.*[6] The title is interesting because Draper did not really think science and religion were at odds. Rather, he thought his Protestant faith (he was a devout

Methodist) was allied with science in a fight against the Roman Catholic Church. The battle Draper really had in mind was between Catholic and Protestant worldviews (or to be more precise, his interpretation of those worldviews). His claim was that science supported his side, and the thrust of his argument was directed toward promoting Protestantism and undermining the Catholics. His book became a major bestseller, and the idea of a battle took hold. The way his battle thesis has played out, however, would shock and distress Draper, for some of those he considered allies have placed in their crosshairs the very Protestants he championed, even using his arguments against them.

The warfare thesis was also advanced a short time later by an academic named Andrew Dickson White, who published a two-volume work entitled *History of the Warfare of Science with Theology in Christendom.*[7] In reviewing this work, recent scholars have found his arguments no better than Draper's, with one reviewer saying White used "fallacious arguments," "suspect or bogus sources," argued by "ridicule and assertion," and "quoted selectively and out of context."[8] (Makes White sound like a politician, which he was.) Dozens of major flaws in this work could be cited, but here is one: White used Copernicus, Johannes Kepler, Galileo, René Descartes, and Sir Isaac Newton as examples of those who were on the side of science in the war against religion. The problem is, each of these great scientists was a dedicated Christian, and none viewed their scientific work as being in opposition to their Christian faith.

This is not to suggest there haven't been conflicts between science and various Dominant Established Religions at times in the past; there most certainly have. These conflicts, however, have involved a Dominant Established Religion gaining worldly power and using that power to suppress competing points of view. This suppression was not focused on scientific ideas, though, but on anything that seemed to threaten the organization's power and prestige. In these political conflicts, the battles were not between "science" and "religion," but between an establishment trying to hold on to power versus those with different ideas who wanted greater freedom to express their views.

This battle has occurred over and over in history. At the dawn of modernity it involved an explosion of new ideas, including scientific ones, and those holding the new ideas felt a need to break away from having to justify themselves at the court of entrenched authority. In this sense, the political struggle in the western world from roughly 1600 to 1900 (in which scientists took part) was a shift in authority from the existing power elites to a new power base, and the Dominant Established Religions of the time were part of the power structure being overthrown.

This challenge to the existing authority structures is what many people mean when they speak of the conflict between science and religion. It is crucial, then, to understand what this battle was—and what it was not. In Europe prior to 1400, political authority resided with kings and their feudal associates; economic authority resided with the royalty and landowners (and a few trading and financial families), and religious authority with Dominant Established Religions. Beginning with the stirrings of the Renaissance, however, and continuing for several hundred years, these power centers were all subjected to questioning and challenge. This assault was often led by religious rebels, such as Martin Luther and John Calvin, who had different religious views from the Dominant Religion of their time. By 1600, the rebellion against authority was gaining ground, and Giordano Bruno, a religious man who had taken vows within the Church, was burned at the stake for questioning its authority.

As the 1600's progressed, many philosophers, such as Baruch Spinoza and John Locke, joined the attack. Over the next centuries, whole countries (like England) and smaller political regions in several countries broke away from the Dominant Established Religions that had been in power. Religious and political groups rose and fell, alliances came and went, and many philosophers lent their voices to the assault on established authority, including some of the greatest (like David Hume, Voltaire, and Immanuel Kant). The ideas of these philosophers were not the same, but they had in common a desire to rethink the relationship of people to authority, including religious authority. As these challenges continued, many scientists (who were called natural philosophers at the time), sided with their philosophical brethren, and thus found themselves in opposition to various religious authorities. Gradually, these accumulating attacks had a dramatic effect, including the breakdown of much of the political, economic, and religious authority of the time. New ideas replaced the old. In the fledgling colonies of North America, Thomas Jefferson, Benjamin Franklin, and many others gave practical application to this evolving thought, including the importance of religious freedom.

The crucial point is that scientists joined, but did not lead, a broad assault on the authorities that had been in place in Europe for hundreds of years. Part of this assault was against a specific Dominant Established Religion, the Roman Catholic Church. As it weakened, Protestant denominations sprang up to replace it in various regions of Europe. Some of these Protestant groups in turn became dominant in their geographic regions, but instead of supporting the freedom of ideas they had at first advanced, they began to mimic the tactics of the Dominant Established Religion they had replaced, trying to control the thinking and beliefs of the people within their sway. In other words, they became Dominant Established Religions themselves, and many philosophers, political leaders, economic thinkers, and scientists began to attack the right of the Protestants to exercise this much authority.

Significantly, though, few of those who led the charge for change against these Dominant Established Religions were opposed to a spiritual understanding of the world or to religion in general. Nor were they opposed to the role of Established Religions in human life; in fact, they believed religions were quite necessary in the realm of values and meanings. What they opposed was rigid control of ideas by the power structures of their time. Their goal was to give individuals more freedom in considering all kinds of ideas: religious, political, economic, and scientific. Occasionally this did lead to a battle between specific scientists and a specific Dominant Established Religion over a particular issue, but none of these skirmishes involved a battle between science and religion in general. The only general assertion that arose from scientists and philosophers was that religion should not play a major role in evaluating the truth of scientific claims.

Escaping the Simplistic

One good way to escape the simplistic caricatures of those who promote the idea of a battle between science and religion is to recognize that both religion and science are extremely complex and multi-faceted. In the world today there are thousands of different points of view with respect to what is important and how people should live, and science and religion crisscross them all in numerous ways. Culture, politics, science, and religion are constantly interacting with each other in intricate ways, with the lines of agreement and disagreement constantly shifting, as does a kaleidoscope when it turns.

For example, there are many differences between the United States and Europe with regard to the "battle" thesis, as well as major differences between the various countries within Europe. In some European countries, especially in Scandinavia (where the political power of Dominant Established Religions was largely uprooted), religious groups are not significant in politics and therefore the idea of a battle between science and religion seldom arises today. When it does, the issue usually revolves around the non-Christian religions of immigrants.

In the United States, conservative religious people have become politically active, so the "battle" is often viewed as between their point of view versus a shifting coalition of moderate and liberal Christians, secular humanists, a majority of the Jewish population, and many smaller religious groups. The crucial thing is that these are cultural and political battles, so it is most certainly not a simple battle between science and religion.

Furthermore, alliances shift constantly, issue by issue. Sometimes conservative Protestants are at odds with moderate-to-liberal Protestants; sometimes conservative Catholics join conservative Protestants, sometimes not; various Jewish groups align in various ways on different issues; and followers of Islam, Buddhism, Hinduism, and many other groups align in dozens of ways. In this complex web, the image of a "battle" is invoked as a political weapon, with some Christians trying to define the enemy as "godless science" in order to rally believers, while those who oppose them attempt to portray themselves as "scientific," depicting *their* enemies as ignorant and opposed to the advance of knowledge. Both images, however, are caricatures, created to gain political advantage.

To move beyond these caricatures, one helpful step is to understand the conflict today as between those with a fundamentalist worldview versus those with a materialistic worldview. This is a real battle, in which religious fundamentalists claim God is on their side, while materialists claim that their views are scientific and represent science in its "battle" against religion. Materialists do this in the hope that all those who value science will be recruited to their views, while the religious side claims God in an effort to recruit all those who feel a religious inclination. But science and materialism are dramatically different things. Science is a method for discovering information about the material world, while materialism is a worldview, a metaphysical belief system that, like all metaphysical belief systems, attempts to explain the ultimate nature of existence and the world. (See the next chapter.)

One of the first things I learned in politics was that much time and effort is spent on trying to define one's opponent. Then I noticed that it is quite common for those who are trying to win converts to *any* cause to do the same—to spend a good bit of time creating a negative caricature of those they oppose. They do this by painting their opponents' positions in the most simplistic and negative terms, so they can then claim all good and all virtue for themselves. This happens all the time: in the schoolyard, among those selling products, between religious groups, and in the artificially-manufactured "battle" between science and religion. Pick up any newspaper in the United States today and you will find several examples.

Skeptico: Why have so many of your examples focused on issues in the United States, rather than the rest of the world?

Wisdom Seeker: Sorry about that. I find it very hard to escape my provincial point of view. I try to remember that my country constitutes a very narrow slice of humanity, but I often find myself focusing on the U.S. because it is the part of the world I know best. But I also try to consider other cultures, having studied many conflicts in other places around the globe. The fascinating thing is that there are almost no battles between science and religion going on anywhere in the world. There are many conflicts in many locales between political, religious, and cultural interest groups, and quite often one or more of these groups will claim that science and/or religion is on their side. But a close examination almost always reveals that the issue is not between science and religion.

For instance, the battle idea in China bears little resemblance to that of Europe or the United States. China had, for two generations, a government "battling" the old religions—Taoism, a Confucian value system, Buddhism, and the widely shared view that the Tao is the primordial source of all that is. Maoism hardly represented science (although it often claimed to do so) as it tried desperately to destroy the ancient belief systems that gave China its framework for living. In spite of the brutal efforts of Maoists, however, core religious ideas continued to provide the underpinnings of belief within which most people lived.

Interestingly, as Maoist thought has weakened in China in the past twenty-five years, these ancient views have re-emerged (in somewhat altered forms), and have blended in complex ways to form a new Chinese framework of thought and understanding. As this has happened, the issues and conflicts that have emerged are different from other parts of the world, and the nature of a "battle" between science and religion, as it is conceived in the United States or Europe is not recognizable in China.

Or consider India, where many fierce conflicts rage. Once again, though, these battles are not between science and religion but, instead, are between Hindus and the followers of Islam, between the rising middle class and the lower classes, between growing numbers of modern Indians versus their more traditional brethren, and so on. In all these conflicts, core assumptions of the competing groups are similar in many ways, and quite different from those in China, or Europe, or the United States.

Australia provides another interesting variation. As European immigration began, no Dominant Established Religion gained significant power, and no single Established Religion recruited a controlling majority of Aussies to its ranks. The country's history as a European prison colony surrounded by indigenous peoples did create a conflict between colonizers and natives, but this was not seen as a battle between science and religion. Further, the absence of a Dominant Established Religion within the colonizing establishment meant that less energy than usual was directed toward religious enculturation. Out of this mix, a surprising current has arisen in recent times: Many young people, raised with little religious encouragement, have become spiritual seekers, actively engaged in exploring Buddhism, Hinduism, mainstream religions, alternative religions, New Age ideas, and even the religions of the indigenous tribes of pre-conquest Australia.[9] They have begun, on their own initiative, the age-old search for answers to the enduring questions that their upbringing did not provide. And, of course, they do not experience a battle between science and religion in the way it is characterized in the American press.

So many more examples could be given. There are major conflicts within various Islamic countries, but none centers around a battle between science and religion. There, the major conflicts are between different religious sects, between modern and traditional points of view, and between various cultural groups. There are issues and conflicts in Canada, but the sides in these conflicts seldom align as "science versus religion," and the way religious issues interact with politics and culture are quite different from their interplay in the United States. Continuing around the world, in each locale we would find conflicts and battles, but we would not find a place where there is a simple battle between science and religion. What we would find are various groups claiming that science supported their political or cultural views, and other groups claiming that the locally popular religion supported their position. But these claims would not match reality, for neither religious leaders nor scientists would have a unified position, but would be found supporting many different positions.

Thought Experiment: Many Different Battles

Imagine for a moment how someone in China, India, Russia, or Australia would think about the relationship between religion and science. The "battle" narrative is understood quite differently in each locale, or is not considered relevant at all. In that light, how do you understand the idea of a "battle"?

In sum, there are many battles in the world today: battles between competing religious groups, conflicts between different ethnic groups, struggles for power between natives and immigrants, stark differences over how resources should be allocated between the rich and poor, and political battles between the privileged and the outcast in various countries. There are battles concerning how to educate the young, over economic issues, ownership rights, abortion, and many other things. Some religious groups have taken positions on some of these issues, but almost always there are other religious groups supporting the opposing side. Focusing on dozens of conflicts all over the globe being reported in the newspapers today, I can find no instance in which science is battling religion. Rather, in every case, both scientists and religionists speak with many voices; they have many different points of view. In those cases when there is rhetoric about a "battle" between science and religion, it is being used in an attempt to gain political and cultural power—the real issue is neither religious nor scientific.

There is, of course, an interest in freedom from religious dogma among scientists, for throughout history, Dominant Established Religions have sometimes sought to impose their views on science. (They have, of course, done this in every area of life and thought, not just science.) When this has happened, some scientists have made common cause against the Dominant Religion with those who supported greater freedom, including religious groups opposing the dominant one. Thus, these battles have not been between science and religion but struggles against religious and political authorities who were trying to exercise controlling power over those who sought freedom to pursue wisdom and truth in their own way. As one example, the desire for freedom from intrusive authority was the ground upon which the founders of the United States established their new nation. Religious freedom was one issue, but so were political freedom, economic freedom, intellectual freedom, and more. The result was the creation of an environment that gave scientists great freedom to pursue knowledge as they saw fit, but this was not the result of a battle between science and religion.

Who Integrates the Answers?

Skeptico: Isn't the goal to find scientific answers to all the major questions? Won't that end the conflicts?

Wisdom Seeker: There are dramatic problems with such an approach. Imagine for a moment that a broad policy question could be split into pieces and parceled out among specialists. Take education, for instance, and the questions of what the young should be taught and who should pay for it. These are important issues in every culture, and because of the importance, many people all over the world have studied them intensely. In the United States, many researchers have studied educational policy their whole careers and have collected enormous amounts of data in support of their views. Different researchers, however, have come to radically different conclusions. No one is more expert than these experts, so who is in a position to decide, in a scientific way, which one is right?

Nor is this the end of the difficulty. Suppose that educational policy were split up into many small questions and specialists in various areas of specialization were given these narrow questions to answer. Even if experts in an area of specialization could agree on answers (which is doubtful), an insoluble problem would remain: Who would be in a position to bring all the small pieces together into a coherent whole? This same dilemma pertains to every field of thought, policy, and action.

Skeptico: Well, who does make such decisions?

Wisdom Seeker: They are resolved by politics and/or governments, by cultural and political power wielded in some way. I have searched but have never found an instance where key questions in a culture have been resolved in a scientific way. (I have found claims for "scientific" answers, but always lurking in the shadows have been personal preferences and agendas.)

Another way to understand this is to consider the functioning of academic committees. It is seldom easy for committees to agree on broad policy questions, and often their discussions do not end by arriving at scientific answers. Rather, disagreements in committees usually end through assertions of power, or skilled leadership, or graciousness by one of the parties, or sometimes through firings or resignations. The issue is this: Within any teeming caldron of differences of opinion (and there are hundreds if not thousands of these in science today), where exactly is the "scientific" position?

I do not mean to single out scientists or academics here: Differences of opinion are a fundamental aspect of human nature, especially with regard to moral, political, and cultural questions. In this context, it is crucial to recognize that there is no such thing as a unified "science" any more than there is a unified "religion" to which we can turn for answers on questions of life and living. Specialized scientists are no better than anyone else at dealing with broad issues, nor are they trained to help the rest of us figure out how to live. This is not a difficulty, unless one posits a mythical "science" to which we can turn for answers.

Still, in many conflicts and controversies there are those who claim to speak for "science" and those who say they speak for "religion." But this is like two kids on a playground having an argument, and just before it comes to blows, one says, "You better be careful, or I'll call in my big brother." The other, not to be outdone, replies, "Ha, I'm not afraid of your big brother. I'll call my big sister; she is stronger than him." In the conflicts we have been discussing, imagine the older brother as Science, and the older sister as Religion.

Science has established great credibility with its many successes in answering questions about the world in which we live. At the same time, religion and the spiritual side of life have had enormous importance in helping people come to terms with values and meanings. It is not surprising, then, that when a controversy concerning ideas, power, or politics breaks out, disputants try to bring science and religion into the battle in support of their views. But this is simply an attempt to use these twin pillars of human life in support of personal or group agendas. (For an ideal image of how it might work, let us return to the playground and imagine the mature older brother and the mature older sister arriving at the scene, laughing, and reconciling the warring younger siblings—then going off to solve a problem together.)

The Broad Perspective

There have been countless wars throughout history but "science" has never taken sides. Nor has "religion." Among thousands of religious groupings, those with a specific doctrine have fought many times, often against each other. Religious groups have supported governments, and just as often they have opposed governments, but I can think of no war in which a religious group was fighting against "science." In fact, both sides in every war use the discoveries of science to gain advantage, and both sides often claim to hold the point of view that "science" supports.

Skeptico: Isn't your focus in that statement wrong? As I understand it, the battle between science and religion is not so much about shooting wars as it is about cultural and political battles.

Wisdom Seeker: Yes, that's true, so let's focus on those kinds of battles in the United States: foreign policy, tax policy, drug laws, economic policy, crime, energy, jobs, gay rights. In none of these areas is there a conflict between science and religion, for the role of science in these debates is not to take sides, but to provide information for consideration by all sides. And people with a religious orientation have as many different points of view on these issues as the population at large.

Skeptico: All right, I'll grant that science does not provide answers to questions about policy in the areas you mentioned, but what about the hot-button issues of abortion, evolution, climate change, and prayer in the schools? Don't they have to do with the battle between science and religion?

Wisdom Seeker: Not really. At first it might seem to be the case, but upon close examination, that is not the reality. Science does not have a position with regard to abortion, and religious people have a wide variety of views. As for evolution, this fight is a political battle about educational policy in the public schools, with religious groups lined up all across the spectrum. Most scientists feel that the current mainstream scientific ideas should be taught, and the majority of religious people agree. Arrayed against this position are those who hold a conservative theological point of view and who would like their theories to be given greater attention in the schools. (They also have scientists in their camp.)

The crucial point is that this battle is not between science and religion, but is, instead, between liberal and conservative political points of view with regard to public policy and education. The conservative side believes their opponents have gained control of educational policy, and conservatives want more power in educational policy. At the same time, moderate and liberal religious people oppose these conservative efforts, and their numbers are probably as great as those who align with the conservative side.

As for prayer in the public schools, conservative politicians have made an effort to arouse voters by making this a political issue, but it can hardly be called a conflict between science and religion, for science has no position on the matter. And, as with evolution, many religious people oppose the more fundamentalist point of view.

The climate change battle is perhaps the strangest of all. Some conservative politicians (backed and funded by a group of business leaders) have attacked the evidence for climate change. The motives of these two allies are different, though: The business leaders want to prevent government regulation and the politicians want to call into question the economic policies of their political opponents. They find common cause on the issue, though, and both positions are understandable from a self-interest point of view. Why some conservative religious people have joined them, however, is more puzzling, for religious groups have no theological reason I can discover to deny climate change or to be against protecting the environment. The only motive I can find is that they feel a need to support the politicians they favor. Nonetheless, whatever their motives, there is clearly no "battle" between religion and science here, especially since a large number of religious folks (probably a majority) are concerned about the dangers of climate change and support actions to protect the environment.

The essential point in all this: There are real battles in the world, but they are almost always political and cultural fights between various interest groups. In these battles, occasionally a specific religious group, representing a small fraction of the world's population, will single out a scientific theory and attack it as part of a *political* fight. They do so in an attempt to gain popular support, often couching the attack in terms of a "battle" between "science and religion," hoping that all those who value religion will join their side. (Like the kids on the playground, they are calling in "big brother" and "big sister" for help.) But always there are many religious people on the other side, no matter what the issue. To get a sense of just how diverse religious opinion is, and has always been, simply bring to mind the countless schisms through the centuries in Catholicism and Islam, or the conflicts between the many different branches of Protestantism, Hinduism, and Buddhism. An old joke (of which I was recently reminded by columnist Terry Mattingly) captures the utter impossibility of any unified religious position on anything. A traveler is crossing a bridge and sees a man about to jump. He asks the suicidal man:

"Are you a Christian?"
"Yes," comes the answer.
"Catholic or Protestant?"
"Protestant."
"Are you a Baptist?"
"Yes"
"So am I. Are you Baptist Church of God or Baptist Church of the Lord?"
The potential jumper yells: "Baptist Church of God."
"Me too. Are you original Baptist Church of God or from the Reformed branch?"
"Reformed Baptist Church of God."
"Me too. Are you Reformed Baptist Church of God, Reformation of 1879, or Reformed Baptist Church of God, Reformation of 1915?"
"Reformed Baptist Church of God, Reformation of 1915."
The traveler immediately turns away, continuing his journey, calling back over his shoulder: "Go ahead and jump, heretic!"

Skeptico: What should scientists and religious people do about the attempt to drag them into all the conflicts you have mentioned?
Wisdom Seeker: I would hope they would resist being co-opted into political battles and continue to advance the search for wisdom and truth—each in their own way.

Skeptico: What if they feel that a deep and important principle is at stake?

Wisdom Seeker: Then I would have them make a clear decision about which side they believe in and how much time and energy it seems wise to invest in that belief, and then do that fully—as citizens, as voters, as members of society.

Science and Life

In *The Varieties of Religious Experience*, William James presents a vision for a healthy relationship between the spiritual and scientific dimensions of life. To achieve this end, he urges scientists to avoid premature conclusions about the spiritual dimension, for "the universe" is much more multi-faceted than "any sect, even the scientific sect," can take into account. He goes on to give many examples of the value of religious experience in individual lives, and shows that mystics through the ages have benefitted themselves, others, and whole cultures as well. Being a scientist himself, he praises scientists and declares that "science and religion are [both] ... genuine keys for unlocking the world's treasure-house." But neither should be thought of as excluding "the ... simultaneous use" of the other.[10]

Many great thinkers have come to the same conclusion. As Will Durant summarized the view of Kant: "Science is organized knowledge. Wisdom is organized life."[11] Kant, in his body of work, intentionally made room for the spiritual dimension to be included in the pursuit of wisdom. In a similar vein, Isaac Asimov observed: "The saddest aspect of life right now is that science gathers knowledge faster than society gathers wisdom."[12] Both understood that when other kinds of knowing lag behind science's discoveries, a serious problem ensues.

To discover a fulfilling way to live, both science and things spiritual have important roles to play, and it is crucial that we find a healthy relationship between them. Putting it dramatically, Alfred North Whitehead said, "More than anything else, the future of civilization depends on the way the two most powerful forces of history, science and religion, settle into relationship with each other."[13] To this end, many of us explore spiritual teachings; at the same time, an increasing number of people all over the world practice the magnificent discipline of science as it continues in its quest to understand the workings of the material world. And these groups are not separate, but overlap continuously—scientists and spiritual seekers are often the same individuals, as was the case with the leaders of the scientific revolution and with the founders of modern physics.

Recognizing this convergence, a good way to think about the relationship between science and religion is to examine how science can best relate to each of the four different but overlapping categories defined at the beginning of the last chapter:

Dominant Established Religions have not opposed science in some broad way. In fact, they have often been among its strongest supporters. Occasionally, though, a Dominant Established Religion has taken a stand against a specific scientific theory. When this has happened, it has always been a mistake, for this involves a confusion of levels of reality and brings harm to both science and religion. At the same time, when scientists have attempted to claim there is a "scientific" position on metaphysical, moral, or philosophical issues, they have made the same mistake in reverse, bringing harm to science and to religion as well.

Established Religions are too numerous to count and have countless points of view. In addition, we humans argue a lot; we fight over land, power, rights, and many other things. In these conflicts, Established Religions often play a role, taking sides on issues of economics, education, government policy, morality, and foreign policy. These positions, however, are always from specific groups (among the thousands that exist) and there are always religious groups supporting the other side. Further, the positions of the various religious groups are constantly changing, with realignments on individual issues going on all the time. In this flux, the positions of various religious groups almost always have to do with political, cultural, and religious issues—they are not fighting with science. The "battle" theme is only raised when one side claims that "science" or "religion" supports its point of view, and the other side falls into the trap of believing this to be the case.

Religions are the paths we follow in search of a fulfilled or meaningful life. There has never been a conflict between science and the attempt to find a fulfilling life for oneself. Sometimes a person will discover something in science that calls into question a specific belief within one Established Religion, but this does not call into question religion itself, any more than a child's discovery that its parents are not always right calls into question the existence of parents. Further, most scientists through history have followed a religious path, and all religious people value and use various aspects of science in their lives.

The Spiritual Dimension connotes the quest to find answers to the deepest questions of existence. It is one of the strongest currents in human history. At the same time, science (the quest to understand the material world as fully as possible) is one of the greatest achievements of humankind. Through the ages, most of us (including most scientists), have had a spiritual interest of one kind or another, and this interest has not been in conflict with science. These two branches of the human enterprise, rather than being in opposition, grow from the same vine: Both are part of the profoundly important search for wisdom and truth.

There is No Conflict

Most of the scientific progress in human history has occurred within cultures that were organized around and successfully operating within specific religious systems. Examples include ancient Greece; Confucian and Taoist China during the dynastic periods; Europe during the late-Medieval and Renaissance period; Protestant England and America in the sixteenth to nineteenth centuries; Jewish communities worldwide at various times; the Islamic world of the Middle

Ages and Renaissance; numerous epochs in India; Peru during the thirteenth to early sixteenth centuries, and many more.

This is the norm: Scientific advances have usually occurred within cultures underpinned by religious systems. When belief systems have broken down, the ensuing turmoil has usually forced a more basic existence and there has been less time and money for the best minds to focus on scientific study. Furthermore, science requires a system of education that only stable societies provide, and stable societies almost always rest on a base of values and meanings given by established religions.

The relationship between science and religion (and art as well) is complicated and multi-dimensional, but it is often complimentary. A healthy religious enterprise incorporates the best scientific ideas into its worldview, as that towering figure of Christian thought, Thomas Aquinas, advised in understanding the Bible: "No particular explanation should be held so rigidly that, if convincing arguments show it to be false, anyone dare to insist that it is still the definitive sense of the text."[14] In modern language, Aquinas was saying that ideas that had been accepted about the material world that came from interpretations of scripture should be abandoned—if they were found to be in conflict with reason or scientific knowledge. He was also saying that *facts about the world* should not be the basis for religious belief, because they arise from a different ground. On the other hand, it seems fairly obvious he thought that religious and spiritual beliefs having to do with meanings and values could not be considered the province of scientific proof.

This distinction has been echoed by leaders in every religious tradition, including in modern times by the Dalai Lama, who said that if science proves a Buddhist idea wrong, Buddhism must change. This does not mean that the Dalai Lama turns to science for spiritual instruction, nor does it mean that every claim made by those who proclaim themselves to be speaking for science must be accorded primacy. It simply means that a healthy and viable religion will constantly incorporate the best of science into its understanding of the world.

Ultimately, science and religion are not in conflict but are complementary pillars supporting the temple of the human enterprise: Science helps us understand the workings of the material world, while religion and the spiritual dimension aid in the discovery of values and meanings.

CHAPTER 7

A BRIEF HISTORY OF MATERIALISM

During college I joined a choral group that practiced every day. In our practices, the stress and strain of my life would often melt away, and I would be lost in the music, or perhaps it would be better to say that I found myself through the music.

I have always loved music. One of the goals of all my travels has been to experience the varied and rich musical traditions of humankind. When I listen in a certain way, all of me is involved—body, mind, heart, soul, and spirit. My very essence is swept up in a union beyond description. Immersion in music carries me into a field that is shared with others but, at the same time, is uniquely personal. This experience does raise a question, however: Who is the "me" that comes alive with music? It seems different from my daily self and yet vitally important, but it is hard to pin down or define.

Although defying definition, this experience is not unique to me. On the contrary, we humans have had powerful experiences with music since our beginnings. And, in special moments, music has always been able to connect us with something beyond our everyday lives. Pythagoras, one of the founders of the Western stream of rational thought, suggested that music was capable of bringing us into contact with the harmony of the universe, and this idea has been confirmed through the ages by millions of people. Furthermore, this experience is available still; is just as accessible as it has always been.

A Magnificent Beginning

Science and music have never been in conflict. In the same way and for the same reasons, science and the spiritual dimension have never been in conflict. How could science be in conflict with the attempt to answer questions about what is ultimately important, how one should spend one's time, or the values by which one should live?

Perhaps surprising to some, science and many religions have lived peacefully together through the centuries. In fact, they have often been mutually supportive. There has been a conflict, however, especially in the last one hundred years, between materialism and a spiritual view of life. And in that time there have definitely been conflicts between various religions and materialism. In order to understand the nature of the modern idea of a "battle," or even to understand the history of Western thought in the last hundred years, the difference between science and materialism must be clearly understood. And the confusion embedded in the oft-used phrase "Scientific Materialism" must be examined.

Materialism is a way of understanding the world, a metaphysical view of how the universe came to be and the role we humans have in it. To understand its ascendancy in the modern era, it is crucial to examine its beginnings, and a good place to start is fourteenth-century Europe. As the Renaissance began to unfold, an idea began to take shape that is still working its way through human consciousness. Until then, every major belief system in the world had assumed there was a spiritual dimension to life—that there was "something" beyond just material things.[e] How that "something" was defined varied enormously from culture to culture and from age to age, but *that* a mysterious "something" existed was present in all.

A few examples of this "something more": Aristotle's "final cause" or "Prime Mover"; the Tao of Confucianism and Taoism; the Gods of Judaism, Christianity, and Islam; the Great Spirit of shamanic

---

[e] The idea that only matter exists had been around much longer—a few ancient Greeks and a few thinkers in ancient India as well as China held that notion—but then the idea did not rise to a level of significance as to have much impact on cultural belief systems.

cultures; the eternal, omnipotent, and omnipresent Brahman of Hinduism; Hegel's "reality" that includes, but is not limited to, all beings, the world, and nature; and the possibility of awakening into the "deathless" in Buddhism. Different as these views may be, all agree that there is "something" beyond the material realm upon which we can base our values, our meanings, and our search for a whole and complete life.

For a few people during the Renaissance, however, a gradual shift of focus away from transcendental explanations and toward explanations grounded in material and mechanistic processes began. This was followed by the great scientific discoveries of the following centuries, and these two currents led a few philosophers to begin to speculate that we would eventually be able to gain complete knowledge of the world—even mastery over it—by understanding material things alone. A handful even went so far as to speculate that nothing could keep us from perfecting life and ourselves once we learned to fully control material things. To arrive at this "perfection," however, we would have to think of ourselves as merely mechanisms—as the highly influential psychologist B.F. Skinner envisioned in his mid-twentieth century novel, *Walden Two*.

But this is getting ahead of the story. The incredible scientific outpouring of the sixteenth century, along with the gradual shift of focus away from the transcendent dimension and to the earthly plane, gave rise to the Age of Reason in the seventeenth century. Gradually the belief began to take hold in some intellectual circles that human reason would be able to bring order to life and solve all the problems of the world. Coming as it did during a time when religious wars were ravaging much of Europe, this was welcome news to an increasing number of people. These wars had brought a growing recognition that religious leaders, especially when in league with governmental authorities, could make terrible mistakes and cause great harm. Some leading thinkers thus began to put their faith in reason and science, hoping these tools would correct many problems occasioned by blind subservience to narrow religious beliefs, as well as problems caused by corrupt religious authorities aligning with those in power.

Out of this ferment came the "Enlightenment"[f] of the eighteenth century, and with it dramatic changes—some of enormous value. The Enlightenment gave Europeans and Americans a new way to think about themselves and the world, and the fruit of that tree was greater individual freedom—freedom of thought as well as of action. From this freedom sprang powerful individual initiatives in art, commerce, science—in fact, in all areas of life. In turn, this burst of initiative by many individuals ushered in a different balance of power, giving those who wished for greater personal freedom the ability to discover truth and make more decisions for themselves, rather than looking to authorities and institutions for answers.

Gradually, as these ideas took hold, they were institutionalized into new forms of government. Jefferson, Franklin, Adams, and the other leaders of the American Revolution were deeply influenced by Enlightenment thought and incorporated many of its ideas into the creation of the United States of America. Even though it was quite radical at the time to suggest that *every* individual had an *equal* right to life, liberty, and the pursuit of happiness, these revolutionary leaders were creating a new government, thus were able to implement many new ideas in the country's founding documents, including a good bit of Enlightenment thought. As these ideas took root and flourished in the United States, they began to flow back to the European shores where they had been given birth. Gradually, and sometimes painfully, these ideas swept away old institutions, and new governments based upon Enlightenment principles were established in much of the Western world—ideas and principles taken for granted in much of the world today.

It is hard to over-emphasize the contribution these three great currents—the Renaissance, the Age of Reason, and the

---

[f] Some scholars treat The Age of Reason and The Enlightenment as synonymous, as two ways to label the same thing, but I prefer the view that the eighteenth century Enlightenment grew out of the seventeenth century Age of Reason.

Enlightenment—made in the formation of the world we know. From this merging fountain flowed technological marvels, economic prosperity, artistic abundance, and dramatically expanded rights and freedoms. These currents gave us modernity, and modernity's fruits include greater democracy; the elimination of slavery in many parts of the world; broader freedom of speech, religion, and assembly for great numbers of people; a widening acceptance of equality and justice for all; greater political and civil rights for women and minorities; and the widely accepted ideal of a fair trial before an unbiased judge or jury. (Although several of these principles were present in ancient Greece and were put into practice to some degree in Roman times, wide acceptance and application only came to fruition in the post-Enlightenment world.)

Spreading Religious Freedom

As this magnificent history unfolded over the course of five hundred years, most of its champions had a spiritual interest, although many questioned some of the views of the religious organizations of their time. Such key figures as Montaigne, Descartes, Francis Bacon, Spinoza, and Leibniz believed that much religious thought was superstition and could not be reconciled with the newly emerging understanding of the world. Yet none of these seminal figures questioned the existence of "something more," something beyond the material realm. They were not materialists. For them, the task was to carve out a greater role for human reason as a counterweight to the superstition and dogma they felt many religions perpetuated.

It is crucial in understanding this history to realize that all the leading figures at the beginning of the scientific/philosophical revolution had a spiritual interest and were religious in one way or another. The questions they raised concerned specific religious teachings, not religion or spirituality in general. Rather than embrace a materialistic worldview, they used the emerging freedom of thought in their cultures to explore and formulate their own spiritual ideas. For instance,

Baruch Spinoza (one of the greatest philosophers of the age) suggested that God and Nature were ultimately one. Some embraced Deism—the belief that God created the world in the beginning and set it in motion, putting in place at that time the laws that govern it to this day. Others followed the trajectory of Francis Bacon, first questioning many religious ideas but ultimately recognizing the value of the spiritual domain—if it could be freed from some of its superfluous attire. The development of Bacon's thought is captured nicely in his essay *Of Atheism*, in which he says that a little science or philosophy "inclineth man's mind to atheism," but going deeper "bringeth men's minds about [back around] to religion."[1]

Ever-Greater Freedom of Thought

In the decades and then centuries following the Renaissance, the gap increased between the freethinking intellectual elites of Europe and the religious institution that had dominated thought there for centuries. It is important to remember, however, that many of the currents of modernity arose within this institution, the Roman Catholic Church. With its commitment to scholarship and a tradition of allowing many different points of view to flourish within its ranks, the Church nurtured and supported the birth of the modern world. In fact, many of the most influential figures that gave rise to the Renaissance, the Age of Reason, and the Enlightenment—as well as the Scientific Revolution—were clerics and church-supported scholars.[2]

At the time, there was a certain degree of freedom for differences of opinion within the Church, but the amount of freedom sought by the leaders of the intellectual and scientific revolutions was great, which led to a growing challenge to the authority of the Church. Simultaneously, reformers within the Church became insistent on the right to hold different views, and they were emboldened to some degree by attacks on the Church's authority by the philosophical elite. Ultimately, some reformers, catalyzed by Martin Luther, broke away from Catholicism entirely, setting in motion the creation of Protestantism. The Protestant rebellion, in turn, kept Church leaders from focusing on the challenge of Enlightenment thinkers, which gave these philosophers more freedom to pursue their ideas without negative consequences. The Church, now engaged in a challenge to its power and authority on two fronts, was increasingly unable to deal with either attack as forcefully as it might otherwise have done.

This is not to suggest that Protestant and Enlightenment views were always in alliance—sometimes they were and sometimes they most decidedly were not. It was, rather, a world in which three great forces moved in relation to each other across centuries—a Dominant Established Religion, rebels within that religion breaking away to create Protestantism, and intellectual elites creating new worldviews not directly tied to either. There were many factions within each of these groups and many alliances between factions arose and dissipated. Specific battles were waged, then faded, and many different combinations of agreement and dissent came together and broke apart. Alliances shifted and changed in various parts of the world. But because two of the combatants were trying to wrest power from the Roman Catholic Church, the Protestant and Enlightenment causes were often mutually beneficial to each other.

In many ways Voltaire, the consummate French intellectual, came to exemplify the Enlightenment challenge to the Church. His battle cry, "Remember the cruelties," was an arrow shot toward the heart of what he perceived to be the corruption of the Church of his time. But once again, it is crucial to remember that his attacks, and those of his contemporaries, were directed against a specific religious organization and not against the existence of the spiritual domain itself. All three parties in this great, centuries-long battle accepted the existence of the transcendent dimension. Their arguments were about the best way to understand it, not about its existence. For example, Voltaire, although not especially religious, was a Deist who believed that reason itself led inexorably to belief in "a necessary, eternal, supreme, and intelligent being."[3] From the point of view of Enlightenment thinkers, then, reason and rationality were not in conflict with the spiritual dimension, but only with particular ideas of Established Religions. One of their tasks in their minds, then, was to work out the right relationship between rationality and spirituality.

To say this in a different way: As the Renaissance gave way to the Age of Reason, which led to the Enlightenment, and as the Scientific Revolution (supported by these currents) moved forward, there was a major shift away from unquestioned acceptance of authority and a movement toward valuing information from direct observation. With this change in emphasis, whole new fields of knowledge arose, which gave a better understanding of the material world and how it worked. Logical analysis became an increasingly important tool, along with the experimental method (which asserted that experiments that could be duplicated should be the measure of truth with regard to the physical world). The new paradigm was saying that experiments and their analysis had to take precedence over dogma and belief with regard to what was considered true concerning the material world.

It must be emphasized again, however, that the central figures who developed these ideas (and in the process gave rise to modernity) were not rejecting the spiritual dimension of life. And they certainly did not think they were in a battle between science and religion. They viewed the arguments going on in their world as between competing religious groups, as competition for power and prestige, or as part of a broad struggle to win greater individual freedom of thought and action. In these disputes, individual scientists took a variety of sides, for science itself was not one of the disputants. In fact, all sides evoked scientific ideas in support of their views. The one commonality of belief among scientists was that in dealing with material things, science was the best way to arrive at knowledge, but this did not lead them to adopt materialism as the most accurate view of the broader reality in which they existed.

The Coming of Pure Materialism

Skeptico: So does anyone claim that all that exists is material stuff?

Wisdom Seeker: Well, yes, but the founders of the great movements we have been discussing did not, because it is an incredible leap from the view that science is the best way to acquire knowledge about the material world to the belief that there is *only* a material world. The fact that some things can best be explained by the scientific method does not suggest it is the best way to explain all things. The discovery that bacteria caused some diseases did not lead to the conclusion that all diseases are caused by bacteria. To move from "some" to "all" is an incredible leap of faith.

Skeptico: But if there is proof, you don't need faith.

Wisdom Seeker: That's right. If there were proof that only material things existed, that would remove the need for faith. But there is no such proof—there are only those who make a materialistic act of faith in their metaphysical assumption.

Skeptico: Well, maybe physicalists or naturalists have improved on the materialist viewpoint—I hear those terms a lot these days.

Wisdom Seeker: In recent decades, the terms *physicalism* and *naturalism* have sometimes been used in place of materialism, making provision for the inclusion of energy as a fundamental component of the universe. But as do materialists, physicalists and naturalists insist that the universe is just material "stuff," plus mindless energy. To all three, the universe is completely explained by mechanistic processes that have no meaning. For all three, there is no inherent point to life, values lack any underlying basis, and there is no room for "something more" beyond the physical or material dimension. As contemporary physicalist Stephen Weinberg put it in his book, *The First Three*

Minutes, "The more the universe seems comprehensible, the more it also seems pointless."[4]

Most materialists, physicalists, and naturalists also make the assumption that the only way to acquire information is through the five senses. In this, as in the belief that everything is material (or physical), they are united, so materialism, physicalism, and naturalism all embrace the worldview of Pure Materialism (capitalized to capture its essence as a faith system). Its founding myth: *Once upon a time a world came into being that was made up only of matter (or matter and energy). This world is the only world there is, and in this world only things that can be measured are "real" and only events that can be duplicated in the laboratory are "true."*

The origins of this faith system are somewhat obscure, but one of its early "saints" is the seventeenth century English philosopher Thomas Hobbes. Hobbes was primarily concerned with political rather than religious ideas, but for him, the only reality was the material world, so all political power had to rest on a material understanding of the world. Almost as an afterthought, he extended this assertion to the religious domain, with the result that he saw religious beliefs as nothing but fantasies.

His religious arguments were fairly easy to refute, but a few thinkers adopted them, mostly as an additional club to be used against the Dominant Established Religions of the time. The overall context was the Thirty Years' War, waged from 1618 to 1648. The war began as primarily a conflict between Protestants and Catholics in central Europe over accession to power in Bohemia (part of the modern-day Czech Republic), but gradually became a terribly destructive conflict that included most of the European continent. To many observers, the massive destructiveness of the war had no redeeming value, focusing a spotlight on the quest for worldly power by the religious establishments involved. This turned many thoughtful people against these Dominant Religions and (coupled with a growing desire for freedom of thought) made Hobbesian materialism seem palatable.

Nonetheless, the movement would likely have died from its flaws except for a stroke of marketing genius by someone in the Hobbesian camp. We do not know who first suggested the strategy, but the idea emerged to name science, the child of the medieval religious establishment, the champion of materialism. Therefore, although it had been raised and nurtured within the Catholic Church, science was proclaimed the arbiter of truth in the new Church of Materialism.

It was a brilliant strategy. Not only was the powerful new force of science claimed by materialists to be in support of their metaphysical position, but a major problem in materialism had been addressed. The problem was this: If all transcendent values and meanings were discarded, on what basis would we humans organize our lives? Hobbes had realized this problem early on, understanding that if everyone simply followed their basic materialistic instincts there would be constant war and conflict. Succinctly capturing the dangers of this situation, he said there would be unending "war of all against all," and that human life would be "solitary, poor, nasty, brutish, and short."

This, however, had not been the story of much of human history, for in many places people had cooperated with each other over long stretches of time, rather than fight all the time. The question that Hobbes thus had to answer: Why, if there are no transcendent values, have people cooperated so often? His answer: Every person who lived in a society that was cooperative had entered into a "social contract," had willingly given power to the governing authority. And once having given away his or her personal power, the individual had no choice but to accept all the actions of the authorities under which they lived.
Skeptico: People had to accept whatever the ruler said?
Wisdom Seeker: In Hobbes' view, yes.

There are, however, major problems with this view, the largest being that there was no time at which people were actually asked whether they wanted to enter into this "contract." (In Hobbes' view, people were born into it and could not change it.) The dilemma that Hobbes was trying to address was this: His theory asserted that the religious and spiritual codes that humanity had used to organize cultures for thousands of years had no real basis, yet he understood that without core organizing principles, peoples' natures would lead to constant war and conflict. What to do? His solution was to make up a new transcendent principle, one that asserted that all those in an organized society had agreed to a "social contract."

What he did not acknowledge (or perhaps did not see) was that to believe in this "mysterious" social contract required a leap of faith no different from the leap of faith made by those with a religious or spiritual point of view. Ultimately, his "social contract" was a transcendent principle, and its existence was pure speculation—there was no proof for it. Hobbes' belief that everyone had entered into a social contract, without knowing they had done so and having no right to resign from it, simply replaced one transcendent theory with another.

Skeptico: Why is it a transcendent theory?

Wisdom Seeker: Because the idea that we are all part of a social contract does not arise from anything material—it is speculative and metaphysical. To assert that everyone (somehow) has forever given over the right to control their own lives to an earthly king or queen (as Hobbes believed) is not a matter of logic, reason, or proof, but a purely metaphysical speculation. Some of the questions left unanswered: How exactly did people first enter into this contract? When did this happen? Who created the contract? As for trying to use his idea today, who gets to define how it is to be understood? Can it be changed in any way? By what process?

Since Hobbes had no useful answers to these questions, his theory was no more rational, scientific, nor defensible than many others that had gone before. Actually, less so. It's real advantage (to him) was that it suited his agenda and his temperament better than the one he was challenging.

Skeptico: Why does this matter? No one in the modern world accepts Hobbes' view.

Wisdom Seeker: That's true. Hobbes' idea of a social contract did not hold up well as humanity moved into modernity. But it is important to recognize his influence, for his challenge to spiritual and religious views was, for a considerable time, a powerful factor influencing those beginning to organize around a materialistic worldview. To recognize that the original ground for materialism was speculative, that it even involved transcendent speculations, helps us to see that it began as, and has remained, a metaphysical theory.

Skeptico: What happened after materialists starting seeing the error of Hobbes' idea? Where did they turn for answers to the key questions about how we humans should live and how we could best live in relation to each other?

Wisdom Seeker: They of course had to find another way to answer these questions, and that is where the marketing genius came in: science should decide.

Skeptico: But as you have just pointed out, no one is authorized to speak for science.

Wisdom Seeker: Yes, this is the very heart of the problem with such a solution, for science is a vast collection of millions of people, each pursuing knowledge in a specific area of expertise. Within this vast network, no group, and certainly no one person, is authorized to speak for "science," especially with regard to questions about culture, society, and how best to live. Anytime power is left up for grabs, however, it creates a tempting vacuum, so a certain number of scientists, philosophers, and politicians since the rise of materialism have declared that they have the right to speak for all of "science."

Which brings us back to "Scientific Materialism," a phrase designed to gain legitimacy for the materialistic worldview, but which is highly misleading. There is nothing scientific about materialism. Materialism takes a metaphysical position with regard to the nature of the universe—without any guidance from science. Science has no position with regard to metaphysical questions. At its beginnings, science was defined as an effort to understand the material world, while the non-material realms were specifically left outside its domain. The tools and methods of science were developed exclusively to explore and explain the material world. It is not surprising, then—if those tools and methods are directed toward questions of meanings, values, and what might exist beyond the material plane—that nothing is discovered. The tools were not developed for such purposes. In fact, to say that the tools of science should be able to find those things is like asserting that a metal detector should be able to locate chocolate. And then saying that if metal detectors cannot find chocolate, chocolate must not exist.

Skeptico: Can science provide any guidance in these areas?

Wisdom Seeker: Science can play a role, but the answers to questions about how to live and what might lie beyond the material world have mostly to do with assumptions beyond the tools of science. Just as there is no scientific position with regard to artistic, moral, or political issues, there is no agreed-upon scientific position with regard to metaphysical questions. Science cannot tell us how to avoid war (or whether we should), the ultimate meaning of life, the best way to raise children, the values by which we should live, how we can diminish the proliferation of weapons of mass destruction, how we can develop the political will to care for the environment, or how we might persuade people to adopt healthy lifestyles. Answers to all of these questions might involve science, but they cannot be answered solely within its domain, for they involve values and beliefs beyond what science knows, and fine scientists support almost every point of view that can be named in all these areas.

Materialism Becomes a Religion

Science is no more at home in a materialist worldview than those that are decidedly religious, so from the time of Hobbes, materialism did not gain many adherents—until the late nineteenth century in England. At that time, a small group of intellectuals, led by Thomas Huxley, began an organized effort to build what Huxley called the "church scientific." (He was being partly humorous, but there is no doubt he was also quite serious.) What Huxley and his followers were actually trying to establish was the "church materialistic," but Huxley could see the marketing advantage of calling what they were doing "scientific." Their main opponent was the Anglican Church, and one of the high priests they claimed for their movement was the brilliant Scottish philosopher David Hume.

Hume was a thinker with few equals in his time—or any other—and one of his most famous works was a withering attack on the "proofs" put forward to justify certain religious beliefs made by the Dominant Established Religions of his time (especially the Anglican and Catholic Churches). His most powerful work, *An Enquiry Concerning Human Understanding*, developed several arguments against religious dogma that are frequently used to this day. Hume, however, was not a materialist, for he had the good sense to notice that the materialist position was equally undermined by his arguments. (Hume died in 1776, however, so he could not protest the "honor" materialists later bestowed on him as one of their own.)

Hume lived in a world in which religious authorities had extraordinary power over education, cultural teachings, and politics; in fact, over every phase of life. One of his key insights was that the emergent ideas of his time were going to have a profound impact on how the world would be understood in the future, especially in the way that many of the religious assertions taken for granted for centuries would be fiercely challenged. In some ways Hume led that charge, for one main thrust of his work was to demonstrate that many of the assumptions underlying the views of the religious authorities of his day were neither rational nor provable. Starting with this idea, he began to sketch out a new way of understanding humanity and the world.

But Hume was also a contrarian—he seemed to enjoy challenging prevailing dogmas wherever he found them. Admiring Hume as I do, I like to think he would have been just as fierce in attacking the materialist dogmas of today, for he was intellectually rigorous and enjoyed pointing out flaws in theories that were not well thought out. Crucially, Hume was not asserting that the transcendent or spiritual dimension did not exist—only that it could not be proven to exist. At the same time, he recognized that *there was no proof against its existence.* What he most wished to do, it seems to me, was free human thought from narrow assumptions wherever they were found, so he challenged the materialistic assumptions of his time as well as religious ones. I think he would have done so even more vigorously today, for many proponents of materialist belief systems in the present time start with assumptions that are neither logical, rational, nor scientifically demonstrable, and go on from there to assert that only their assumptions are right and all others are wrong. (My sense is that Hume would not have been pleased to be included in such a camp.)

Many further examples could be given of historic figures whom the "church materialistic" looks to as its founders, but "founders" who, when their views are examined carefully, do not actually adopt or endorse materialism. (Various books give many examples, such as: *Reality* by Peter Kingsley, *The Empiricists* by R.S. Woolhouse, *The Devil's Delusion: Atheism and its Scientific Pretensions* by David Berlinski, *The Meaning of Life* by Terry Eagleton, *Science and the Modern World* by Alfred North Whitehead, *The Passion of the Western Mind* by Richard Tarnas, *Science Set Free* by Rupert Sheldrake, *Science and the Akashic Field: An Integral Theory of Everything* by Ervin Laszlo, and *Quantum Questions: Mystical Writings of the World's Great Physicists* by Ken Wilber.) In short, materialism was most distinctly *not* what the founders and leading lights of the Renaissance, the Enlightenment, and the Scientific Revolution had in mind as the end result of their efforts.[g]

Thought Experiment: Are the Assumptions of Materialism True?

If you are interested in whether the assumptions of materialism can be demonstrated by reason or proven by facts, you can determine this for yourself. Simply ask: Do I understand the basis for these assumptions? Can I state the proofs that they are true?

Skeptico: I don't think I can do that, but I am sure someone must be able to.

Wisdom Seeker: How can you be so sure? But the larger point is: If you cannot articulate definitive proofs for materialism and yet you accept it as true, you are making an act of faith just like those who believe any other religion.

Skeptico: What is the core assumption of materialism, in your view?

Wisdom Seeker: The assumption of materialism is that tiny bits of matter, through countless random/chance events, somehow managed to organize themselves into planets, stars, and galaxies. Even more surprising, these infinitesimally small, non-living and purposeless bits of stuff then organized themselves into complex forms of life. But this was only the beginning. Next, they created consciousness. Not stopping there, they went on to create reason, art, science, values, music, poetry, love, the urge to profound sacrifice, and a sense of meaning in some of their most intelligent creature creations. Even that was not enough, so these mindless and purposeless particles finished off the job by endowing many of their most highly evolved creatures with a belief that they could experience a feeling of union with others, with

---

[g] An interesting side note is that Aldous Huxley, grandson of Thomas Huxley, became one of the best-known proponents in the twentieth century of the importance of a spiritual worldview, especially with his book, *The Perennial Philosophy.*

nature, and with something greater than themselves. Now *that* is a truly miraculous creation myth!

An example of belief in this myth comes from the renowned molecular biologist Francis Crick, who famously said of all human beings: "You, your joys and your sorrows, your memories and your ambitions, your sense of personal identity and free will, are in fact no more than the behavior of a vast assembly of nerve cells and their associated molecules."[5] In making this statement, he seems to think he is being scientific, but this is pure metaphysical speculation. Further, it is quite dogmatic, asserting something as true that is highly speculative. Such statements carry materialism dangerously close to the territory of becoming a Dominant Established Religion, even including attempts to force others to adopt their beliefs through shame or intimidation.

It is possible, of course, to choose to believe in materialism, just as one can choose to believe in various other ways of understanding the world. But, as with all other worldviews, there is no proof for it, which becomes vividly clear with the realization that wise, thoughtful people through the ages (including many scientists) have adopted quite different views. Many do so today. A few of the alternatives: (a) consciousness gave rise to the material realm; (b) guiding principles existed from the beginning of the universe to give shape to the organization of the material world; (c) things evolve in a meaningful direction; (d) a creative force was present at some point in the past; and/or (e) forces beyond explanation by materialism are active today.

Like materialism, each of these views is a metaphysical theory that tries to explain the origin and operation of the world in which we live. Each has arguments in its favor, but all rest on assumptions that cannot be proven. Yet many materialists contend that their views are the only possible approach—without recognizing that this assertion is based on an act of faith in favor of the materialist myth.

Reason is often evoked as a support for materialism, but being rational, if it means anything, means considering for oneself which metaphysical view seems the most accurate—without being intimidated by the assertions of others. If we are to be rational, each of us must decide this issue for ourselves, because the very nature of metaphysical theory is that it goes beyond the knowable facts, even goes beyond the capacities of reason. Ultimately, metaphysical theories provide the framework within which "facts" make sense and reason is exercised. Every set of facts—and the reasoning process itself—has to function within a context that gives definition and meaning to how one will understand the facts and use reason. This means that, insofar as we are reasoning beings, our metaphysical theories are the sea within which we swim. The facts and the reasoning of physics make sense within the framework of physics, but that framework is not very helpful in understanding poetry or romance. The Australian aborigine and the TV climatologist might be equally good at predicting the weather, but their facts and their reasoning are quite different.

This is critically important because, in arguments about belief, a trump card often thrown on the table is the cry, "You are not being rational!" or "Reason demands." But these imagined trump cards are nothing but bluffs—they are raw assertions by those who throw them out, with the hope that everyone will believe that they have a card that they do not really possess. The actual situation is quite different. Rational beings come to many different metaphysical beliefs, and in this realm, reason and science do not take sides. Materialism, then, just like all the world's religions, requires an act of faith for acceptance. Materialists who claim reason and science as their allies are simply asserting that everyone should accept their myth as *the truth*, and further, that we should all base our lives upon their particular act of faith about the nature of reality. There is no rationality here nor anything scientific.

In his refutation of materialism, the influential nineteenth century philosopher Georg Wilhelm Friedrich Hegel pointed out that it is fine and helpful to take measurements of an object—when what you want to know concerns the physical nature of the object. He went on to say, however, that such measurements tell you little about what is actually important about the object.

Skeptico: What does that mean?

Wisdom Seeker: My understanding, growing out of Hegel's thought, is that physical measurements give you only the physical characteristics of an object; they do not tell you anything about why the object is important to you or why you chose to measure it in the first place. In other words, physical measurements do not tell you why you chose to focus on that object, when there are thousands upon thousands of other objects you could have focused upon. Measurements do not tell you anything about the motivation for doing the measuring.

Ultimately, we care about an object because of its meaning for our lives, yet it is not possible to measure meaning with physical tools. An object's relevance—its meaning—involves ideas about it, expectations for it, wants and needs associated with it. This is the starting point for all measurement, but these things are personal and subjective; they are not found in the material realm. In other words, the motivation of a person conducting a measurement leads to the measurement, but that starting point is a subjective wish or desire. Even the most practical scientist making the most finely tuned measurement is doing so because of decisions about what she wishes to know and why she thinks that is important—and such decisions are not objective. Once a goal has been set, the remaining decisions can be somewhat objective, but picking what one will investigate is always personal and subjective. Furthermore, measurement results tell us nothing about the most important aspects of a scientific experiment, the *meaning* the results have for the scientist and for those who are interested. For that, we must look to the interpretation of the results, and interpretations lie in the realm of thoughts and ideas, which are beyond the measurements themselves.

To use an analogy from mathematics: The meaning or significance of a mathematical formula is not found in the material dimension. Mathematical formulas might be *about* matter, but their meaning and significance lie in concepts beyond the material realm and cannot be discussed in materialistic terms. For instance, one aspect of the famous Einsteinian formula, $E=mc^2$, concerns matter, but this formula was not and will never be found through an examination of matter. The formula is not "in" the matter, but in the mind. Its predictions about the material realm can be tested in the material realm, but the concept itself and the motivation to produce it are not there. Further, the formula arose from a history of mathematical concepts that were not contained in matter but were transcendent to it, concepts that developed over time in the consciousnesses of many different minds. In the same way, the physical properties of a painting tell us nothing about the experience the painting will engender in those affected by it. So it is with music, where sound waves can be analyzed in the physical dimension, but the *experience* of the music is in an entirely different realm.

Thought Experiment: Where Is the Music?

One day a violin was found on a captured pirate ship, stored in a way that indicated it had great value. Those who captured the ship, however, had never seen a violin or any other stringed instrument. The discovery created great puzzlement: Why was this thing considered precious? Brilliant researchers were assigned to investigate its use and value. They studied the violin in the laboratory for years, weighing it, dissecting it, creating a precise description of its physical characteristics— cataloging its shape, texture, and molecular structure. But they were unable to provide answers concerning its meaning and value. The researchers plucked the strings of the violin and scraped them with a stick during their investigations. They even measured the strings' vibrations. These measurements, though, did not give them an *experience* of music, for violin music is much more than the vibration of a string. When a violin is played for a receptive audience, then, where is the music?

Those who appreciate violin music do so within a system of thought, feeling, and experience developed over centuries. A culture must develop and train composers to write a certain kind of music, and musicians must be taught to play it. Anyone who is to have a positive experience is taught to appreciate that music. (I remember having a very negative response the first time I heard classical Chinese music.) It is only when a fine instrument is played by a talented artist to receptive listeners that the essence and meaning of a violin reveals itself. (For the listener, this must of course be a subjective experience.)

How music affects us has never been explained by materialism and quite likely never will be. When a piece of music can create a shared sense of beauty and harmony among thousands (even millions) of listeners separated by centuries, something is at "play" that transcends the material plane. When many different people are moved to a shared feeling of pleasure, beauty, joy, or sorrow—in ways that cannot be measured by the most sophisticated machines—the best guess has to be that there is a realm beyond the material.

Skeptico: But that's where the brain comes in!

Wisdom Seeker: Ah, yes, the brain! But there is a difference between the brain and the mind. The physical brain is made up of matter, such as neurons, but if you put a neuron under a microscope—no matter how strong the microscope—you will not find a thought or feeling. If you put one thousand neurons under a microscope—still no thought or intention will be found. If you put one trillion brain cells under a microscope you will not find a thought, an emotion, or a motivation. You can measure activity in the brain, but no one has yet measured a thought or discovered how the matter in the brain formulates feelings or dreams. Or creates the motivation to write a book about materialism.

You can, of course, put someone's head in an MRI machine when thoughts and feelings are occurring and measure physical activity going on in the brain. But the only thing you have found is a physical *correlate* to thoughts and feelings. This physical correlate is related to thought, but it is not thought itself. When you measure brain activity, you **have not** found a thought. Nothing in the MRI readout can tell you what a thought is, where it is located, or what particular thought or feeling is occurring in the subject. The subject has to tell the researcher **whether** she was thinking and **what** she was thinking. And, of course, an MRI machine cannot tell whether a thought is creating brain activity or brain activity is creating thought.

As an analogy, imagine a TV set playing in a room.[h] If you examine the electronic circuits of that TV, you can find physical activity in the circuits. If you measure the movement and intensity of that physical activity, however, you will still have no clue about the **content** of the program on the screen and no information about the source of that content. Thus the electronic activity is a physical *correlate* to the TV program, and a necessary part of the process, but the content of the program is originating far beyond the electronics.

In the same way, the best guess of some neuroscientists is that the mind, and the world of thoughts and feelings and motivations in which we live, is more than the physical brain. There is great controversy about this, of course, but a significant number of the best researchers have concluded that the mind is different from the brain and that thinking cannot be understood as "nothing but" electrical/chemical activity.

This view is supported by the fact that the stories we live within, the stories that give meaning and motivation to our lives, have never been captured by physical measurements. Our minds weave thoughts and feelings together to create our stories, but as far as anyone has been able to tell, these stories are not material or physical things. When we are thinking, the brain's machinery operates, but the **contents** of our thoughts and feelings do not show up in the readouts from any machine. A researcher studying an MRI readout cannot tell you about the contents of your thinking process, just as those studying the electronics of a TV cannot tell you about the **contents** of the

---

[h] This analogy is not original; I have heard and read it many times, but haven't been able to trace it back to its originator. The philosopher Leibnitz might have inspired it with some of his images, but of course, television did not exist in his time.

program on the TV. The contents of our minds—ideas, images, feelings, motivations, and dreams—seem to be of an entirely different nature than the electrical and chemical activity that we can study through physical measurement.

This fact creates a particular dilemma for the materialist: The motivation to write books and give speeches in praise of materialism does not seem to come from the material about which they sing. Motivations have never been discovered in matter. A rock does not seem to have an urge to persuade other rocks to adopt a materialistic viewpoint. As far as we can tell, rocks do not care if other rocks agree with them. Motivations exist in the world of emotions, of elaborate systems of thought and feeling that give rise to intentions, ambitions, fears, hopes, and dreams. Nothing we have discovered in materialistic research gives any clue about how a lump of matter can create motivations, ambitions, or the desire to write a book promoting materialism.

Another way to understand the limits of materialism is given by philosopher Ken Wilber, who suggests that there are four distinct areas, four quadrants that must be taken into account if we are to comprehend our world and ourselves. The four are:

1) The inner experience—the subjective experience of feelings, thoughts, and ideas. The experience of "I."
2) Shared experiences with others—experiences that arise from relationships, from living within cultures and within shared meaning systems. The experience of "We."
3) The realm of matter—the objects out there, the material universe. The "It" with which our senses interact.
4) Finally, there are the systems of organization of the material world, the systems that structure the relationship of material things to each other, such as when we think about planetary systems, biological systems, or information systems. Wilber has labeled these systems, "Its." (Are these systems out there in the world, or do

our organizing minds create them? We will leave that question for another time.)[i]

In Wilber's model, each of these areas has equal importance, and none can be collapsed into or reduced to the other. Further, each is always present and each must be taken into account if we are to understand human life and human experience. Looking at the overall picture in this way, it becomes clear that materialism deals only with Quadrant Three and some aspects of Quadrant Four—and has great value in helping us understand these quadrants. But materialism is not equipped to deal with Quadrants One and Two, which is where we find the experience of music, love, values and meanings, motivations, and most spiritual and religious experiences. No wonder materialism has had such a hard time dealing with these things.

How then can we explore Quadrants One and Two—the domains of I and We? Through one of the most mysterious things in the universe: consciousness, the subject of the next chapter.

---

[i] The presentation of Ken Wilber's quadrants that I find most helpful is in Chapter 5 of his book, *Sex, Ecology and Spirituality: The Spirit of Evolution* (Boston, Massachusetts: Shambhala Publications, 1995).

CHAPTER 8

Science and Consciousness

"In my hunt for the secret of life, I started my research in histology. Unsatisfied by the information that cellular morphology could give me about life, I turned to physiology. Finding physiology too complex I took up pharmacology. Still finding the situation too complicated I turned to bacteriology. But bacteria were even too complex, so I descended to the molecular level, studying chemistry and physical chemistry. After twenty years' work, I was led to conclude that to understand life we have to descend to the electronic level, and to the world of wave mechanics. But electrons are just electrons, and have no life at all. Evidently on the way I lost life; it had run out between my fingers."[1] — Nobel Laureate Albert Szent-Gyorgyi

Perhaps the greatest scientific mystery of all time is consciousness, yet it keeps slipping through the nets we set to catch it. Given its central importance, it is no wonder we have been trying to understand consciousness for a long time. But just as life continually slipped through Albert Szent-Gyorgyi's grasp as he searched for it at many levels, consciousness keeps doing the same, no matter the methods we use in our search. The surprising, almost shocking reality is that we don't seem to understand consciousness any better than did the ancient Greeks, Indians, or Chinese. Through the centuries, many thinkers such as Plato, Confucius, Buddha, Shankara, Rumi, Dogen, Teresa of Avila, Shakespeare, Dostoyevsky, Carl Jung, and Helen Luke (to name but a few) have had theories of consciousness that are as profound and insightful as any today. Their theories are different, and there are pluses and minuses to each, but this is true of all modern theories as well. To me, no theory today is more reasonable or believable than the best of the past.

Skeptico: How can you say that? I read all the time about the progress we are making in brain research.

Wisdom Seeker: We know a lot more about the brain today, but there is a distinct difference between the brain and consciousness.

Skeptico: What do you mean? I read a book by the philosopher Daniel Dennett called *Consciousness Explained,* and he said consciousness could be completely explained by brain activity.

Wisdom Seeker: He is almost certainly mistaken. One of the great neurobiologists of our time, Roger W. Sperry (who won the Nobel prize for his work on the brain), said the evidence does not support a "materialist and behaviorist doctrine" concerning the nature of reality, which is what Dennett offers. On the contrary, Sperry's view is that, "Instead of renouncing or ignoring consciousness," the way forward is to give "full recognition to the primacy of inner conscious awareness as a causal reality." Continuing, he said:

> The swing in psychology and neuroscience away from materialism, reductionism, and mechanistic determinism toward a new, monist, mentalist paradigm restores to the scientific image of human nature the dignity, freedom, responsibility, and other humanistic attributes of which it has long been deprived in the materialist-behaviorist approach.[2]

In the same vein, Sir John C. Eccles, a neurophysiologist who won the Nobel Prize in Physiology/Medicine, used the phrase "promissory materialism" to highlight the fact that brain research has not even begun to solve the riddle of the human mind:

> I maintain that the human mystery is incredibly demeaned by scientific reductionism, with its claim in promissory materialism to account eventually for all of the spiritual world in terms

of patterns of neuronal activity. This belief must be classed as a superstition.[3]

In other words, promissory materialism is the claim that researchers will find, sometime in the future, a material basis to explain the total functioning of the mind—without any current evidence to support that claim. This, for Eccles, is a "superstition without a rational foundation." He continues:

> The more we discover about the brain, the more clearly do we distinguish between the brain events and the mental phenomena, and the more wonderful do both the brain events and the mental phenomena become. Promissory materialism is simply a religious belief held by dogmatic materialists ... who often confuse their religion with their science.[4]

Skeptico: But what about all that evidence that Dennett points to?
Wisdom Seeker: He has almost no evidence, just assumptions and assertions. All that anybody has shown is that there are physical activities in the brain that sometimes correlate with various emotions, ideas, and memories. But correlation is not causation. Roosters often crow in the early morning, and then the sun rises. This has led some tribal peoples to the conclusion that the crowing of the cock causes the sun to rise. Most people believe, however, that this is an example of correlation rather than causation—that the crowing is not the cause of the rising of the sun. Correlation often occurs when two events are mutually impacted by a third factor that ties them together, which is the case with the sun and the crowing rooster. In just this way, measurable brain activity is often correlated with thoughts and feelings, but I have never seen any evidence that shows that brain activity **causes** the thoughts and feelings. Some people (of the materialist tribe) speculate that this is the case, but they have never demonstrated anything but correlation.

To support the causation thesis, for many years an effort was made to show that specific areas of the brain are associated with specific feelings and ideas. The latest research, however, indicates that many areas of the brain are involved with feelings and ideas, and it has so far been impossible to tie the arising of a thought or feeling to a specific location in the brain. In fact, recent research points in the opposite direction, suggesting there is a broader, more general source for thoughts and feelings than simple neuronal firings.

This is important to each of us because nothing is more essential in understanding the nature of human life and the best way to live than consciousness. That you are conscious means you are aware of your existence, aware of feelings and ideas and plans, and able to consciously consider how you will react to them. On the other hand, to define consciousness as nothing but neuronal firings and/or chemical activity severely reduces what it means to be human and limits our perceived capacity to participate in the creation of our own lives.

Let me rush to say that I do not know what consciousness is, and I cannot be certain that it is not created by the brain in a mechanistic way. What I know for sure, however, is that no one has demonstrated this to be the case, and that there are many other ways to understand consciousness. In this open space, where no one knows what is really true, each of us has the opportunity to decide for ourselves the view we will organize our lives around.

Skeptico: Are you sure that science hasn't explained consciousness?

Wisdom Seeker: Absolutely sure. No one has been able to explain consciousness, which is the reason Professor David Chalmers calls it "the hard problem" of both science and philosophy.[5]

Skeptico: But I have read a lot of articles by people who think they understand it.

Wisdom Seeker: I didn't say there aren't a number of people who *claim* to have figured out consciousness. But of the many current theories being promoted (and there are many), none is widely accepted. Disagreements about what consciousness is and how it works fill magazines, journals, and conference schedules. Part of the difficulty is that consciousness must be present before any research on consciousness can begin—for there to be a research project, someone must have the conscious thought: "I will do this research project." In the same way, the existence of consciousness is absolutely necessary before science can begin in any shape, form, or fashion. (This being the case, I am often struck by the difficulty of trying to make a scientific argument against the existence of consciousness. It is similar to asking a person to read an article claiming that language does not exist.)

The fierce disagreements in the scientific community about consciousness become clear in browsing the reports of conferences on the subject, such as the "Toward a Science of Consciousness" conference sponsored by the University of Arizona.[6] For twenty years, many different presenters have asserted with great confidence specific theories about consciousness, only to be refuted moments later by other experts with conflicting theories (presenters who have equally impressive credentials). It is puzzling how all these experts, attending the same conference, can be so confident about their views when other experts at the same conference have powerful arguments to the contrary. Shouldn't such a situation lead to a little less certainty? For some reason, however, this topic generates strong convictions. It is similar in ways to how people feel about their religions, where there are many differing and unprovable views, with lots of people feeling strongly about their theories in spite of the great diversity of opinion.

Significant Disagreements

One the key disagreements about consciousness between knowledgeable people involves whether each person has an individual, separate consciousness. That we do is the materialist point of view, but many people disagree, including Erwin Schrodinger, Nobel Prize winning physicist. His view: "To divide or multiply consciousness is something meaningless." And his proposal: "The unification of minds … in truth there is only one mind"[7]—which of course has been the understanding of various wisdom traditions throughout history, including several streams of Hinduism.

Another disagreement concerns how long consciousness has been present. One view is that consciousness is a recent development in the evolution of the human brain, but many knowledgeable observers think otherwise, including Nobel-winning biologist George Wald: "Mind, rather than emerging as a late outgrowth in the evolution of life, has always existed." His view: That mind is "the source ... of physical reality,"[8] which has a strong correspondence with both Hinduism and Buddhism.

Still another conflict, mentioned earlier: Some researchers believe that consciousness is created solely by neuronal and chemical activity in the brain. Others, however, think that focusing on these mechanistic actions alone is like focusing on the electronics of a computer and ignoring the software. For a computer to function, there must be a program, the software, written by a human that tells the electronics what to do.

Skeptico: Caught you! Computers can write programs for other computers.

Wisdom Seeker: Sure, but only if a program written by a human being tells it to do so. In every chain of events leading to a computer action, at the beginning of the chain there is a human being who has set in motion the action and defined the purpose of it. Therefore, if human mental activity is to be compared to a computer, consciousness is the programming, which is separate from the hardware, the brain. The reason this distinction must be made is that if you measure the signal in a brain neuron, you have not found consciousness. Even if you measure the signals in a hundred thousand connected neurons, you will not have found consciousness, but simply electrical and chemical activity. When a person is experiencing the color green, the neuronal signal is not green, nor can it be identified by a machine as being a green signal. The mind, in some mysterious way, takes the signals it receives and creates images and ideas.

Skeptico: So what is the mind?

Wisdom Seeker: The way I think of the mind is that it is where the things most associated with being human reside: memory, consciousness, the creation of ideas and images out of neuronal signals, creativity, the capacity to reason, the ability to make choices, deep and powerful feelings like love, compassion, and kindness, the ability to override base urges and do what seems right and good, and the part of us that can be touched and moved by art and music. All that, however, does not pin mind down, for mind is a mystery. We do not know what the mind is. You might say it is the seat of consciousness, but that is simply to replace one mystery with another. What we do know is that our experience of life and living—the color green, love, beauty, and most everything else of importance in our rich and varied lives—have not been found to reside in the signals of the brain; our experience is created when the mind organizes and transforms those signals. How? No one knows.

When researchers measure signals passing through neurons, they are not measuring consciousness, but merely signals in the brain. Researchers do not know whether consciousness is present except by asking the people being measured what is going on inside their experience—they must ask for a subjective report from a conscious person, and only then can they begin to correlate the signals measured in the neurons with feelings, thoughts, and experiences. Machines simply cannot tell whether a neuronal signal amounts to consciousness or not. Neuronal measuring machines find the same signaling in the brains of rats and cows as they find in human brains. Are those animals conscious? I take no position on this question, but it seems clear that machines can only measure electrical and chemical activity in the hardware, not the consciousness that determines whether the signals have coherence or meaning. No machine can judge whether or when neuronal activity amounts to consciousness. Further, when my neuronal activity is measured, no machine can tell whether my conscious thought is centered around literature, science, or religion.

Several years ago, as I was reflecting on the experience of love, the reality of the limits of what can be learned through brain measurements began to sink in. When I am experiencing love, those examining my brain with a machine have no more understanding of my feeling experience than if a lion or a turtle were in the machine. A researcher who does understand my experience of love does so from his or her own past subjective experience of love, not from the machine's readout. Further, those who truly wish to understand the experience of love will have to step out from behind all machines, into their personal life, and experience it for themselves. A machine that provides objective data just won't deliver an understanding of the subjective experience. As the poet Rumi put it in "Each Note":

> Advice doesn't help lovers!
> They're not the kind of mountain stream
> you can build a dam across.
> An intellectual doesn't know
> what the drunk is feeling!
> Don't try to figure
> what those lost inside love
> will do next!

The Mystery of Memory

Another great mystery closely connected to that of consciousness, but in some ways different, is that of memory. Discovering what memory is, how it works, and how it relates to the brain has proved virtually impossible for researchers.

Skeptico: Ha! Caught you again! I read an article in a recent issue of *Nature* saying that MIT researchers had found that "memories reside in specific brain cells."[9]

Wisdom Seeker: I read that article, but most knowledgeable researchers do not agree with it. Besides those I have already quoted, one of the most respected neurologists in the world, Professor Rudolf Tanzi (who holds the Joseph Kennedy Chair in Neurology at Harvard University), said in a recent speech that memory doesn't seem to "live in the brain."

The article you mention in *Nature,* though, is a very good place to examine some of the mistakes often made by researchers who jump to unsupported conclusions about memory. In that article, the researchers start with the **assumption** that memory resides in the brain, and then, *presto,* their assumption leads them to the conclusion that memory resides in the brain. This is a great example of circular thinking rather than scientific discovery.

In this particular project, the researchers create a conditioned reflex in a mouse and then define that reflex as memory in general. A conditioned reflex has some things in common with memory in general, but the two are **not** the same thing. If you reflexively pull back your hand from a spider you suddenly see beside your hand, the motivation for that action does not encompass the full range of the nature of memory. Even less does a conditioned reflex in a mouse represent the full range of memory in a human being (although the article suggests that it does). Humans sometimes act in a reflexive way, just as mice do, but memory is much more than reflexive action. To create reflexive actions in a mouse and then make the gigantic leap to the conclusion that this explains how human memory works is, well, it is a fantastic and unsupported leap. It is like assuming that when a camel falls to its knees, it is praying.

This article in *Nature* is an excellent place to see one of the most striking problems in consciousness research: the tendency of many researchers to define consciousness simplistically rather than dealing with its true complexity; to define it in a reductionistic way so it can be studied more easily. The problem they are trying to deal with is that studying consciousness is different from any other scientific pursuit, because consciousness is the tool with which scientific research is done. In essence, to study consciousness requires turning around and examining the instrument being used in the study. This is why it is such a "hard problem," and why consciousness remains a mystery after centuries of research and study.

When the researchers in the *Nature* article designed their experiment, they were using human consciousness to create the experiment. If they had wished to truly study consciousness itself, they would have had to study why *they, themselves,* were motivated to do the experiment in the first place. If they had wished to study memory, they would have had to explore how *they, themselves* remembered all the things they had learned during their lives and been able to put all those memories together in a coherent way so as to be able to create the experiment. All this would have been necessary to truly get at human memory and consciousness. This is why studying consciousness is so much more difficult than studying other things—it cannot be isolated as an object in the material world. To get around this difficulty, one approach is to define consciousness simplistically as a material thing, which is the approach of the study in *Nature*: It starts with a reductionistic, materialistic view that a mouse's reflexive action is the same as memory. But as Arthur Schopenhauer saw many years ago, "materialism is the philosophy of the subject who forgets to take account of himself."[10] Experimenting with a mouse's reflexes has some value, but it is a far cry from dealing with human memory, or with consciousness, and the value can only be gained if the researchers understand the limits of a reductionistic approach.

Understanding Consciousness

Skeptico: All right. You are making a good point, but what about your statement that many people in the past had an understanding of consciousness at least as profound as ours today. How can you say that?

Wisdom Seeker: Studying the brain is very popular today, but that does not mean we have made much progress in understanding consciousness. Brain function, yes, but consciousness, no. In fact, even our understanding of brain functioning is quite controversial. Recently the New York Times ran an article, "The Trouble With Brain Science," that discussed an "indignant open letter to the European Commission, which is funding the Human Brain Project." This project is "an approximately $1.6 billion effort that aims to build a complete computer simulation of the human brain." The "indignant" letter was signed by hundreds of neuroscientists from all over the world, charging that the undertaking was "overly narrow" in the way it was approaching the problem and that it was not "well conceived."[11] The Times article summarized the dilemma:

> Are we ever going to figure out how the brain works? After decades of research, diseases like schizophrenia and Alzheimer's still resist treatment. Despite countless investigations into serotonin and other neurotransmitters, there is still no method to cure clinical depression. And for all the excitement about brain-imaging techniques, the limitations of fMRI studies are, as evidenced by popular books like "Brainwashed" and "Neuromania," ... well known. In spite of the many remarkable advances in neuroscience, you might get the sinking feeling that we are not always going about brain science in the best possible way.[12]

It is a common prejudice in the modern world to think that we have the most advanced understanding on many topics, yet at the same time we are beset by murder, crime of all sorts, and poverty. (This is certainly the case in the United States, at least). We pride ourselves on all we have learned, but an incredible percentage of us are anxious, depressed, hypochondriacal, or addicted to drugs (legal as well as illegal). We talk about the progress we have made, yet many of us are increasingly lonely, alienated, obese, and can't sleep. We criticize past cultures but spend an increasing amount of our time on trivia: mindless TV shows, pornography, violent movies, and messages posted by famous, self-centered people on the internet.

At the level of relationships, divorce is rampant, single parents are increasingly the norm, and many young people are finding their personal connections in gangs or in the artificial world of the internet rather than with family members or friends they see in the flesh. Speaking of families, there are healthy and nurturing ones, but far too many are characterized by alienation, emotional distance, and frustrated feelings. At the community level, we glorify our culture and recommend it to others, but much of our educational system is broken, our health care system is a mess (and our leaders are unable to agree on any of the possible paths that might fix it), and our political system is reduced to hostile camps that demonize each other.

There are, of course, many fine people in our culture and there are many creative ideas for making the world a better place, but in numerous ways we are not doing so well. Beyond our shores the world is filled with war, poverty, hunger, disease, and tribal strife—and "we the people" of the world seem to be unable to do much to alleviate these problems. We try, but things do not seem to be getting much better.

Skeptico: Wow, you paint a bleak picture!

Wisdom Seeker: One view of where things stand in our world is definitely bleak. There is a positive view as well, though, and I think it is also true: There has been progress in many individual locales in numerous ways. It is important to honor the progress, but it is also important to honestly face the difficulties if we are to effectively deal with the problems.

Skeptico: I can see that, but I don't see how your point has much to do with whether we have a better understanding of consciousness than people in the past.

Wisdom Seeker: The relationship lies in the fact that most of the problems today have to do with consciousness—with how we understand what it means to be a human being, how we go about finding fulfillment, and how we relate to each other. In the modern world we have learned how to manipulate matter to an impressive degree, and we can manufacture and transport enormous amounts of physical goods. We have learned much about how the brain works. These achievements, however, have not solved the problems that have to do with consciousness: having good relationships with the people close to us, living in peace with those outside our own circle, and finding what is meaningful to organize around so that we are not overcome with depression and despair.

Many cultures in the past did not come close to providing the material comforts for the majority of their people that we do today, but they were able to provide stable and healthy systems of understanding for their members over long stretches of time, and they were able to create an environment in which a deep sense of meaning and fulfillment was more common than it is today. In this regard, many cultures in the modern world are not doing as well as a significant number did in the past. There have, of course, been lots of dysfunctional cultures in past centuries, plenty of times and places where I would not have wanted to live. (And we like to compare ourselves to those cultures in order to feel good about our own progress.) But all over the world there have been cultures that provided good environments for people to live out their lives in meaningful and worthwhile ways. For several hundred years this was the case in ancient Greece, in large segments of the Roman Empire, in China under several of the dynasties, in India, in numerous tribal and indigenous cultures, in Bali (right up to today), and many, many others. Compared to these healthy past cultures, we are not doing very well in terms of happiness, meaning, and fulfillment, and our problems have a lot to do with our failure to develop a mature understanding of what is necessary to be a healthy, conscious human being.

Modernity has delivered a great deal of individual freedom, much more than many cultures in the past, and that is a valuable prize. It is likely, though, that our freedom has made solving the problems of loneliness, meaninglessness, alienation, and despair more difficult. If we are to keep our hard-won freedom and still make progress in solving the problems of the modern world, the best approach I see is through an increase in individual consciousness. It is probably no longer possible in much of the world to improve things by insisting that the majority accept the meanings given by authority figures—the genie of freedom has escaped from that bottle. But if having meanings and values imposed by authorities is not an option, the only way forward is for individuals to become more conscious of what is really important and to set off in that direction with energy and determination. One necessary piece of the puzzle, though: These efforts must be guided by a dose of wisdom, including the age-old belief that there are meanings and values that we all share. For societies, the only real hope is that sufficient numbers of us will follow this path and become conscious enough to make good communal decisions.

Skeptico: That sounds right, but you are being abstract. Be more specific.

Wisdom Seeker: In much of the modern world we have emphasized personal ambitions and desires, neglecting the advice of wisdom figures throughout history that doing so leads ultimately to unhappiness. We have focused on acquiring material goods but given short shrift to finding meaning (reversing the emphasis of many cultures in the past). We have emphasized individualism, often at the expense of relationships with other people. We have concentrated on creating "free time" and then, rather than treating it as precious, have squandered it on trivia.

E. F. Schumacher (whose *Guide for the Perplexed* was quoted in Chapter 4) foresaw these dangers in the middle part of the last century, saying:

> In the absence of sustained study of such "unscientific" questions as "What is the meaning and purpose of man's existence?" and "What is good and what is evil?" and "What are man's absolute rights and duties?" a civilization will necessarily and inescapably sink ever more deeply into anguish, despair and loss of freedom. Its people will suffer a steady decline in health and happiness, no matter how high may be their standard of living or how successful their "health service" in prolonging their lives.[13]

Schumacher says that if one's focus is narrowed to the "material aspects of the Universe" it will make "the world look so empty and meaningless that even those ... who recognize the value and necessity" of a deeper wisdom will not be able to "resist the hypnotic power" of the narrow vision. In other words, they will likely organize around simply trying to get more and more stuff. They will "lose the courage as well as the inclination" to pursue deeper wisdom, wisdom that other cultures have acquired.

The problem, as Schumacher sees it, is that science for manipulation has increasingly ignored the higher levels of our being and denied all worldviews except materialism. The consequence is a self-reinforcing loop in support of a worldview that disregards all higher levels and is therefore—no surprise—unable to find any evidence for the existence of such levels. As this worldview has gained ascendency, he suggests, the road to recovery has gradually been closed and the higher aspects of our being are used less and less to produce true wisdom. The great danger he sees is that if this goes on too long, our ability to recognize true wisdom will "atrophy and even disappear altogether." If this happens, the problems we face will increasingly seem overwhelming; they will remain unsolved and seem increasingly insoluble, even as our efforts to solve them become "more frantic." Ever the economist, Schumacher then notes that, as this process plays out, our material possessions may continue to increase, but the quality of our lives and the fulfillment we experience will decline.

Schumacher's conclusions have a direct bearing on the relationship between science and religion. He certainly does not defend the excesses of Dominant Established Religions; he even goes so far as to suggest that it is quite possible to live complete and fulfilled lives without Established Religions. Finding a relationship to the transcendent, however, is quite another matter: "It is not possible to live without religion, that is, without systematic work to keep in contact with, and develop toward, higher levels." Failing this, the only remaining option is to focus on "pleasure or pain, sensation, gratification, refinement or crudity."[14] But taking this path leads to the downward spiral he so vividly describes and that he fears might define our future.

Coming at these issues from a different angle, psychiatrist Carl Jung reaches a similar conclusion, noting that we have lost valuable wisdom that other cultures possessed:

Among all of my patients in the second half of life—that is to say, over thirty-five—there has not been one whose problem in the last resort was not that of finding a religious outlook on life. It is safe to say that every one of them fell ill because he had lost that which living religions of every age have given their followers, and none of them has been really healed who did not regain this religious outlook. This of course has nothing whatsoever to do with a particular creed or membership of a church.[15]

The crucial point is that the issues Jung, Schumacher, and so many others raise are directly related to consciousness. How we understand ourselves and our world will be the single largest determinate in our ability to find meaning and fulfillment in our own lives, as well as in solving the problems of our communities and countries. This is where we can learn from the wisdom traditions of the past, for some had a better understanding of the role of consciousness and how to work with it than most people and many cultures do today. If the wisest figures in human history were able to gaze upon the culture of the United States in the current era, they would likely shake their heads in kindly despair and wonder—that a country with so much opportunity has so many problems and so many people who are anxious, addicted, angry, or depressed. They would conclude that the understandings upon which many in our culture are organizing their lives are much too limited and narrow.

Skeptico: What do you mean, "limited and narrow"?

Wisdom Seeker: Limited and narrow because we are ignoring much of the accumulated wisdom of human history and calling that progress. We are defining ourselves as machines and marveling at the "sophistication" of our understanding—but thinking of ourselves as biomechanical automatons is not sophistication; it just sets us up for meaninglessness. Machines do not have meaning. This reductive view disregards the hard-won wisdom of the past: the understanding that consciousness is precious and that its increase is the pathway to meaning and fulfillment. The view of the wisdom traditions is that—through discipline, effort, commitment, and faith—a human being has the capacity to find wisdom and to become loving, compassionate, free, at peace, and even joyful. Many wisdom teachings even assert that we are capable, through a transformation of consciousness, to participate in the highest reaches of "Being" itself. To jettison this rich understanding of what it means to be human seems incredibly limited and narrow.

Skeptico: Exactly who are you talking about—all those in the past who had such a sophisticated view of consciousness?

Wisdom Seeker: Some who come to mind from the distant past include Jesus, the Buddha, Socrates, Confucius, Lao Tzu, Teresa of Avila, Rumi, Patañjali, Bodhidharma, Hildegard of Bingen, Al Ghazali, Shankara, Chuang Tzu, Dogen, Plotinus, and Shakespeare. In the last century or two, William James, Rabbi Adin Steinsaltz, Ramana Maharshi, Emily Dickinson, Roberto Assagioli, the Baal Shem Tov, Fyodor Dostoyevsky, Evelyn Underhill, Anandamayi Ma, Carl Jung, Ramakrishna, Hazrat Inayat Khan, Leo Tolstoy, T.S. Eliot, Ralph Waldo Emerson, Mahatma Gandhi, Aldous Huxley, Martin Heidegger, Herman Hesse, George Gurdjieff, Shunryu Suzuki, Henry David Thoreau, J.R.R. Tolkien, Joseph Campbell, and Victor Frankel. Certainly all of these folks did not have a complete understanding of consciousness and they did not all agree with each other. Each, however, had a fairly sophisticated understanding of human consciousness that is worth considering today.

Modern Developments

One of the most striking things about we human beings is our capacity for positive change, especially when guided by conscious choices and when we pursue our visions with determination and commitment. Cultures rise and fall, advance and decline, but no matter the times or the difficulties, individuals always have the possibility for growth and development. In the modern world, the search for wisdom (at least among a few individuals) continues apace, and there are hopeful signs. In this quest, science is playing an important role, with some leading scientists turning their considerable talents to exploring the deepest questions that consciousness brings to the fore, even focusing on the importance of consciousness itself for understanding ourselves and our world. Sir James Jeans, one of the twentieth century's pioneering physicists, defined the broad context in which this search is taking place with an enigmatic statement: "The universe begins to look more like a great thought than a great machine."[16] If this is correct, then science is increasingly studying the "thought" of the universe. If carried out with the proper respect for the knowledge of the wisdom traditions of the past, this will prove immensely valuable.

At the level of consciousness, then, there is no reason that the goals of science and the goals of the wisdom traditions cannot be aligned, for both are attempting to understand the "thought" of the ultimate reality. At this level, science and things of the spirit begin to meet—and perhaps even to merge. This connection is made vivid by the realization that the ability to consider and reflect on science, as well as on the deepest questions concerning wisdom, can *only* begin when consciousness is present. Both explorations require consciousness: consciousness that one exists, that there is a world to be explored, and consciousness of others with whom one can exchange and confirm discoveries. Both spiritual inquiry and science rest on this foundation. Consciousness is the one essential for exploring the "thought" of the universe, whether in science or in the wisdom traditions. Consciousness, then, is a threshold between science and the spiritual, a doorway through which the two can fruitfully build a relationship.

Skeptico: Perhaps together they will figure it all out!

Wisdom Seeker: Perhaps, but a touch of humility is in order. Throughout history, no matter how much we have understood about consciousness, mystery has always remained. Consciousness entices, but defies us as well. Ultimately, it always seems to elude capture by our theories. We have been trying to catch it in our nets of thought for thousands of years, but we still do not understand it. Even worse, when advances are made in one direction, something always seems to be lost in another. When a new piece of the puzzle is understood and put in place, another piece that had seemed solid is brought into question. The process can be likened to a family working on a complex jigsaw puzzle together: sometimes for a new piece to be added, it is discovered that a previously added piece has to be removed because, although it seemed to fit, it really didn't belong where it had been placed. Could it be that consciousness stands in relation to human thought in such a way that it cannot be known by that thought? We look out and see the world; we look inside and discover our own thoughts, images, and feelings. But how do we look at that which is looking?

Reflecting on these issues over a hundred years ago in an essay entitled *Does Consciousness Exist?*, William James came to the conclusion that our personal awareness is all that we really have. All else is derivative. In other words, fundamental awareness does not consist of a "me" that sees something "out there." Rather, awareness is but a single point. The starting point of every observation is not something out there that a "me" can study, for all that can finally be studied is the perception or image of the thing in the mind of the observer. Things cannot be separated from the awareness of them. Something being studied and the person doing the studying are stuck together like the two sides of a hand. Physicist Max Planck was getting at the same thing in *Where is Science Going?* when he said, "Science cannot solve the ultimate mystery of nature. And that is because, in the last analysis, we ourselves are part of nature and therefore part of the mystery that we are trying to solve."[17] Echoes of the centuries-old Zen insight: Reality is "Not Two."

Thought Experiment: Where Is the Flower?

Close your eyes and bring to mind an image of a flower. Where is that flower? Now look at an object out there in the "world." Where is that object? Close your eyes a second time and bring to mind the object at which you just looked. How is its location different from the flower you brought to mind? You have been trained to think of objects you look at as "out there," but all you know for sure is that you have an image of the object in your mind. You can *know* that you have that image, but how can you *know* that there is an object "out there" that corresponds to it? You cannot bring the object into your mind and compare it to your image. You can bring another image of the object into your mind, but then you are comparing two images, both inside your mind. Where, then, is the object you think is "out there"? Are there actually two things, an object and your image of it?

James' philosophy, of course, was also very practical (he helped create the school of pragmatism), so he was in no way advising against practical action. His view was that we should be practical and treat our perceptions as real when undertaking actions; we should act "as if" the things we were perceiving in our everyday lives were really "out there." But when it came to ultimate realities, he realized that consciousness did not allow us to separate the observer from the observed, so it might always be impossible to capture the mystery of existence with our concepts.

Skeptico: Tell me again why it is so hard to get a handle on consciousness.

Wisdom Seeker: When we define consciousness as something "out there" to be studied, we create an illusion, a phantom that we chase endlessly but never catch. When consciousness is made into a concept, that concept is created by our minds and is not consciousness itself but a will-o'-the-wisp that has no substantiality. To study that concept, then, is not to study consciousness, but something artificial we have created. To paraphrase Pogo, we have met consciousness, and it is us. Or to borrow from that great ninth century Indian sage, Shankara: You can cut many things with a knife, but you cannot cut a knife with that same knife.

A scholar and scientist who has reflected deeply on the importance of consciousness and on the convergence of science and spirit (as well as their relation to art), is Ervin Laszlo.[j] In a series of books from *The Whispering Pond* to *Science and the Akashic Field,* he describes how science is coming to understand that everything in the universe consists of interconnected fields, and that ultimately each thing is connected to everything else. This includes the human body, and his theory incorporates the new understanding that our bodies, at the most basic level, are **not** made up of atoms or particles—but of

---

[j] Laszlo had an early career as a classical musician, then a prestigious scientific career teaching at several major universities in Europe and America. He has written a number of books elaborating a new general evolutionary theory, and he developed the idea of the "fifth physical field" to try to imagine the existence of an absolute dimension beyond time and space.

waves or vibrations that are continuously receiving and transmitting information to and from its field faster than a biochemical mechanism could possibly function. Interactions are happening on many different levels and at speeds that cannot be explained by materialistic, biological, or mechanistic concepts.

This leads Laszlo to the conviction that consciousness is not a byproduct of the brain, nor produced by neurons, but that consciousness pervades the universe as one interrelated whole, a whole that constitutes the universe and all the living fields and systems in it. He notes that as one opens to music, there is a sense of being part of a larger universe, of uniting with something larger than oneself. Those who have had the good fortune to have this experience with music, he says, are more likely to recognize the sense of connection that can be felt when we open out and experience a connection to the larger consciousness in which we exist. He is in very good company. William James said, "Our lives are like islands in the sea, or like trees in the forest, which co-mingle their roots in the darkness underground."[18]

Both Laszlo and James thus express the belief that we are separate on the surface but connected underneath, and this is exactly the message that many wisdom traditions have given us. From a different perspective, mathematician and philosopher Alfred North Whitehead came to the same conclusion, saying that space is "prehensive,"[19] by which he seems to have meant that everything is connected and that every part can, in some way, know every other part. Somehow, each part of the universe is in connection with, continually influencing and being influenced by all the others.

In the same vein, physicist David Bohm discusses at length in *Wholeness and the Implicate Order* that there is an underlying order to the universe, beneath the "explicate order" that we normally see, and at this underlying level everything is connected. Further, when we are able to deeply experience this implicate order, which Bohm believes is possible, we are connected to everything and everyone, and this in turn creates the possibility of a much better relationship with other beings and with all of nature. For Bohm, the individual is ultimately not a hard physical object separate from other objects; a better analogy would be that we are each like whirlpools in a great stream. As part of the stream, each of us is part of the interconnected flow of energy of the whole, but we also have our own individual movement within the whole. Expanding his image, if all of existence is one mighty river, clear lines of demarcation do not exist between the individual self and the flow of existence; we each might be separate mini-currents, giving rise to the experience of individuality, but boundaries between ourselves and the river are fluid, shifting, indistinct.

Skeptico: What does that mean for how I should live?

Wisdom Seeker: If you come to understand yourself in this way, you will develop a more full and rich understanding of who you really are. This, in turn, will lead to the possibility of becoming a more full and complete human being. But the one tool that is essential for this development is …

Skeptico: I know: *Consciousness.*

Wisdom Seeker: Good guess, Skeptico! Now, with this as background, we can explore at an even deeper level how science and things of the spirit can "settle into relationship with each other" in a harmonious way.

CHAPTER 9

SCIENCE AND SPIRIT IN HARMONY

I like solving problems—one reason I studied engineering in college. Dealing with a problem can be straightforward and analytical, but it is not always so. Numerous times in the past, when stuck on a problem I couldn't solve, I turned to my "sleeping mind."

In case you are interested, the method is simple: Get ready for bed, but before sleep comes, think through the issue you are trying to resolve. Following this method, it is amazing how many times I have awakened the next morning with a way forward clear in my mind. Where did the answer come from? What is the "sleeping mind"? I do not know. But as earlier chapters have documented, both science and art have ridden this mysterious way of knowing for a long time.

On a parallel track, through the years I have visited many spiritual places. Occasionally there have been moments when a door opened and the world appeared fresh and new. In those moments, a deeper understanding took up residence inside me. How did this happen? Another mystery. But these two mysteries seem related: There is a similar feel between practical insights that arise around sleep and understandings that arise in spiritual places. The similarity does not seem accidental, though I cannot explain it. For me, however, both mysteries have great value and are due respect.

What would it mean to take seriously the challenge quoted earlier by philosopher and mathematician Alfred North Whitehead: "More than anything else, the future of civilization depends on the way the two most powerful forces of history, science and religion, settle into relationship with each other."[1] (Whitehead includes in his use of the word "religion" what I think of as the spiritual dimension. The two are often equated, but there is an important distinction to be made. As discussed more fully in Chapter Five, the essence of the distinction is that opening to the spiritual dimension means grappling with the fundamental questions about ultimate reality and life, while engaging in a religion means working with a specific set of answers to the spiritual questions.)

To take up Whitehead's challenge, how might we proceed? For me, the first step is to realize that both religion and the spiritual dimension have to do with the deepest questions of existence: How should I live? What is truly important? What will give my life meaning? These are different questions from those associated with science today, but for most scientists throughout human history, these questions were quite relevant.

Consider the lives and thought of Rene Descartes and Isaac Newton, both of whom had as much to do with the creation of modern science as anyone who could be named. In *Discourse on the Method of Rightly Conducting the Reason, and Searching for Truth in the Sciences*, Descartes laid the foundation for scientific thought today, providing a way to think about problems and a method for arriving at proofs that could be tested and compared. Descartes did not singlehandedly create these approaches, of course, but his book, which expanded the thought of others, became the focal point for the discussion and dissemination of key ideas.

It is fascinating, then, to discover that one of the primary reasons Descartes developed his method was to prove the existence of God. (And, using the logic he is famous for developing, the same logic that became a cornerstone of modern science, he succeeded to his satisfaction.) It is equally interesting to learn that Descartes' inspiration for his life's work came from a dream. Both these things make clear that, although Descartes has come to symbolize the modern philosophic and scientific revolution, he was deeply interested in spiritual questions and fully open to non-logical ways of gaining knowledge. For Descartes, there was no conflict between science and things of the spirit; instead, there was a deep and even necessary connection between them.

A poll in 2005 selected Sir Isaac Newton as the greatest scientist of all time.[k] His *Principia Mathematica*, first published in 1687, is still considered by many to be the single most important work in the history of science. His revolutionary insights became foundational blocks for modern science, and generations of scientists have believed Newton to be without peer.

Would it surprise you to discover, then, that Newton was a deeply religious man and believed that a transcendent force was responsible for the creation of the world? His succinct view, recorded in his non-scientific papers: "Gravity explains the motions of the planets, but it cannot explain who set the planets in motion."[2] Even in the *Principia*, his scientific masterpiece, he said, "This most beautiful system of the sun, planets, and comets, could only proceed from the counsel and dominion of an intelligent and powerful Being."[3] Although the idea that the world is a "clockwork universe" independent of Divine activity is often attributed to Newton, he specifically rejected this notion. He even warned against using his ideas to portray the universe as a machine or clock free of spiritual influence. Rather, Newton thought his work provided clear evidence for Divine activity in the world.

Although a number of writers in the past have tried to portray Newton's spiritual interests as unimportant, new research definitively shows that this was not the case. In recent years the full extent of his spiritual writing and the motives behind his entire body of work have been carefully examined, and the resulting picture is that he read the

---

[k] A few years ago there was an article naming the one hundred most significant human beings who have ever lived. In the top five were four religious leaders and Newton (who was number two on the list).

Bible daily, wrote two and a half million words on religious and spiritual topics (much more than he wrote on science), and believed his spiritual writings to be as important as his scientific achievements. In fact, it has become clear in recent years—as a full understanding of his spiritual work has emerged—that Newton did not see his scientific and spiritual work as separate.

After a detailed review of his massive spiritual and philosophic writings, J.E. Force and R.H. Popkin conclude in their book, *Newton and Religion: Context, Nature, and Influence,* that Newton's overarching goal was to bring scientific ideas into harmony with his religious, spiritual, and philosophic understandings. Their conclusions are reinforced by a current project at Cambridge University that aims to make all of Newton's spiritual and alchemical writings available to the public. From these efforts, the clear theme that is emerging is that Newton's underlying plan was to reveal what he believed to be the *prisca sapienti* (primal knowledge) of the universe, and at this level of knowledge he felt there was no separation between science and spirituality.[4] In other words, Newton's spiritual and scientific work comprised one grand endeavor. In his mind, everything fit together as a unified attempt to understand the nature of the universe, increase our understanding of the Divine plan at work in that universe, and explain humanity's role in the unfolding of that plan.[5]

Of course, Newton was wildly unconventional in his scientific thought—a major contributor to many of his breakthrough insights. Because of this unconventionality, however, he was frequently criticized by the scientists of his day. He was equally unconventional in his spiritual thought, which at times put him at odds with the Dominant Established Religion of his time. And detractors follow him still; in modern times he has been roundly criticized for spending so much time in the study and practice of alchemy, since alchemy is considered about as respectable as voodoo by many people today. But Newton himself believed that his alchemical studies were the source of much of his scientific insight,[6] so it is a bit strange to think of him as the greatest scientist of all time while dismissing his view of how he arrived at his scientific breakthroughs. Do we really know more about how Newton was able to do what he did than he himself knew?

The crucial point, then, is that Newton saw no conflict between the spiritual, religious, alchemical, and scientific areas of his life and thought; rather, all fed and enhanced each other. We do not have to agree with his conclusions, of course, but it is important to acknowledge that the "greatest scientist of all time" did not see a conflict between science and religion; indeed, he believed that all of his scientific work was of a piece with his broader understanding of the religious and spiritual domains.

It is also important to emphasize again that although Newton was deeply religious, this did not prevent him from having serious disagreements with the Dominant Established Religion of his time. As a radically independent thinker, Newton did not accept the beliefs of the establishment but instead spent a great deal of time developing his own spiritual views. Because of this, he was reluctant to publish many of his spiritual and philosophical works during his lifetime. Being a very public figure, though, it was hard to hide his beliefs, so Newton was often under suspicion by the orthodox and was accused, among other things, of being a Rosicrucian. Notice, however, that he felt free to publish his scientific but not his religious ideas. This is a clear sign that the religious authorities of his day were not fighting with scientific thought, but rather were focused on enforcing their religious views, which occasionally overlapped with scientific ideas.

Newton and Descartes are important, not only because of their genius but also because of their interest in spiritual questions. In this, they are representative of almost all the important figures of the scientific revolution. Many of these key figures questioned the conventional answers of the religions of their time (sometimes publically, sometimes in private). Many had views that were different from the views of the Dominant Established Religions where they lived. They did not, however, think their spiritual interests could be separated from their scientific work; on the contrary, they thought it was

central to all they were doing. For instance, Johannes Kepler sometimes felt himself possessed by a "divine frenzy" when doing research
and believed astronomers were "priests of the most high God with
respect to the book of nature." Copernicus thought astronomy to be
"more divine than human." Galileo believed his discoveries arose
through "God's grace enlightening his mind," and Newton himself
wrote ecstatically of his scientific explorations: "Oh God, I think thy
thoughts after thee!" (The above quotes are all from *The Passion of the
Western Mind.*[7])

And just as they valued things spiritual, the leaders of the scientific
revolution understood the importance of dreams and intuition, even
saw them as sources of knowledge that could make crucial contributions to scientific exploration. For all these figures, then, science and
the spiritual quest were inseparably entwined in the search for wisdom.
As historian Karen Armstrong put it in *The Battle for God*: "Many of the
explorers, scientists, and thinkers at the cutting edge of change believed
that they were finding new ways of being religious rather than abandoning religion."[8] As said before, we do not have to accept their views
as "the truth," but it seems unwise to dismiss the cumulative thought
of so many great minds, especially when they are in close agreement.

It Is As It Always Was

Skeptico: But don't the best scientists of the modern world see things
differently from those earlier ones?

Wisdom Seeker: No, not really. Albert Einstein, perhaps the most
honored scientist of the twentieth century, concluded after a lifetime
of reflection that there was an organizing principle in the universe
from which meaning and values came:

> To know that what is impenetrable to us really exists, manifesting
> itself as the highest wisdom and the most radiant beauty which our
> dull faculties can comprehend only in their most primitive forms—
> this knowledge, this feeling, is at the center of true religiousness.[9]

This sounds almost like Plato, as well as many other wisdom teachers. Einstein joined them in the belief that, when we catch a glimpse of the mystery, we experience it as beauty, and when we have an insight about that realm, it feels like wisdom. Einstein even sensed, with the mystics, that the wisdom of science and the experience of beauty are not separate. There is more. Einstein thought science arose from this mystical domain: "The finest emotion of which we are capable is the mystic emotion. Herein lies the germ of all art and all true science."[10] Einstein thus makes clear the connection between science and the spiritual dimension and even suggests that the core motivation to do science comes from an emotion—the same emotion that fuels the spiritual search. As quoted earlier, Einstein went even further, elevating the spiritual domain to greater importance than the scientific realm he had made the focus of his life work:

> Humanity has every reason to place the proclaimers of high moral standards and values above the discoverers of objective truth. What humanity owes to personalities like Buddha, Moses, and Jesus stands for me higher than all the achievements of the inquiring and constructive mind.[11]

Robert Oppenheimer, who led the program to develop the atomic bomb in the United States, emphasized that the broad understanding of the world emerging from modern physics was not new, but was "an exemplification, an encouragement, and a refinement of old wisdom."[12] This view was fueled by his studies, which led him to see that the ideas being developed in physics corresponded to currents in Western spiritual thought, and had a "central place" in many Buddhist and Hindu concepts of the universe.

Dean Radin notes something similar in his book *The Conscious Universe*, suggesting that mystics resemble scientists in several ways:

> Numerous scientists, scholars, and sages over the years have revealed deep, underlying similarities between the goals, practices and findings of science and mysticism. Some of the most famous

scientists wrote in terms that are practically indistinguishable from the writings of mystics.[13]

Skeptico: That's impressive, but Einstein and Oppenheimer seem like a long time ago to me; maybe their views are obsolete. What about scientists and scholars today?

Wisdom Seeker: In a study of faculty members from colleges across the United States (conducted by the Higher Education Research Institute at UCLA in 2003), it was discovered that 81 percent considered themselves "spiritual persons." And in a study conducted by Neil Gross of Harvard and Solon Simmons of George Mason University in 2006 (designed to represent the 630,000 professors teaching full-time in United States colleges and universities), only 23.4 percent selected: "Do not believe in God" or "Don't know whether there is a God."[1]

Skeptico: Well, 23 percent is a lot.

Wisdom Seeker: That's true, but in examining that 23 percent more closely, it becomes clear that the phrasing of the question forced those with a Neoplatonic view, Buddhists, and even those who agree with Einstein into the 23 percent. If the question had been phrased differently, such as, "Do you think there is a spiritual dimension to life?"—I think many of that 23 percent would have answered in the affirmative.

A crucial understanding is that most everyone who professes *not* to believe in God is rejecting a particular human definition of God—either the one they were given when growing up or a definition being pushed toward them by a religious group with which they disagree. Karen Armstrong, historian and scholar of religions, illuminates this idea by noting that when religious landscapes are shifting, those who advocate new ideas are often seen as atheists by defenders of the old faith. Anyone who rejects an Established Religion becomes subject to that charge, so the first generations of Christians, Jews, and Muslims were all called atheists by the Established Religions of their times. Or

---

[1] These polls included all faculty members, but studies suggest that scientists as a group are similar in their answers to faculties in general.

consider Socrates, who was sentenced to death for "not believing in the gods"—yet his words show a deep commitment to the gods, as he understood them. He just had a different view than his accusers, who were a part of the Established Religion of his age.

The key point is that most "atheists," according to Armstrong, are denying "a particular conception of the divine." And in one sense their denial is partly right, for any human definition of *that which cannot be put into words* is inevitably flawed. Couple this with the modern tendency to rebel against authority, and those who say they "do not to believe in God" are often simply asserting their individualism by picking out a particular conception with which they can disagree. A speaker I once heard, who believed in the existence of a divine dimension, said to an "unbeliever" in the audience who kept arguing: "Sir, nor do I believe in the God you have set up not to believe in."

Skeptico: If someone asked, "Do you believe in God?" what would you say?

Wisdom Seeker: For me, the only honest response would be to say: "Which definition of God are you talking about?" All definitions are human creations and interpretations. Those who choose to believe in God have created their own definition or accepted someone else's in which to believe. And anyone who chooses "not to believe" has chosen a definition to oppose. Often, those whose purpose is to oppose have simply created a "straw God" that is easy to denounce.

Thought Experiment: Which God Do You Believe In, or Reject?

There are many ways to define God. What is your definition, either the one you accept or the one you reject? What do you think about all the others?

Rediscovering the Mystery

Many arguments about beliefs and about religion are caused by the inadequacy of human definitions, for all definitions that profess to pin down ultimate reality are partial and limited (in science as well as in religion). This does not mean that discussions about the nature of ultimate reality or thinking about the possibility of a transcendent dimension lack worth. If undertaken in the right spirit, these activities are quite valuable, and both science and religion have significant contributions to make; both are capable of bringing forth wisdom from the sea of the unknown. At this level of inquiry, there is actually a deep connection between science and things of the spirit. Both are fishing in the same waters, are trying to catch understanding from that vast sea of what is unknown to us. Ultimately, however, both leave many questions unanswered, and mystery remains.

Skeptico: I can see how spiritual questions arise from the mystery of existence, but I'm not convinced that's true of science.

Wisdom Seeker: Every time science answers one set of questions, new questions inevitably arise. There have been periods when some scientists thought they had all the key pieces of an understanding of the physical world in place, but they were soon disabused of that notion. At the beginning of the twentieth century, a number of scientists proclaimed that all the key questions had been answered, but shortly thereafter physics upset that apple cart, in the process reminding us just how mysterious the physical world really is.

Since the dawn of modern physics, the deeper it has penetrated, the greater the mystery it has uncovered. In the last few decades, physics has *not only* failed to provide simple answers; it has pictured the starry heavens above and the quantum level below in a way that is almost defiant of rational understanding. For instance, the most accepted theory today concerning the composition of the universe is that it is made up mostly of "dark matter" and "dark energy," and these two "mysteries" (what else to call them?) account for more than 96 percent of all that exists.

Their names, however, begin with "dark" precisely because we cannot see them or find them with our instruments—we can only infer their existence. This dark stuff is a great mystery, evoking comparisons to the "ether" that was thought to fill the universe from

Aristotle's time until the end of the nineteenth century. At that time, the "ether" idea was supposedly buried for good, but it has refused to stay buried; it has returned as the two "darks." Like the undiscoverable ether, there is no direct evidence for their existence; we simply assume they exist because we need them to make our theories work.

Dark matter is presumed to exist because something has to be generating the gravitational forces we cannot account for in the universe. Dark energy is assumed in order to explain the accelerating expansion of the cosmos; the current theory says the stars and galaxies are being continually pushed away from each other for reasons we do not understand. But if 96 percent of what exists is totally unknown to us, the world is a mystery. And it raises several fundamental questions: Does the physical world we know interact with this unknown realm? Is the "dark" realm governed by laws we recognize? If there is an energy exchange between the known world and this unknown realm, what does that mean with relation to our presumed "laws" of the conservation of matter and energy? We do not know the answers to these questions.

There is also the current theory describing reality at the smallest level, which is called superstring or M-theory (see Chapter Two). If it is correct, at the most basic level there is no matter as we normally think of matter: There are only vibrations. The core idea is that the building blocks of the universe are infinitesimally small vibrations, called "strings," but these strings are not "matter" in any normal sense of the word. Further, no instruments can detect them—and therein lies a major problem for science.

Lee Smolin, a noted researcher at the Perimeter Institute for Theoretical Physics, points out that there is no empirical evidence for the existence of these "strings" and that no one has been able to propose an experiment that the community of physicists thinks can verify their existence. This is dramatic, for to accept superstrings as the building blocks of the universe (as many have done) without even a proposed experiment to verify their existence means going against a core assumption of science: that a theory must include a proposed way to discover whether it is valid or not.

Karl Popper is most responsible for developing this idea, arguing that even though a lot of theories are accepted that cannot be demonstrated through a positive test, a new theory must at least contain a possible "falsifiability" experiment. In other words, someone must come up with a plausible way—at least imagine how, at some point in the future—a test could be performed to discover if the new theory were wrong. Otherwise, if there is no way to prove that a new theory is true, or even that it might be false, what is the difference between such a theory and a fairy tale? But no one has been able to suggest a way of determining whether string theory is false.

As mentioned in Chapter Two, I have had a fondness for string theory since reading a description by Professor Michio Kaku: "It's a bizarre theory that says that all matter really consists of tiny vibrating rubber bands, or strings." (Another way to think of them: tiny vibrating waves of energy.) "Different vibrations of these strings could be considered musical notes, with each note corresponding to a different particle." His conclusion: If these strings exist, "the universe is a symphony of strings—cosmic music—resonating through eleven-dimensional hyperspace."[14] This is, of course, hard to conceptualize—even the best physicists have a hard time doing so. Superstrings, if they exist, are quite a mystery.

Assuming the existence of superstrings brings up another dilemma. Stanford theoretical physicist Leonard Susskind, one of the originators of the original idea, says that the number of possible "vibrations" of the strings is 10^{500} —an unimaginably large number. The implication of this is that the number of different particles in the universe is also an unimaginably large number. But only a tiny fraction of this number actually seem to exist. Why so? No one knows. All we know from the theory is that the universe is made up of a very limited number of notes among the incredibly large number that could be playing, and no one has any scientific idea why some notes are played and others are not. Yet life as we know it is dependent on these specific notes being played, rather than others. All of this is quite mysterious.

One further example: Brian Swimme (mathematician, director of the Center for the Story of the Universe at the California Institute of Integral Studies, author of four books on cosmology, evolution, and religion, and producer of a twelve-part movie series entitled *Canticle to the Cosmos*) suggests that the material "stuff" we take for granted doesn't exist continuously in the world we know. Rather, the infinitesimally small "things" that make up our world—whether particles or vibrations—constantly merge back into the "quantum vacuum" *trillions of times a second* and then reemerge again! (He reaches this conclusion on the basis of the work of physicist David Bohm.) In other words, the building blocks of the material world are constantly disappearing from "existence" in the material world and then "foaming forth," reappearing with equal rapidity into the world we see and touch. Thus, the world we take to be solid is a constant flux from materiality to non-materiality and back again.[15]

If this is so, what happens to these small "things" during the nanoseconds in which they are "merged back" into the quantum vacuum? Where are they? Do they become part of dark matter? Do they return to dark energy? Are they subject to normal physical laws during this time? No one knows. But this theory could help explain some of the mysterious features of quantum particles, such as their seeming ability to transfer information over tremendous distances faster than the speed of light.

These modern issues and questions in science are fascinating, and I am not qualified to judge their final truth. I do not think anyone is. They are recounted here simply to demonstrate that modern science is repeatedly coming face-to-face with the mystery in which we exist. To paraphrase storyteller Michael Meade, physics is constantly veering back toward metaphysics—from which it came.

Skeptico: Don't you think that if we wait a little longer, all will be explained—that the next breakthrough will bring an understanding of what ultimate reality *really* is?

Wisdom Seeker: Not likely. Reading back through several hundred years of scientific discoveries, it is common for a new theory to generate headlines that say that the deepest mysteries of the cosmos have been solved—followed (in a few years, or a few weeks) by a new mystery. Then comes a new "answer," and the process is repeated over and over again. We like this game and the feeling it gives that we are making progress. To add a dash of humility to the mix, just think back to the issue of gravity discussed earlier. Newton demonstrated that gravity was affecting the Earth and every object on it, but he was perplexed until the end of his life that he was not able to give an explanation for *how* it works. He tried and tried but could not find an explanation for the *how*, so he focused his efforts on explaining gravity's effects. Even today, no one has solved the mystery of *how*.

> ### Thought Experiment: How Does Gravity Work?
>
> Do you know how the moon reaches down and creates the tides in the oceans? If not, you are not alone. No one knows *how* this happens; only *that* it happens. We call it gravity, but naming is not explaining. How does gravity work?

All this leads to an unmistakable realization: The unknown constantly reappears at the boundary of our knowledge, no matter how much information we acquire. Perhaps this is because every system of knowledge begins with assumptions, and knowledge acquired through any set of assumptions cannot capture the whole. Assumptions make the information manageable but do so by excluding as well as including. In other words, an answer only works within its set of assumptions, not within other sets of assumptions. This means that beyond the knowledge acquired by any system of thought there will always be things that are unknown and unexplained. This is part of the reason for the continual flux in science, and a major reason that science is perpetually exciting. It also leads to these conclusions: Scientific knowledge is not close to answering the fundamental questions about the nature of the material world; it is even less prepared to answer the deepest questions about life and living; and it certainly cannot be used to confirm or reject religious or spiritual beliefs (except when those beliefs have strayed into the territory of how the physical world should be understood).

Vladimir Nabokov, novelist and practicing scientist (he was a lepidopterist and a Research Fellow at the Harvard Museum of Comparative Zoology, where he made a significant discovery involving blue butterfly speciation), summed up the dilemma: "The greater one's science, the deeper the sense of mystery." In this vein, an article in *Newsweek* a few years ago was talking about quarks, considered at the time to be the ultimate "small things." The article, written when string theory was emerging in the popular mind, observed that even quarks might be composed of something smaller and that there was "the disturbing possibility that the universe will never surrender its ultimate material."[16]

I was not disturbed, but amused, for I have come to accept that there is much we do not know and very likely much we will never know. It is even likely, as Niels Bohr suggested, that the "real" world toward which quantum mechanics points is a trickster. He noted that any time we try to pin down and separate into discrete objects the world we think we see "out there," those objects (which we have actually created in our minds) refuse to maintain their substantiality. John Gribbin (who holds a doctorate in physics from Cambridge) summarized the view developed by Bohr and his colleagues: "Everything we call real is made of things that cannot be regarded as real."[17] Or as Einstein put it, there is a unified field of existence, and "matter" cannot be taken from that field and made separate from it.

Einstein's startling image means that what we call matter does not consist of objects, even infinitesimally small objects, but is rather an *intensity*. Philipp Frank summarizes Einstein's view as saying that, "The mass of a particle is actually nothing but a field of force that is very strong" (at a particular point). This means that what we perceive as the *motion* of an object that has mass is "nothing but the change of a force field in space."[18] Therefore, in the new physics, there are not two things, "field and matter;" instead, if Einstein is right, the field is the only reality and matter is but a greater intensity in the field. No wonder we are having such a hard time finding the basic "particles" from which, according to past assumptions, the world is made.

Meeting in the Mystery

Skeptico: You keep using the word "mystery." I don't have a very positive view of that word, but apparently you do. What do you mean by it?

Wisdom Seeker: "Mystery" is understood by different people in various ways. One narrow view is that it is a confusion that needs to be cleared up. A negative view is that it is mumbo-jumbo used to manipulate the naïve. The way I use it, however, is to point to that which lies beyond our understanding. Mystery in this sense is something we can engage with and be changed by, but which we cannot tie down with neat definitions or master with the intellect. Seen as representing that which lies beyond our understanding and control, mystery is linked to things of great importance, such as love and existence itself. As French quantum physicist Bernard d'Espagnat put it, "Mystery is not something negative that has to be eliminated. On the contrary, it is one of the constitutive elements of being."[19] Understanding mystery in this way, it becomes the ground where science and things of the spirit meet; it is the starting point and province of both.

To explore the mysteries of existence, science focuses on the physical world. As it goes about its business, however, it inevitably comes to the edge of the mystery in which we exist; it is constantly bumping into questions it cannot answer. For their part, organized religions and individual spiritual quests focus on meanings, values, and our place in the greater scheme of things—all of which eventually lead to the mysteries of life and existence. Thus, as science and religious/spiritual undertakings proceed, they come to a point of intersection. And this is valuable for both—if they are willing to approach such occasions with humility and respect for each other. Many of the wisdom traditions advise just such a path. For instance, St. Augustine said: "Let us, on both sides, lay aside all arrogance. Let us not, on either side, claim that we have already discovered the truth."[20] The Hindu tantric tradition points in the same direction when it says that two veils hide the truth: ignorance and self-righteousness. In other words, if you self-righteously believe that the truth you have found for yourself is true for everyone, this creates as much blindness as does pure ignorance.

Skeptico: If someone wanted to try to live toward the harmony you are talking about, what would they do?

Wisdom Seeker: Those interested in the spiritual side of life would relinquish all attempts to judge scientific discoveries about the physical world through religious theories. Instead, they would cultivate a deep respect for the marvels science has wrought and for the hard-earned knowledge it has achieved concerning the workings of the material world. They would honor all the contributions science has made to life on earth and recognize that science even has the capacity to serve as a doorway to spiritual growth and insight. The fact is, many scientists have experienced their work as a practice similar to and sometimes entwined with spiritual seeking. Since both are fueled by awe and wonder at the mystery of existence and both require great dedication and discipline, there are indeed many similarities. Science can even be a meditative practice, if approached with an open mind and heart. Ultimately, science can become "a tremendous spiritual vocation," as Charles Tart wrote and as the lives of many scientists through history demonstrate.

On the other side of the relationship, to move toward harmony the scientific community would recognize that spiritual knowledge cannot be judged by science. All assertions about spiritual things rest on metaphysical beliefs, and science is not equipped to provide spiritual or metaphysical judgments. Insofar as religious organizations are operating in the world, however, these organizations can be studied by the methods of science; intellectual disciplines can study how an organization is operating, evaluate its successes and failures in the world, and measure the effect it is having on individual lives. But science cannot judge what the goals of life should be, the meanings a person should choose, what values people should live by, or the validity of metaphysical views that attempt to bring an experience of fulfillment, happiness, or joy. As one of the greatest philosophers of the twentieth century, Ludwig Wittgenstein, said: "Even when all possible scientific questions have been answered, the problems of life remain untouched."[21]

Winston Churchill was neither a scientist nor much of a spiritual seeker; he was not even a religious person, recounting in his biography how his readings in his college years and shortly thereafter turned him against religious thought. His attitude changed, though, when he went to war. In a time of crisis in war, he found himself praying—even though he did not know to what he was praying. He then remembered a version of Pascal's phrase, "The heart has its reasons which reason does not know," and adopted that as an operating principle. Realizing it need not be a problem if the head and the heart "did not always run ... together," he began to give both head and heart value in his life, saying,

> It would be very foolish to discard the reasons of the heart for those of the head. Indeed I could not see why I should not enjoy them both. I did not worry about the inconsistency of thinking one way and believing the other. It seemed good to let the mind explore so far as it could the paths of thought and logic, and also good to pray for help and succour, and be thankful when they came.[22]

By adopting Churchill's openness, scientists will be able to join Einstein in honoring all those who have contributed to the spiritual development of humankind. They will also be free to honestly acknowledge, rather than ignore, the spiritual interests of scientists like Newton, Kepler, Galileo, and Copernicus. They will be able to acknowledge, maybe even understand, the reports of numerous great scientists who said that their spiritual pursuits, in some mysterious way, contributed to their scientific discoveries. Who knows, such open-mindedness might even enhance their own scientific endeavors, as it seems to have done for many scientists.

As science, religion, and things of the spirit develop mutual respect, they become allies, and this eventually leads to the recognition that without taking each into account, life is impoverished. Einstein captured it perfectly: "Science without religion is lame, religion without science is blind."[23] Even that iconic hero of non-believers, Charles Darwin, did not believe they needed to be in conflict, saying in a letter: "It seems to me absurd to doubt that a man may be an ardent Theist and an evolutionist ... I have never been an atheist in the sense of denying the existence of a God."[24]

David Loye, who wrote a fascinating book on Darwin's broader beliefs (*Darwin on Love*), noted that Darwin's final understanding of human existence was not organized around "survival of the fittest" but around the importance of love. In Darwin's first book, *The Origin of the Species*, he was primarily focused on the forces that affect the animal kingdom, but when he dealt more extensively with humans in *The Descent of Man*, he continually focused on the importance of love, and in that book stayed open to the mysterious source of love's arising. (He mentions "survival of the fittest" only twice in *Descent* but speaks of love ninety-five times.)[25] Darwin's conclusion seems to be that love is one of the central forces involved in the development of the human species, and needless to say, love is the word most commonly used by the wisdom traditions to try to hint at the underlying mystery of existence.

Skeptico: I have to admit that Darwin wrote a number of things that do not fit with how he is portrayed by my fellow skeptics, but you won't be able to deal with one of my heroes, the Scottish philosopher David Hume, so easily.

Wisdom Seeker: As you say, Hume is often brought in to challenge religious views, and he made some striking arguments against specific religious ideas. But he, like Darwin, did not hold the views frequently attributed to him. His arguments were directed against specific claims he felt to be unjustified by the Established Religions of his time. (He also questioned the basis of scientific knowledge, saying we could not really know the causes of things.) That he was not opposed to the spiritual in general, but to specific claims by specific Established Religions becomes crystal clear in his introduction to *The Natural History Of Religion,* where he says: "The whole frame of nature bespeaks an Intelligent Author; and no rational enquirer can, after serious reflection, suspend his belief a moment with regard to the primary principles of genuine Theism and Religion."[26]

The Union of Science and Spirit

The practice of science often leads to awe and wonder at the mystery of creation and sometimes to an experience of harmony with all that is—states usually associated with spiritual experience. Conversely, spirituality can lead to powerful experiences of knowing, including knowledge of the material world, and the history of humankind is filled with stories of people who came to know things about the material world while in altered states of consciousness. Breakthrough insights too frequent to count have come to scientists through dreams, visions, and unexplainable moments that resembled spiritual experiences much more than they resembled the scientific method. For example, Thomas Edison used radical self-manipulation techniques to stimulate insights that have had a profound impact on the modern world.

Because of the importance of these kinds of insights, wisdom traditions through the centuries (such as Chinese Taoism, the Greek mystery schools, branches of Indian Yoga, various esoteric traditions, and shamanic cultures all over the world) have developed techniques to access this other way of knowing. Through these techniques, much knowledge has been gained, and the results have been used both for spiritual development and to increase humanity's knowledge of the physical world. Examples abound, from Newton's alchemical experimentations to the health benefits gained by millions through the practice of Tai Chi or one of the other martial arts, all of which grew out of the insights of Taoist sages. Of special importance is the way many cultures have acquired knowledge about medicinal plants from this other way of knowing, and we are still mining this rich vein of knowledge to this day. (Perhaps as many as half of all modern drugs were discovered in part by working with what older cultures had discovered about the medicinal use of plants and minerals.)

Within the Christian contemplative tradition, this other way of knowing has also had great prominence. In her book *Mysticism*, Evelyn Underhill describes a direct path to this state: "All that is asked is that we shall look for a short time in a special and undivided manner at some simple, concrete, and external thing." Continuing, she says that the thing chosen can be almost any object, the crucial point being that you must not pay attention to anything else but "concentrate your attention on this one act of loving sight" so that "all other objects are excluded from the conscious field." The trick is to stop thinking and "pour out" your attention toward that one object, to "let your soul be in your eyes." Then:

> This new method of perception will reveal unsuspected qualities in the external world. First, you will perceive about you a strange and deepening quietness, a slowing down of feverish mental time. Next, you will become aware of a heightened significance, an intensified existence in the thing at which you look.[27]

Following this method, you discover that "the barrier between its life and yours, between subject and object, has melted away." In this way, mystics through the ages have gained knowledge about the world and many scientists have done the same. As recounted in Chapter Five, many scientific breakthroughs have arisen in this way, and spiritual adepts such as Teresa of Avila and Hildegard of Bingen have taken insights gained in mystical states and applied them very successfully to creating organizations in the world, building monasteries, writing music, and developing ways to improve the health of the people around them.

In the modern world, having looked beneath the surface of the supposed conflict between science and the spiritual domain, many spiritual leaders have recognized the commonalities and concluded that science is an ally and friend. Pope John Paul II and the Dalai Lama, two of the best known and most respected spiritual figures of the modern era, both came to this conclusion and shared a deep interest in scientific ideas. (Until John Paul's death in 2005, the two talked at length on a number of occasions about science and other topics, developing a mutual respect and friendship.) Importantly, they both made determined efforts to bring their spiritual understanding into harmony with the best scientific thought of their time.

Still another area of commonality between science and the spiritual is the fact that many practitioners of both experience what they are doing as something to which they have been called. Called by whom? By what? Very hard to say—this is another mystery. That famous "atheist" of the last century, British mathematician and philosopher Bertrand Russell, said of his own motivation: "I have wished to know why the stars shine. And I have tried to understand the Pythagorean power by which numbers hold sway above the flux."[28] Thus even this committed non-believer believed in an unseen order that held sway above the "flux" in which we normally live.

Russell goes further: "In the union of love I have seen, in a mystic miniature, the prefiguring vision of the heaven that saints and poets have imagined."[29] These words would be completely at home if coming from the pen of a mystic, and further, in citing Pythagoras, Russell is entering the spiritual realm, for Pythagoras was a mystic and religious teacher, as well as an early scientist. Not only that, Pythagoras believed his scientific and religious views were inseparable. He thought that numbers represented the Divine realm, and it was this Divine realm that held "sway above the flux" of the material world.

Spirituality was an integral part of the Pythagorean vision, and Russell had to know this, for he was a life-long student of philosophy.

He wrote several books on its history. Thus, Russell had to have known this crucial fact about Pythagoras, so his reference to a "Pythagorean power" integrating and bringing harmony to everything cannot have been accidental. I think Russell knew full well the implication of what he was reflecting by referring to Pythagoras in this way. Of course, these words were written very late in his life, so by the time he wrote them, his views had changed a lot from those of his early years.

This is not to suggest that Russell was retracting his criticisms of the Established Religions with which he disagreed; he doesn't do that. But his words imply that he had developed an understanding of the distinction between the specific doctrines he opposed and a spiritual sense not tied to those specifics. Perhaps what happened to Russell is reflected in this observation by the great physicist Werner Heisenberg: "The first gulp from the glass of natural sciences will turn you into an atheist, but at the bottom of the glass God is waiting for you."[30] Of course, Heisenberg did not hold a conventional view of "God," as his other writings make clear:

> In the history of science, ever since the famous trial of Galileo, it has repeatedly been claimed that scientific truth cannot be reconciled with the religious interpretation of the world. Although I am now convinced that scientific truth is unassailable in its own field, I have never found it possible to dismiss the content of religious thinking as … part of an outmoded phase in the consciousness of mankind, a part we shall have to give up from now on. Thus in the course of my life I have repeatedly been compelled to ponder on the relationship of these two regions of thought, for I have never been able to doubt the reality of that to which they point.[31]

It is thus abundantly clear that many of those who, from a simplistic point of view are supposed to be "battling religion," are doing no such thing. Rather, most physicists, scientists, mathematicians, engineers, and technologists are instead in the company of Einstein, Newton, Descartes, and so many others—they see the value of developing a spiritual perspective and have undertaken a personal quest to gain such an understanding for themselves. Many do disagree with the assertions of particular Established Religions, especially religions that make an effort to control the scientific enterprise, but this is very different from being at odds with all things spiritual or even with all religions.

Skeptico: I'm still thinking about that quote from Heisenberg you just mentioned. Did he mean that both religious thinking and scientific truth point to the same final reality, or that each pointed to separate realities, but that he could not doubt the reality of either?

Wisdom Seeker: I have puzzled over that and am not sure, but in either case, his words emphasize the importance of honoring both science and the spiritual domain. Heisenberg came to believe, along with so many others, that the discoveries of science were not in opposition to the Real and the True and the Good. On the contrary, countless scientists, philosophers, theologians, and spiritual seekers through the ages have come to the realization that the world, and our life in it, is a great mystery, and this mystery is the nexus at which science and things of the spirit meet.

Skeptico: Careful, discussing science in terms of mystery makes some people nervous.

Wisdom Seeker: I know, especially those who want to think of science as always being fact-based and objective. But a full understanding of science must include this part of its nature, as well as an understanding that all knowledge is ultimately based on assumptions.

Skeptico: What do you mean by that?

Wisdom Seeker: Let's move on to the next chapter, and I will try to explain.

CHAPTER 10

ON THE WINGS OF ASSUMPTIONS

I love to travel. When flying across an ocean I assume the plane is trustworthy and the pilot is competent. I further assume that the pilot will be able to find the one tiny spot on this vast earth we are looking for where we are supposed to land.

I have rented cars all over the world (it is an adventure to drive in Japan, Jamaica, Greece, South Africa ... and Ireland). All over the world I walk up to a counter, give someone who does not speak my language a small card with numbers on it, and assume they will give me the keys to a $50,000 car.

Stepping into a rental car and pulling out onto a busy highway, I accelerate to a fairly high rate of speed (not that high, at least at first), and do not slow down at intersections if I see a small green light. I make the assumption that other drivers will not venture into my path if there is a green light; that this symbol means the same thing to the Balinese as it does to me. I do this even though I know that cars in some countries often run red lights—I have seen it happen many times myself (especially in Egypt ... and Paris). Nevertheless, I assume this will not happen to me; if I did not assume this, I would have to stop at every intersection and proceed very cautiously.

On the first day of a trip I often stop at a little machine, put a piece of plastic with numbers on it in a slot, and assume that the machine will spit out money in the local currency. I assume it will connect with my bank account several thousand miles away and that the two banks will only take a "fair" fee … even though I do not know what a "fair" fee is. The assumption that I can acquire local currency in this way is so strong that if it doesn't happen, I will end up stranded in a foreign land without funds to pay for food or shelter.

The Basis for Human Life

Our lives ride on assumptions just as an airplane rides on the unseen air. When we look toward the horizon, the air is the medium through which we look. We can see clouds or birds in the air, but we cannot see the air itself (except perhaps in a few cities where the smog makes the air visible). As with the air around us, we live and move through the medium of our assumptions—quite often without seeing them or noticing that they are there.

We walk into restaurants all over the world and assume people we do not know will make a reasonable effort to serve sanitary food. We logically know that some will not make this effort, yet we walk into unknown restaurants all the time, even in strange lands, and assume that the food is reasonably safe and will not make us sick.

We assume that most people who enter into a sport or game will attempt to play by the rules, and we assume that if they don't, we have a right to correct their behavior. We even assume that everyone else—judges, referees, other players, observers—will help us enforce the rules.

To have functioning economies, we assume that most people will abide by the agreements they make and fulfill the obligations they undertake. We must assume most people will do these things, including the simplest exchanges, if an economy is to be viable. We know some people are corrupt, but we assume that most are not. If we did not make this assumption, each of us would have to do everything for ourselves each day.

I once let a doctor bombard my head with radiation to reduce a tumor (although there were many potential dangers), assuming he knew exactly how much radiation to use and the precise spot toward which to direct the beams without harming my brain. Millions of times a day we humans let someone with a knife (usually a person we hardly know) cut open our bodies, cut into our hearts and vital organs, saw our bones—with the assumption that this is a good idea and that they know what they are doing. We assume they will make a reasonable effort to help us get better, rather than experimenting on us or rushing through the procedure just to get our money.

From the time we are born we are encouraged to make a wide range of assumptions, and small children seem to inherently assume that their caregivers will take care of them. They even demand care with their cries if it isn't forthcoming. Some caregivers do not take care, though, but as babes we do not know this, so we assume they will try to meet our needs. As we grow, we assume that the way these powerful figures are doing things is the right way; later, we might rebel, or even be repulsed by the way they acted, but when we are young we tend to assume that their ways are right and if something is wrong, it is likely our fault.

Then, as we get older and move out into the broader world, we mostly assume that people are telling the truth most of the time. We assume that our loved ones are sincere and not manipulating to get what they want from us most of the time. These are remarkable assumptions. Why do we make them when we know, in fact, that people do lie with some frequency? There seems to be in us some deeply ingrained assumption that other people will tell the truth much of the time. Furthermore, if we did not make this assumption, human relationships—as well as culture as we know it—would not be possible.

We humans are assuming beings. There is no proof for many of the things we take for granted, nor would it make sense to spend a lot of time trying to find proofs for them. We assume much, and human life rests upon these assumptions.

What About the Factual Stuff?

Skeptico: Okay, I can see we make a lot of assumptions, but some things are based on facts, like science.

Wisdom Seeker: Is science ultimately based on facts?

Skeptico: Of course it is. Everything in science has to be proven.

Wisdom Seeker: Does science start with facts or with assumptions?

Skeptico: With facts … I hope.

Wisdom Seeker: Sorry, but that isn't the reality. Science does not begin with facts. To practice science a person must be enculturated into a system of assumptions. Every field of science is sustained by a set of assumptions, and there is no way to function in any area of science outside of its assumptions. Anyone who tries to do so is simply ignored. The assumptions provide the bedrock and the boundary; they make it possible for that science to exist—but also create limits concerning what it can do. Crucially, no field of science can provide proof for its core assumptions. As mathematician extraordinaire Kurt Gödel made clear in his *first incompleteness theorem*, if you start with certain axioms, you can use those axioms to prove theorems that result from those axioms, but you cannot use those initial axioms, or any theorems that grow out of them, to prove the initial axioms.

In other words, the results of scientific discoveries can never be used to prove the assumptions on which those discoveries were based. The ideas and theories that flow from the starting assumptions are valid within the system, but have little or nothing to say about the framework of the system itself. In a sense, the strength of science lies in the limitations its assumptions provide—by limiting what is included, science can do certain things very well. To gain this benefit, however, science must accept its starting assumptions on faith; it can provide no proof of their truth.

As an analogy, baseball managers, like scientists, operate within a system. When new participants enter the world of baseball, they enter a system of established rules. To be a successful baseball manager, a person must have an extensive knowledge of how to operate within those rules. That person, however, does not need to know how the game of baseball started or the reasons the rules were originally designed as they were. A successful manager does not need to know why there are four bases instead of five or three strikes rather than four. In fact, it would likely be a detriment if a manager started questioning the assumptions of baseball during the course of a game. To be successful, a manager only needs to know the rules that are in place.

Thought Experiment: Inside and Outside the Assumptions

What would happen to a baseball manager who began to question why there were four bases instead of five, or three strikes instead of four during a game?

In science, as in baseball, there is no need for scientists, in doing their job, to look beyond the assumptions they have been given. If a baseball manager wants to understand the reason there are four bases instead of five, he will have to undertake a completely different field of study than that involved in becoming a successful manager. The same is true for science. Scientists who wish to understand the assumptions of science will have to undertake study in many areas besides science; they will need history, philosophy, sociology, anthropology, psychology, economics, etc.

Further, young scientists will often find themselves ostracized if they start questioning the core assumptions when learning to be a scientist. Every field of endeavor has a way of enforcing its assumptions, a way to keep those in the field in line so that it can operate in a coherent manner. Even when a fully accredited scientist suggests publicly that the assumptions of the field might be wrong, it creates an outcry. For such a rebel, money for research often dries up, publishing opportunities fall away, job opportunities evaporate, and sometimes even the current job is threatened. (And sometimes the questioning is simply ignored by everyone in the field, which might be the most painful outcome of all.)

Why does this happen? Not because scientists think of themselves as the "science police," but because they have been enculturated to believe that their assumptions are "the truth." They have succeeded in their careers by having faith in the assumptions and thus believe that a rebellious colleague just does not understand the most basic ideas in the field. There is a quick, automatic consensus that the rebel is either poorly educated, incompetent, or a bit crazy. And sometimes they are—but not always.

This is not malicious; it is how every field of endeavor perpetuates itself, from baseball to science to religion. Science, in fact, is admirably self-correcting—with errors that occur within the assumptions. Intentional fraud is eventually exposed. Erroneous results based on the natural human tendency to find evidence in support of one's own views are gradually overcome (although this can take a long time).

It is very different, however, concerning errors that arise from the assumptions themselves. As Thomas Kuhn suggested in his revolutionary book, *The Structure of Scientific Revolutions*, changing a set of assumptions in science requires a paradigm shift. Further, such a shift will occur only after a long process in which more and more anomalies build up—data that does not fit into the old system. As the anomalies grow, the old order will fight fiercely to defend itself from change, will fight to defend its assumptions. Eventually, however, there will be a massive tipping of the scales into a new order, a new scientific paradigm. A fascinating example is the firestorm of derision that greeted Louis Pasteur, little more than a hundred years ago, when he concluded that germs spread disease and that health practitioners were spreading disease to their patients. (He was right, of course, but this did not keep doctors from resisting his ideas for a long time.)

Changing core assumptions in any field is a difficult and painful process. This was certainly the case as Copernicus, Kepler, and Galileo tried to turn the scientific thought of their time toward the view that the Earth revolved around the Sun. A few hundred years later, as physicist Max Planck was trying to turn the scientific community away from Newton's view of the universe and toward the quantum model, he observed that, "A new scientific truth does not triumph by convincing its opponents and making them see the light, but rather because its opponents eventually die, and a new generation grows up."[1] In other words, those who are invested in any paradigm do not often change their views; change comes only as they gradually die and no longer occupy the positions of power. Only then can new ideas be established. This is dramatically the case with the core assumptions that are in place in each field of study.

Skeptico: Are you saying I should not accept the assumptions of today's science?

Wisdom Seeker: Not at all. Until a scientific paradigm shifts, you are right to use it as the best means for discovering truth *in its area of expertise.* At the same time, it is valuable to look with a keen eye at the assumptions upon which any knowledge is based in order to understand its weaknesses as well as its strengths. This will help you remain open to new ideas and to broader possibilities. When it comes to how you will live your life, the implications of this insight are especially important. The assumptions within which you live provide a structure for living, and that is critical, but at the same time those assumptions constitute the walls of your prison. This means that for intractable problems, both in science and in your own life, going outside the "norm" is the only way to really solve those problems. As a popular quote often attributed to Einstein has it: "We cannot solve our problems with the same thinking we used when we created those problems."

Many Successful Sciences

To develop a broad perspective on what science can and cannot do, it is important to remember that scientific ideas are ever-changing and that many previously accepted scientific ideas have been proven wrong. Further, it is crucial to come to terms with Thomas Kuhn's evidence that science is not a process of building a more and more accurate paradigm, but that occasional transformations of thought upend core ideas of accepted truth by changing the paradigm.

One way to get at this is to recognize that different cultures have had very different scientific paradigms. The Greeks, Romans,

Egyptians, and Chinese (to name but a few) had scientific systems based on very different assumptions than we have today, but each built great civilizations with large cities and incredible buildings; each created sophisticated tools and marvelous art. And, of course, each of them had significantly different assumptions from the others.

With regard to medicine and health, many cultures have had very different assumptions than we have in the West today, yet some of those cultures had good health and great longevity. For thousands of years the Chinese had a different view from ours concerning how the body works, yet during long stretches of time (during periods when peace and prosperity reigned in China), life expectancies were as great as ours today. In ancient Israel, following a different set of health assumptions, there was an expectation of longevity: The Talmud says that the age of eighty brings "a new, special strength of age." And the ancient Hindu Vedas suggest that "the natural duration of human life" is one hundred years.

Dr. Alexander Leaf (who was the Jackson Professor of Clinical Medicine at Harvard Medical School for many years and in 1995 won the highest honor the Association of American Physicians can give) reported in his book *Youth in Old Age* that several societies with totally different medical assumptions than our own had great longevity. He visited several of those cultures and found a surprising number of people who were still alive past the century mark, some of whom were quite active and healthy up to one hundred and ten years of age and beyond.[2]

All this makes clear that very different assumptions can be successful—in medicine as well as in other areas of science. Different sets of assumptions have different strengths and different weaknesses; each system works well in some ways but not so well in others. Importantly, when a set of assumptions is replaced, some things are gained while others are lost. It is hard, however, for those within a paradigm to accurately evaluate its strengths and weaknesses. When we look at the assumptions of cultures in the past, it is easy for us to point to what we consider mistakes. Yet people in past cultures would likely see the mistakes in our assumptions more clearly than we do. In that light, isn't it likely that some of the assumptions we live by today will seem mistaken to people in the future, even some of our assumptions in science?

Skeptico: If there are mistakes today, why haven't they been corrected?

Wisdom Seeker: The natural tendency of every person and every group is to focus on the evidence that supports their point of view. Dr. John Ioannidis, who studies research methods and results, wrote an essay in 2005 documenting the problem entitled: "Why Most Published Research Findings Are False." His conclusion: "False findings may be the majority or even the vast majority of published research claims." This is not primarily due to intentional dishonesty, he says, but results from "poor study design or self-serving data analysis."[3] In other words, the facts on which researchers focus and the way they interpret those facts are significantly clouded by their biases.

The problem might be even deeper than that. Kevin Dunbar and Jonathan Fugelsang, researchers at Dartmouth College, believe that resistance to taking in new information that contradicts what we already believe is "hardwired into our brains." When presented with ideas that are contrary to what we currently believe, the parts of the brain that focus on finding errors become very active. We do not, however, seem to focus on what is wrong with our own ideas, but turn our powers of criticism toward the unwanted thought. And, not surprisingly, their research suggests that this happens with scientists just as it does with everyone else.[4]

Skeptico: If someone were an especially brilliant scientist, with the best training in the world, would that person still have this problem?

Wisdom Seeker: Yes. Even the most brilliant people are subject to this tendency. In fact, they will often use their brilliance to try to prove their point of view to be correct. It is very rare for any of us, scientist or otherwise, brilliant or not, to be willing to question the core assumptions into which we have been enculturated. And if we have built our careers on those assumptions, the resistance to change is enormous.

An additional problem is that the vast body of scientific knowledge is undergirded by many assumptions, and even if the most brilliant scientist wished to prove to her satisfaction the truth of these assumptions, she would not be able to do so. There are too many; there would be dozens of assumptions she would not have the time or training to test for herself. This being the case for even the most brilliant scientist, it is even more so for the rest of us. I do not know how to measure the speed of light, locate a black hole, find a quark, isolate DNA, or do the ten thousand other things that would be required to test the ideas of modern science. I can only assume that the main body of scientific thought our culture is using is true; there is no other approach I can take. Recognizing how much rests on assumptions, though, encourages me to stay open to the possibility that some of it is wrong. I can in fact be almost certain that a lot of it will change.

Consider how radically the assumptions in science have changed in one hundred years, how the assumptions of one hundred years ago are radically different from those of two hundred years ago, and how those are very different from the assumptions of three hundred years ago. Is there any reason, then, to believe there will not be an equally radical change in the next one hundred years? William James saw this clearly, asking if what we know represents more "than the minutest glimpse of what the universe will really prove to be when adequately understood?" His answer? "No! our science is a drop, our ignorance a sea. Whatever else be certain, this at least is certain,—that the world of our present natural knowledge is enveloped in a larger world of some sort of whose residual properties we at present can frame no positive idea."[5] This was true in James' day, and the emergence of the mysterious quantum world means it is equally true in ours.

Skeptico: You are making me very frustrated. What am I supposed to do with all this information?

Wisdom Seeker: Assume that the broad body of scientific knowledge of today is adequate for today. Have faith in your scientists; trust that most are sincere and are committed to finding the truth, and that in their areas of specialty their cumulative knowledge is the best available. At the same time, do not take this knowledge to be the final truth. Stay open to new ways of thinking and new ways of seeing. As Shakespeare reminds us in Hamlet:

> There are more things in heaven and earth, Horatio,
> Than are dreamt of in your philosophy.[6]

Also, keep in mind that if our perceptions of material reality are affected this dramatically by our assumptions and mental constructs, it is likely that our perceptions about things that are harder to measure—feelings, relationships, values, perceived dangers, and opportunities—are affected even more. In these areas, where the essential elements of living happen, it is even harder to know anything for sure, and our understanding is even more likely to be based on assumptions that cannot be proven. In this terrain that has so many unknowns, it is not surprising that we often project our views onto the world we encounter, rather that seeing it clearly.

For instance, if I am angry but bottling it up inside, I am more likely to perceive the people I meet as angry. On the other hand, if I am optimistic, I will tend to see opportunity on every hand, even in the most difficult circumstances. If I am feeling kind and compassionate, I will frequently experience tender feelings from others. And when feeling fearful, I will frequently encounter situations that seem dangerous. As Shakespeare put it in Julius Caesar, "A coward dies a thousand times before his death, but the valiant taste of death but once."[7] Considering projection in its broadest sense, an ancient saying, attributed to the Talmud, captures the heart of projection: "We do not see things as they are; we see things as we are."[8]

Have All Past Paradigms Been Wrong?

Having core assumptions as the bedrock of science is crucial to its success. Science would be impossible without assumptions. The same is true in all other areas of life; assumptions provide the foundation from which everything in life proceeds. Assumptions are the common ground from which practitioners in any field communicate with each other, share their results, and test new developments. Our assumptions, however, no matter how necessary, are not facts, nor are they "true" in some final way. To add to the problem, every assumption creates limits for what can be known; there are limits to what each paradigm can understand and explain.

This is a major reason the knowledge given by science keeps changing. Copernicus, Galileo, Bacon, Descartes, and Newton ushered in a radical set of changes. Another change is happening now, with the advent of quantum mechanics (which grew out of the unanswered questions created by the previous paradigm). Changes are inevitable, but they can happen slowly, especially as scientific discoveries interact with worldviews. As Ken Wilber suggests, modern thought has barely begun to incorporate the implications of quantum theory into its understanding of the world.

Skeptico: As this happens, will the new worldview be an improvement?

Wisdom Seeker: Hard to say. It is common for every group to believe that their assumptions are better than those held by others. It is also true that new assumptions usually become established because they deal with some issues better than those they are replacing. But new assumption sets also deal with some issues less effectively than the old system, because some things have to be left out to make the new system coherent. History is filled with examples of new paradigms that seemed promising but proved to be less effective in some areas than the old systems they replaced. This is true of political systems, educational systems, moral systems, artistic systems, economic systems, and scientific systems as well. Ancient Greece and Rome had remarkable achievements in many areas of human endeavor, but their assumptions gave way to other assumption systems that were better in some ways—but inferior in others. Some periods in China, India, the Islamic world (and many other locales) reached a pinnacle of development and then fell back to a more primitive level of sophistication and understanding—only to be followed by another new and advanced system a few generations later. Which was better? It depends on what you value.

Another way to understand the lesson of changing paradigms is to look at cultures of the earliest peoples around the globe. Many early cultures had nothing to compare to the intricacy and sophistication of modern science, but people in those cultures were often happier, less depressed, had less anxiety, and had more stable, lasting, and fulfilling relationships than the average person today. I have visited cultures where this is still the case, in places such as Bali, villages in Asia, small towns in Europe, and tribal societies in Africa. Through the eons, in many places on the planet, people have been better than we are today at living in harmony with nature, creating healthy communities, preventing crime, educating the young into a shared life, and maximizing the number of happy people. Of course, these things were the focus of their systems of thought, as opposed to some of the things we concentrate on today.

Skeptico: But I have read many horror stories about primitive cultures in which those people were bloodthirsty savages, and also miserable!

Wisdom Seeker: You must be careful what you read. Many of those accounts are based on stories sent back to justify the subjugation, exploitation, and even the massacre of native populations by those who wanted to take their land and resources. Further, many of those who perpetuate these accounts have a very specific agenda: They want to show that their ways are much better than those of people in the past.

Skeptico: But weren't some older cultures pretty bad?

Wisdom Seeker: Certainly. But those who emphasize how bad things were in the past usually ignore or downplay the numerous examples of earlier peoples who had happy and healthy lives.

Skeptico: Aren't many of the people living in remote places today, those who are hanging on to their old ways, doing poorly?

Wisdom Seeker: Yes, but many of these cultural groups once had highly successful societies. The problems we see today usually stem from these groups having been conquered or overrun by Western cultures. Cultures have also deteriorated through the centuries due to changing climates, natural disasters, and the erosion of key organizing principles, so it is not hard to find examples of dysfunctional societies in the past. But there have been many, many highly functioning societies through the long history of humankind, some of which had important things we have lost.

Science and the Problem of Assumptions

Looking at the broad sweep of history in this way, it is clear that modern science has delivered many benefits, but sometimes these were purchased at the price of deleterious effects. Examining the causes of both the good and the bad, specialization stands out. Early scientists tended to have wide-ranging knowledge in science as well as many other fields, including philosophy and spiritual ideas. A significant number were also artists. Today, specialization in narrow disciplines brings benefits but creates problems as well. Among the difficulties: How can the many specialized discoveries in various fields be brought into relationship to each other? The problem is magnified a hundred-fold when we try to understand how the insights and discoveries of all these specialized disciplines can be related to the living of a fulfilled and meaningful life. How can all the pieces of our specialized knowledge be integrated into a coherent whole?

Skeptico: Who is equipped to do this?

Wisdom Seeker: Basically, no one. Most scientists don't trust philosophers or spiritual figures to do it, although in the past the task of integrating the broad range of human concerns was their province. The pendulum has now in fact swung to the other extreme, with some materialists asserting that science should be made the sole arbiter of truth in all areas. In essence, they claim that science should assume the role of a Dominant Established Religion for our time. Ironically, though, this claim is made as scientists become more and more specialized, so that no scientist is equipped to deal with all of science, let alone the larger issues of life and living.

To me, it is a puzzle why people insist that science can deal with the broadest questions of life when no one in science is being educated to do so. It is doubly puzzling when those who claim the mantel of truth for science on all topics disparage the disciplines that made holistic thinking through the centuries possible: philosophy, metaphysics, psychology, and theology. A minimal knowledge of history shows that those scientists who made significant contributions to the broader questions of life had a deep familiarity with and interest in all these areas of thought.

Skeptico: What should a scientist who is interested in the broader questions do today?

Wisdom Seeker: The first step would be to understand the difference between science as a method and materialism as a worldview. It is quite valid for scientists to vigorously defend the value and methods of science, which is one of the most marvelous things ever created. But problems arise when materialists assert that science should be the final arbiter of truth in all areas of life, as Sam Harris does in *The End of Faith: Religion, Terror, and the Future of Reason.*

Materialists have every right to argue in the marketplace of ideas that they have the "final truth" about the world. When they claim that science supports their views, however, they have ventured into the land of the absurd. William James, more than a hundred years ago, captured the essence of the reason for this perfectly:

> Science means, first of all, a certain dispassionate method. To believe that it means a certain set of results that one should pin one's faith upon and hug forever is to sadly mistake its genius, and degrade the scientific body to the status of a sect.[9]

Those who argue that materialism and science are the same thing—and that because "science" works, the materialistic worldview must be correct—are lost in a fog of confused thinking. They do not seem to grasp that materialism is a worldview, a metaphysical assumption.

Like it or not, human life requires a metaphysical theory within which to exist. As British philosopher Mary Midgley said, it is a necessary condition of the thinking process:

> To have a metaphysics is to have a conceptual structure of one's world picture, a general map of how the world is and how it can possibly be. Metaphysical doctrines include obviously necessary things like views about causal necessity ... about the reality of physical objects and the possibility of knowledge, about the proper way to think about mind and matter, time and space, and—of most interest to most of us—views about human nature and human destiny. They are the most general presuppositions of our thought, without which it would remain a hopelessly shapeless collection of scraps.[10]

There is just no way around the fact that each person lives within a metaphysical worldview. This is not a problem, but when a person fails to understand that he or she lives within a worldview—that can be a big problem. E. A. Burtt (Susan Linn Sage Professor of Philosophy at Cornell University in the middle part of the last century) made the crucial point that any attempt to argue that a human being is **not** embedded in a metaphysical system **is itself** a metaphysical position. For this reason, those who try to deny the importance of metaphysics enmesh themselves in "an exceedingly subtle and insidious danger":

> If you cannot avoid metaphysics, what kind of metaphysics are you likely to cherish when you sturdily suppose yourself to be free from the abomination? Of course it goes without saying that in this case your metaphysics will be held uncritically because it is unconscious; moreover, it will be passed on to others far more readily than your other notions inasmuch as it will be propagated by insinuation rather than by direct argument.[11]

In other words, if you don't even know you are embedded in a metaphysical position, you will think your assumptions are "the truth" and will think everyone should just accept your views because *you* think they are true.

Which brings us back to the crucial distinction between science and materialism. Science is a method for dealing with the material things around us, and it has worked exceedingly well in taking us to the moon, creating vaccines, building cities, creating amazing information networks, and providing creature comforts. It does not, however, provide answers concerning values, meanings, love, justice, or what one should do with one's time. Materialism does attempt to answer these fundamental questions, but its answers have not proven very successful up to now (as in the Soviet Union or Marxist China), and they are certainly not supported by science.

Assumptions and Decisions

Skeptico: If no one can tell me what is "really true," how do I go about making the key decisions of my life?

Wisdom Seeker: My suggestion is to honor the core assumptions of the culture in which you were raised, or the one in which you have chosen to live, while refraining from "hugging forever" the belief that it is "the truth." Appreciate the assumptions within which you live, but hold them lightly, staying open to ever-deeper wisdom and to broader understandings. Core assumptions have shifted many times before in every area of thought and action, and new systems have emerged and prospered. This will happen again. In the meantime, it is appropriate to use the assumptions of the paradigm in which you live—but, as best you can, stay open to expanding horizons for yourself and your world.

Skeptico: You make it sound easy.

Wisdom Seeker: No, it isn't easy. I am constantly torn between wanting something solid to believe in and discovering that much is unknowable within the finite human perspective I inhabit. There is such a strong urge in me to want to know what to expect, what is real and true, and yet the most solid truth I have discovered is how much I do not know.

Skeptico: That captures my frustration pretty well. What do we do about those feelings?

Wisdom Seeker: Try to remember that we do not need to know "the ultimate truth about reality" to have fulfilling and meaningful lives—we only need to keep opening into the largest understandings we can discover. Hopefully, what seems right, true, and good will keep growing and expanding for you, for me, and for anyone else who seeks to become wiser as they grow older. My work seems to boil down to these two tasks: Make the best decisions I can on the basis of what I know right now, and live as faithfully as possible from those decisions until greater wisdom arises and leads me to new decisions. That is all I can do. I can't force myself to know more than I do, and I can't force myself to have more wisdom than I have. I can only make the best decisions I can on the basis of what I know now, while allowing what I know to continually grow and change.

Of course, being open to change in one's basic beliefs is scary. To overcome the fear, I keep reminding myself that fixed and rigid beliefs usually grow out of fantasy, a fantasy of having found certainty. All I have to do to remember this is to ask myself whether I agree with the views of all those who proclaim that they have "the truth." H. L. Mencken's witty line about this contains much wisdom: "There is always an easy solution to every human problem—neat, plausible, and wrong."[12] The more I examine the easy answers on offer, the more I realize that fixed, rigid beliefs lead to imprisonment rather than to liberation. When ideas conflict, we wish to know which alternative is true, but reality does not seem to organize itself that way. As Niels Bohr put it: "Profound truths" can be "recognized by the fact that the opposite is also a profound truth."[13]

Skeptico: Can you be more specific? How does that work in decision-making?

Wisdom Seeker: I try to stay open-minded until I have to make a specific decision. When a decision is necessary in a particular area of my life, I take into consideration everything I understand up to that moment and make the best decision I can using both head and heart. Simultaneously, I hold open the possibility that I might not have understood the whole picture. As much as is possible, I leave room for future changes in relation to what I have decided.

Skeptico: But some decisions cannot be changed! If I am trying to decide about a trip or a job, I have to pick one or the other.

Wisdom Seeker: Absolutely. The constant challenge is to live your decisions and commitments fully, while knowing that change will likely be called for in the future. The essence of a courageous, fully-lived life is the ability to live your truth with energy and vitality while recognizing how little you know, and even accepting that, at some point in the future, some of your core assumptions will prove to have been wrong.

Skeptico: Can you boil that down to specific advice for me?

Wisdom Seeker: When you need to decide something, consider the possibilities as fully as possible and decide, then act with confidence on the basis of that decision, knowing that you have done the best you can. At the same time, be willing to acknowledge that there is much you did not know and that the decision might have been wrong. This gives you greater freedom to change as you move forward—as opposed to the path of trying to convince yourself that you were right from the start (which just locks you into a failing trajectory). Such an approach will help you avoid compounding an initial mistake by sticking too long with that mistaken path. By staying open to change and corrections, while at the same time remaining responsible for the decisions you have made, you will become a master sailor, constantly correcting course as the winds and seas shift and change around you. On such a path, with humility as rudder and courage as sail, you can live fully in the absence of certainty.[14]

Skeptico: That sounds sensible. I am glad you avoided talking about the need for faith. Talking about faith troubles me.

Wisdom Seeker: Sorry Skeptico, you can't avoid faith. I wasn't avoiding it up to now, just saving it for this point in the story. Hopefully it will not trouble you too much if we talk about it; perhaps doing so will even be of value for you.

CHAPTER 11

IS YOUR FAITH CONSCIOUS OR UNCONSCIOUS?

Some of my favorite stories concern that humorous and crazy-wise character, Nasrudin, whose escapades have supplied teachings for cultures all over the Middle East. In one particular story, a pesky neighbor, known for borrowing things and not returning them, approaches Nasrudin as he stands by his front gate.

"I need to borrow your donkey," demands the neighbor.

Hesitating a second, Nasrudin says politely, "I'm sorry, but my donkey isn't here."

At that moment, the donkey—which is in the barnyard behind the house—brays.

Incensed, the neighbor bellows: "I thought you said your donkey wasn't here!"

Nasrudin pulls himself up to his full height and says in a calm and dignified voice, "Who are you going to believe—me, or a donkey?"

Active and Passive Acts of Faith

One definition of faith is to believe in or have devotion to ideas, people, or things for which there is no proof. Or, to paraphrase Voltaire, faith consists in believing something that is beyond our understanding.[1] Since each of us was enculturated into certain beliefs from the time we were born, each of us has, from our earliest days, been indoctrinated to have faith in some things as opposed to others (ideas, institutions, religions, people, economic systems, governments, etc.). We were all taught to accept the beliefs of the world into which we came. And we all did so—at least for a time. Not only that, but the beliefs we were given were embedded in a web of rationalizations developed by the culture to justify those particular views. Then, when we interacted with the people around us, the accepted beliefs were constantly reinforced as being obviously right and true. As this process unfolded, these beliefs were not proven, but rationalized— although every culture likes to think its positions rest on solid proofs. To see that your culture's beliefs do not rest on proofs, however, it is only necessary to present them to someone from a different culture. When you do, you will quickly discover that people from other cultures do not see your beliefs as proven at all, but simply as opinions and theories backed by unproven assumptions.

We each grow up within a culture, and when we are young, the beliefs and opinions of our culture are reinforced by praise when we respond in the "right" way, and discouraged by looks, negative comments, exclusion, and sometimes punishment when we stray from the common view. Within each family, young people are given strong encouragement to emulate individuals who exemplify the family's views. Combining this family influence with broader cultural reinforcement comprises an indoctrination process that we all undergo. In this way, all children begin life within a belief system that I call their *passive act of faith*, or **unconscious faith**. From this starting point, as we get older many of us simply go along with the powers that be in our world—parents, teachers, extended family, ministers, cultural heroes and heroines. This process is mostly unconscious, with most of us in our early years simply accepting the patterns and beliefs in which we find ourselves embedded.

Then, as we reach maturity, many of us continue along within these passive acts of faith. There are good reasons for this: It is easier to go along than risk becoming an outcast; it is easier to accept what the head of an academic department, a boss, a person we have fallen in love with, an important colleague, a minister, or a significant family member says than to deal with the consequences of raising questions. After all, we have to live in a shared world with these folks.

Going along in this way, however, is decidedly an act of faith, for there are constantly bits of information that come toward us that do not fit into the belief system into which we were enculturated. To continue along the encultured path, therefore, requires that we discount or ignore a certain amount of information that is coming in—information there is no factual or rational reason to discount or ignore. We have, of course, been given rationalizations about why we should ignore this information (the "proofs" of our culture). But these rationalizations fall far short of any reasonable standard of proof. Rather, they serve as filters, and by letting some things in and keeping other things out, our culture's rationalizations create, to a great extent, our view of the world.

Many of us go through our whole lives in this condition: going along, taking the road of least resistance, and making the necessary compromises to live our lives within the system we were given. In such a life, our passive acts of faith are hidden in the unconscious— they are beliefs that are taken for granted. This does not keep us from having to make choices, of course, for every culture has conflicts and contradictions within itself that necessitate individual choices. Following this path, however, does provide a basic framework and a sense of stability and security—which is the reason a significant percentage of the hundred and eight billion people who have ever lived have chosen to live this way. (Statistician Carl Haub estimates this to be the number of humans who have lived during the last 50,000 years.)

In the modern world, though, following this path is much more difficult, for there are many systems colliding with each other, and we frequently encounter those with ideas and opinions different from our own. Even if these "others" do not live next door, we are

bombarded with their views through modern communication systems. In such an intensely pluralistic world, what shall we do? Do we
try to ignore all other points of view? Do we make an effort to accept
the assurances of those in our system—in spite of our doubts? Or do
we actively grapple with the questions and doubts for ourselves?

In this fertile atmosphere, some find the challenge to question and
explore stimulating—they seem to have been born with an inquisi-
tive nature, came out of the womb questioning cultural assumptions
and ready to challenge authority at the drop of a fact. Others begin
to notice anomalies building up in the system they were given, until
finally something explodes within and a shift is unavoidable. Still others go along on the prescribed path until they are jolted out of their
passive faith by a crisis. There are many different reasons, then, to begin
to consciously consider our acts of faith, to stop ignoring the donkey
in the courtyard.

Skeptico: These acts of faith sound a lot like the assumptions you
talked about earlier. What's the difference?

Wisdom Seeker: Good question! Our assumptions lead to our
acts of faith, and drawing a clear line between the two is frequently
impossible. There is a clear distinction of great importance, however, which is between active and passive acts of faith, between
conscious and unconscious assumptions. Passive acts of faith follow from embedded, unconscious assumptions. Conscious acts of
faith occur when we thoughtfully consider our assumptions and
decide either to continue using the ones we were given or to organize around others.

Skeptico: What's the difference between faith and belief?

Wisdom Seeker: The two words are closely related, as revealed by the
fact that each is used prominently in definitions of the other. Some people do make a distinction, though, and you can define them differently.
But as they are used in common speech, they are often interchangeable.

Skeptico: If you were making a distinction between them, what
would it be?

Wisdom Seeker: I would use the word *belief* for something one simply thinks is true, without much reflection, and I would use *faith* to point to a more active process—to times we choose where we will put our trust, times we decide more consciously where we will make our commitments. In other words, if you think you know something, you do not need faith with regard to it. I know I like ice cream, so I do not have to have faith with regard to liking ice cream. The trouble is, there are many things we believe (we think we know) because we have been indoctrinated to think that way. Most of us have been encultured to believe in a particular form of government, a particular religion (or to have skepticism about religion), and we have been given a particular way to determine what is true. Many people "believe" that certain things are true without seriously questioning those beliefs. A person might fervently believe that his favorite football team is the best and deserves to win, while another might staunchly believe that her preferred political candidate is the best and deserves to win—without giving the opposing team or candidate serious consideration. These are unconscious beliefs, or to use my earlier definition, passive acts of faith.

Another way to say this is that accepting things without working them through for oneself is what I mean by passive acts of faith—not very different from belief. Devout Muslims, Christians, Communists, or believers in any other system may quite fervently believe that their understanding of reality is the truth. It would also be accurate to say that they have faith in their system, so faith and belief are not very different in this sense.

Skeptico: So what is the difference?

Wisdom Seeker: This is where I make a distinction between conscious and unconscious faith. Fervent believers have unconscious faith, for they hold beliefs without consciously considering the alternatives. For me, this kind of faith is very similar to belief. But there is a real difference between unconscious faith and what I think of as conscious faith. People are only ready to move into conscious faith when they recognize how hard it is to be sure about anything and accept that there are few clear answers to the most important questions life throws at us. If a person reaches this point and is willing to face the difficulties head-on, and is also willing to consider with an open mind and heart where to place her faith, she is ready to harvest the fruits of a conscious life.

Thought Experiment: Imagining Conscious Faith

Imagine a person who actively chooses to consider all the factors that affect a situation as fully as possible, then acts with determination on the basis of his best sense of what is right and true and good. Imagine doing that yourself, even though there is no proof that what you have chosen is true. Imagine acting with courage on what you have chosen, while remaining open to change. That is conscious faith.

Skeptico: How does trust fit in?

Wisdom Seeker: Once again, making a clear distinction between faith, belief, and trust is difficult; in common usage they often slide into and overlap with one another. The way I think of trust is that it involves a positive act of faith. To trust another person is to believe that person will do the right or the good thing when interacting with me—at least most of the time. To trust a group of people is to hold a positive view of the motives of that group. Trust, like faith, can arise in either a passive or an active way. If I trust my parents without thinking about whether that is wise, that is passive. On the other hand, if I wrestle with whether to trust someone or something and then decide to do so—in spite of the danger of being disappointed or being let down—that is active. For me, as I said before, the important distinction is between passive and active. The more a person comes to a healthy relationship with the complexities of life, the more likely it becomes that that person's acts of faith, trust, and assumptions will be consciously chosen.

On Becoming More Conscious

Skeptico: What will happen to my relationship with the world around me if I start to make more conscious choices?

Wisdom Seeker: Being more conscious does not lead to one specific result; much depends on our individual natures, the culture in which we were raised, and the culture we are living in now. Some highly conscious people decide to follow the guidance of the culture they are in as best they can, some decide to change cultures, and others stay in the old culture as rebels within it. Each choice has its positives and its negatives.

Those who consciously choose to follow the guidance of a culture must deal with the contradictions they see within it, so when contradictions surface, they must make a choice. Will they ignore the contradictions or point them out to others? When an inner voice or intuition tells them to follow a different path, will they break away and listen to this "different drummer," or will they continue to follow the old way as best they can?

Skeptico: I will be a rebel!

Wisdom Seeker: That is a noble choice, but it is also fraught with difficulties. Will you rebel within the system and try to change it, or will you pull up stakes and leave, joining the age-old search for greener pastures? Whichever you choose, you will constantly face questions about whom to believe, for there will always be views held by those you respect that are in conflict with your own. If you pay close attention, you will even discover many conflicting views within yourself.

Skeptico: Then I will find a group that fits my views.

Wisdom Seeker: That is also a fine choice, but I can assure you that in a short time, if you remain conscious about what is going on, you will discover contradictions within the new culture as well. Then you will again be faced with the question of whether to accommodate the contradictions, attempt to change the new culture, or move on once more.

Skeptico: So how do I decide what to do?

Wisdom Seeker: First, engage your reasoning to evaluate the situation, then consult your intuition for guidance. Often, though, the answers that arise will not be very clear, so you will have to make another act of faith. As you do this, the crucial thing is to remember the distinction between a conscious and an unconscious act of faith. To say this in a different way, no one can escape making acts of faith with regard to the belief systems within which they live. Each of us was indoctrinated into a system of belief and each of us lives in a culture that is shaped by one or more of humanity's belief systems. Further, we humans are by nature social beings, so most of us spend a lot of time interacting with others. Needless to say, we do this on the basis of cultural systems.

We can change systems, but that is simply switching allegiance from one brand to another. We might rebel against the beliefs we were given, but rebelling against something is to live in relation to it—a rebel is defined by what he or she is rebelling against. Furthermore, rebelling is an act of faith that the old system is wrong. Even those who burrow into lonely caves in the Himalayas do so within a set of beliefs about what they are doing and why, based on acts of faith about what is important for their lives.

Further, without exception, acts of faith to go off alone have always been influenced by cultural systems that shaped the thoughts and feelings of the person making that choice. Isolated monks have not escaped their enculturation (unless they reach the state of complete enlightenment or oneness with the transcendent that a few have reported). Nor have they escaped the necessity for making continuing acts of faith, for at any moment they can change directions, leave the cave, go back into the village and resume a worldly life (a significant number are reported as doing just this).

Skeptico: Say more about the difference between active and passive faith; I am still confused.

Wisdom Seeker: Some people go along with the ideas and beliefs of the people around them, while others accept some things but challenge others. In the short term it is usually easier to go along, but this does not lead to the development of an internal compass. Those who just go along are constantly looking to others to tell them what to believe: This is passive faith. It is almost impossible to stay completely in passive faith as one gets older, however, for choices inevitably arise. An especially vivid example would be when friends or family members undertake illegal activities. When this happens, do we watch silently or do we voice our concerns? Do we report them to the authorities or do we support them—actively, or covertly by our silence? Even those following the path of passive faith are sometimes forced to make these kinds of choices.

Usually, though, conscious faith begins when an awareness arises that there are differences between what you believe and what your culture says you should believe. Everyone, at one time or another, has had such feelings, although there are wide variations in how we respond. Some of us push this sense that a conflict exists down, away from consciousness, and hold fast to what the culture says we should believe. Others of us more consciously consider the conflicts, and begin to choose on a case-by-case basis the views we will organize around. This can lead to spending time and energy trying to change those laws, customs, and values that seem wrong, or even to breaking the ones that seem unjust. This is choosing to make one's acts of faith more consciously.

A person might also consider carefully the conflict between personal beliefs and the culture's views, and decide to uphold the culture's point of view. This, too, is a conscious act of faith; it is putting one's faith in the value of the community's wisdom, as exemplified by Robert E. Lee. He did not believe in all the assertions of the Confederate States when they broke from the Union before the American Civil War, but he decided nonetheless to fight with his friends and neighbors because they represented his culture and his culture's view of what was best. (For his consciousness in this decision, he was deeply respected by his enemies as well as his friends.)

Ultimately, no matter the path we take, there will be conflicts between some of our beliefs and values and those of the people we know best. We can perhaps minimize the conflicts by trying to accept everything the majority of people around us believe, but even this is not always possible, because the important people in our lives will at times disagree. Another, and potentially greater danger is exemplified by the example of growing up in a Mafia family. Mafia families (in both senses of that word) live by a clear set of values, and one such value is to keep anything that happens within the family from outsiders. This is strongly encultured (becomes an unconscious choice for most members) and leads to those raised in Mafia families helping to cover up crimes, and even to committing shocking ones.

This is an extreme example, but in a sense we all live within currents that mold our choices in the same way, and we all face moments when our enculturation is in conflict with our deep sense of what is right and wrong. When this occurs, we can either adhere to our conditioning without confronting the conflict—a passive choice or decision—or we can consciously consider what is going on and make a more conscious choice. Becoming more conscious brings this reward: It allows us to participate at a different level of our being in the creation of our own individual lives.

Skeptico: But if I choose to do what I feel is right, no matter what the people around me are saying, how is that an act of faith—if I really, truly believe I am right?

Wisdom Seeker: Because you cannot be sure. To follow what you feel or believe is right is an act of faith; it is simply to assume you are more likely to be right than those with a different view. You might be right, but no matter how strong your conviction, there is no way you can know for sure. You might be motivated by an unconscious urge, you might have been persuaded by a clever charlatan, or you might have gotten caught up in being a rebel without recognizing it. For myself, I can think of several times I started with clear and pure motives, came to a strong conviction about something, then gradually realized I had been unaware of significant information—and therefore had come to a strong conviction that turned out to be wrong.

Thought Experiment: The Powerful Desire to Be Right

Have you ever argued for a position, even after you sensed it might be mistaken—because you did not want to admit to someone else you might be wrong? Or perhaps you did not want to admit it to yourself.

Skeptico: Have you ever done that?

Wisdom Seeker: I have done it many times, especially in my political days, arguing for a candidate or position although some part of me did not believe what I was saying anymore. In other areas of my life I can remember sticking with an original, mistaken view after I had begun to sense it was wrong—because I was unwilling to admit my mistake. I can even remember being quite righteous about a view I now see as being motivated by deeply buried feelings or old enculturations.

The problem is, when I am driven by these kinds of unconscious views, there is no way to know whether they are right or wrong; whether they are good for others or for myself. They might be right, but how can I know that to be true if I am simply following what I was taught? Most of those who do the biddings of a Mafia kingpin think they are acting in a proper way. If I simply follow what I was indoctrinated to believe, how can I know whether my views are healthy or unhealthy? And how is my position different from that of a member of a Mafia family?

Skeptico: I am safe from that; I rebelled against what I was taught long ago.

Wisdom Seeker: Not so fast; you might be safe from one danger but are quite likely trapped by another. In rebelling against what you were taught, your motivation is probably no different from that of a teen-ager in rebellion mode.

Skeptico: Well, maybe that is partly true. How do I avoid it?

Wisdom Seeker: Make your acts of faith as conscious as possible. Weigh alternative choices carefully. Evaluate the possibilities as best you can in relation to their potential outcomes in your life, in the lives of the people you care about, and even for the greater world in which you exist.

The criteria by which all acts of faith must be evaluated, ulti-mately, are these: What is my deepest intention and how does that fit with what seems truly important in my life? What fruits are my decisions producing in my life and in the lives of others? What kind of person am I becoming? If your acts of faith are unconscious, if you are trapped behind the bars of your rationalizations and self-justifications, answers to these questions will seem easy, for you will have no perspective from which to view yourself clearly and hon-estly. If you find these questions difficult to answer, you are likely becoming more conscious in your decision-making and in your life.

But I Have Proof!

We are all embedded, to some degree, in belief systems that are supported by rationalizations and justifications. Of course, most of us do not think of our arguments as rationalizations and justifications, but rather as powerful evidence, if not proof for our views. Followers of every belief system construct proofs for their positions, whether they be Catholic, atheist, Communist, Muslim, Hindu, Jewish, Protestant, Buddhist, evolutionary theorist, or those of a politically correct persuasion. The fascinating thing is that proof systems only work for those already in them. Those outside, those who operate under a different set of assumptions, are almost never persuaded by the evidence presented by another system.

This becomes obvious with the realization that there are many different belief systems in the world, each with its own evidence and proof, but no system has persuaded large numbers of people in other systems to change. In fact, the number of different and conflicting belief systems in the world has gradually increased throughout history, and is still doing so today. This suggests that, of all the proofs developed over several thousand years, none have been successful in persuading a majority of us; otherwise, most everyone would be congregated around the ideas accepted as proven. This failure of proofs is true in disagreements between people of different religions, between the religious and the non-religious, and even between factions within each religion. For instance, within Christianity there are many different factions with many different beliefs, and the arguments are not diminishing in spite of the fact that each group feels like it has "proof" of its position. It is even the case that what one generation within a faction accepts as true will change in the next generation, with new beliefs arising and the old ones—that seemed so solid—passing away.

All this does not mean that developing justifications to support one's beliefs has no value. Although such arguments seldom persuade outsiders, their real goal is to strengthen the resolve of those within the system, to help those within feel better about the acts of faith they have already made (whether conscious or unconscious). For those who have accepted the assumptions of a system of thought, the proofs within the system "make sense." Those outside the system, those who have not accepted the assumptions, seldom find the arguments convincing. That's why those outside are seldom converted by another system's "proofs."

Individuals do convert from one system of belief to another with some regularity, but these conversions are not in any particular direction, are not moving humanity toward a common point of view. If this were the case, if one view were winning, it would suggest that one view had the best arguments. But that isn't what is happening. Instead, there has been a great deal of movement back and forth from one belief system to another through the centuries. Further, groups that continue over long stretches of time frequently redefine their beliefs to such an extent that earlier generations professing the same name would not recognize the new system.

The overall pattern is that old systems disappear, new ones arise, and large groups split into factions. People move from one system to another; various systems have bursts of growth and then recede; new belief systems are born and gather adherents. Thus, as mentioned before, there are now nineteen major world religions, but these are made up of two hundred and seventy denominations, which in turn are made up of tens of thousands of sub-groups—all with their own evidence, proofs, justifications, and rationalizations. In addition, in the world today, there are belief systems that delight in debunking the proofs of all religious points of view. Needless to say, these many positions are not moving toward agreement in the modern world; all these groups are not consolidating, so there is no reason to think that the proofs of any of them are proving effective, except in creating shifts of allegiance on the margins.

What is more, when people do move between systems it is seldom because of proofs, but rather because a person has a dramatic experience (such as Paul's conversion on the road to Damascus), or because someone becomes disillusioned with the group to which she or he previously belonged. Or, occasionally, a change is spurred by an encounter with the energy and presence of a charismatic teacher. Sometimes people change because they feel emotionally welcomed and supported by a new group; sometimes they do so because they hope for social or political advantage. What seldom accounts for these changes is evidence and proof, for the starting assumptions of each system have to be accepted— whether atheistic or religious, materialistic or moralistic—before proofs can work.

The failure of proofs is made explicit by the fact that countless dialogues have occurred over thousands of years between the best and the brightest of many different belief systems, yet there are few reports of leaders of one system accepting the "proofs" of another and converting. Dialogues continue apace today, but we seldom read of Jewish Rabbis converting to Islam, Baptist preachers becoming

Hindus, Buddhist monks becoming Pentecostals, or a Richard Dawkins-inspired materialist converting to Catholicism. We do encounter many stories of leaders within one system developing a better understanding of another, and sometimes incorporating the best ideas of another system into their own. And there are many reports of friendships developing between the leaders of different belief systems. It is incredibly rare, however, to read about leaders of one system accepting the "proofs" of another and abandoning their own.

Thought Experiment: The Effectiveness of Proofs

In a serious conflict with another person over core beliefs, how often have you been able to persuade that person by offering proofs of your point of view?

Skeptico: Okay, I understand why arguments justifying beliefs mostly help people feel better about what they have already chosen. But I have to say, for someone who doesn't think that making arguments or offering evidence has much value, you spend a lot of time doing both. Why do you go to the trouble, if arguments, evidence, and proofs have so little value?

Wisdom Seeker: I didn't mean to suggest they have no value, just that seeking answers to the most important questions of life do not usually start with evidence and proof. Accepting that, I share my thoughts and feelings because they might have value, especially for those whose thoughts and experiences incline them in a direction similar to mine. Millions of people are searching, seeking, trying to understand at any given time, and the thoughts, feelings, and experiences of another can be of great value, especially when there is an overlap in emerging views.

Skeptico: Have your arguments ever changed anyone's mind?

Wisdom Seeker: A number of people have thought about things I have said and shifted their views. These changes, however, were not because of proofs, but because the ideas I presented resonated with views that were already emerging in them. In a similar way, I have often shifted my views when listening to the ideas and feelings of another. In this process of exchange, the tools I have found most valuable are openness, kindness, consideration, and listening to the other with respect. I have never found arguments very effective, either for my own understanding, or in helping another. And I cannot think of a single "proof" about how we should live, what the world is like, or how we should spend our time that someone has given me that has been decisive in and of itself. Deep truths do not take root in us through arguments or proofs alone, but must be confirmed by experience, must be validated by a growing sense of what feels right and true and good—and this always involves intuitions and feelings as much as thoughts and thinking.

Consequently, I have little faith that arguments alone will persuade those who have a fixed point of view. There are, however, many people who are open, curious, and seeking—who are searching for a new and deeper understanding. That is the kind of person I wish to be, and that is the kind of person to whom I am speaking and writing. For myself, that is also the kind of person to whom I pay attention, and doing so is the best way I know to grow in wisdom and understanding.

Ultimately, this journey is not about defense of an established position, but about finding and then sharing with others the clearest and deepest understanding we can attain in a lifetime of seeking. In my own journey, I hope my awareness has grown as I have aged, and I believe that by exchanging thoughts and feelings with those who are also learning and growing, all of us will be carried to a deeper awareness of what a fulfilled life might be—and to the wisest acts of faith possible.

I Am a Skeptic!

Skeptico: All that is well and good for those who need to make acts of faith, but I am a skeptic. I don't need to make any acts of faith.

Wisdom Seeker: Oh Skeptico, don't you see that believing you don't need to make acts of faith is an act of faith? Don't you remember that the starting point for both science and reason is an act of faith? Nobel Prize-winning physicist Max Planck, one of the greatest scientists of all time and the founder of quantum mechanics, said: "Anybody who has been seriously engaged in scientific work of any kind realizes that over the entrance to the gates of the temple of science are written the words: Ye must have faith. It is a quality which the scientist cannot dispense with."[2]

Skeptico: Are you sure he said that?

Wisdom Seeker: Yes, I am pretty sure; it is widely quoted. But since I didn't hear him say it myself and an editor could have inserted it into his book (*Where is Science Going?*) without his permission, I must admit that quoting it here involves a certain amount of faith in the fact-checking systems and honesty of modern publishing. I make these assumptions in spite of the fact that those in power have sometimes manipulated the publishing process, and there are often errors in books.

Skeptico: Well, I will research that quote myself.

Wisdom Seeker: That's a great idea. As you do, look for this one also—although I am afraid you will not like it either: At the beginning of his book, *Science and the Modern World*, the great mathematician and philosopher Alfred North Whitehead discusses the underpinnings of modern science and concludes that "faith in the possibility of science ... is an unconscious derivative from medieval theology."[3] As I mentioned in Chapter Six, medieval theology asserted that every occurrence has a cause and every cause is governed by a general principle. Whitehead says these beliefs are central underpinnings of modern science. He goes further, asserting that belief in a world where you can scientifically determine the cause of things is not rational at all. (What is the rational argument for it?) Whitehead says this belief was handed down from the medieval clerics, who based their conviction that such an order existed upon faith that God had established the universe in just that way.

Skeptico: Now you have gone too far! You must be putting words in Whitehead's mouth!

Wisdom Seeker: I urge you to read it for yourself. But be warned, he has much more to say. For instance, "Science has never shaken off the impress of its origin. ... It has remained predominately an anti-rationalistic movement, based upon a naive faith." In other words, it is not rationality that underlies the scientific belief that we live in an orderly universe, but an act of faith (although it is an unconscious one for most scientists). Einstein understood this clearly and made a conscious decision to put his faith in the belief that a "sublimity and marvelous order ... reveal themselves both in nature and in the world of thought."[4] He also said:

> My religiosity consists of a humble admiration of the infinitely superior spirit that reveals itself in the little that we can comprehend about the knowable world. That deeply emotional conviction of the presence of a superior reasoning power, which is revealed in the incomprehensible universe, forms my idea of God.[5]

Because of their belief in an ordered and rational universe, medieval theologians stressed the importance of reason as the backbone of their faith, and scientists in the following centuries adopted that same faith, as well as the medieval assertion of the importance of reason. Then, as philosophers led by David Hume (I know you like him, since he was one of the greatest skeptics of all time) began to point out that such a position was actually irrational, scientists continued to organize around it anyway—in defiance of the powerful arguments put forward by Hume and reinforced by Immanuel Kant. Hume, of course, is best known today for his fiercely critical attacks on the Dominant Established Religions of his time, but another of his arguments was that we cannot really know the cause of things because we have no mental tool to *see* cause and effect. All we can observe is one thing following another, but one thing following another does not prove causation, so we actually have no way to know true causes. (My example of this principle is that a rooster crowing every morning before sunrise does not mean the rooster's song *caused* the sunrise.)

Hume's thought was then taken up and refined by Kant, who made a convincing argument that we think there is causation because our minds organize the world that way—not because the world out there, the "thing-in-itself," is a certain way. In other words, we do not discover causation "out there" in the world but create it in our minds. Science, however, ignored Hume's skepticism and Kant's assertion and placed its faith in the medieval notion that we can know the material world directly. Further, it adopted the belief that the world has an unseen and constant order that can be discovered though the investigations of science. There is no proof for this assumption; it is an act of faith.

Skeptico: I am at a loss for words. I am not sure whether I want to read any of that.

Wisdom Seeker: Don't be troubled, Skeptico. Your skepticism is a valuable tool. There is much to be said for developing a skeptical eye with regard to all arguments; many people are manipulative and the world is filled with sales-pitches for beliefs that are flawed. Not only that, it is quite valuable to be skeptical of oneself: We all have hidden motives, self-deceptions, unrealistic expectations, and delusions. Skepticism has an important place—but it does not provide a plan for living. It can unmask errors, but it does not provide a basis upon which to make positive decisions about how to live. If, for instance, you need to decide about whether to take a job, it is valuable to be skeptical—up to a point—concerning the words of a potential employer. But if you stay in skepticism throughout the process, it will be difficult to settle on any job, and when you take one, you will enter it with an attitude that will not be conducive to success (assuming you are hired, which is unlikely if you go through the interview process with a skeptical attitude). Søren Kierkegaard captured the twin dangers with the observation that we are fooled (or fool ourselves) in two different ways: By believing what isn't true, or by refusing to believe what is true.

This wisdom is especially relevant in one of the most important areas of human life: relationships. If you are to have good relationships with others, if you are to develop love and friendship, it simply will not work to respond at every turn with "I am skeptical!" Nor will skepticism work in choosing the values you will live by. When carried too far, skepticism becomes a weapon that blasts away at all those with whom you disagree, in the process destroying everything in its path, including your own hopes and possibilities.

Skepticism helps us see errors—in the claims of others as well as in our own point of view. Used wisely, this can move us closer to wisdom and understanding. Continuing endlessly to find flaws, however, does not work as a method for discovering the positive possibilities of life; for that you must make an act of faith in some direction.

Thought Experiment: Being Skeptical of the Skeptics

Have you noticed how skepticism is often used to attack the beliefs of others, but is seldom directed by the skeptic toward his or her own point of view? How often are skeptics skeptical of their own beliefs? How often are skeptics skeptical of their act of faith that skepticism is the most accurate point of view?

Most skeptics are skeptical of others without holding themselves to the same standards. In an essay in 1893, Sir Leslie Stephen said of the skeptics of his time, "The so-called skeptics are just as much believers as their opponents."[6] He went on to say that skeptics assign superiority to their preferred views, but usually their positions have no more proof behind them than the positions of their opponents. This "attacking" form of skepticism occurs all the time between dissenting groups, including between different religious groups. Each side directs "withering scorn" and charges of "superstition" toward the other without noticing that the same charges could just as easily be hurled toward them and their beliefs.

Skepticism has a useful role in debunking unhealthy and dysfunctional beliefs in every field, from science to religion, but skepticism is not belief-free. Biologist Rupert Sheldrake (from whom I learned about Leslie Stephens, quoted above) notes that most skepticism "is a weapon serving belief or self-interest. ... The more militant the skeptic, the stronger the belief."[7]

Skepticism can point out ideas that do not work, but offers no guidance for making the positive choices we must make in our lives. It helps us eliminate flawed possibilities, but when we need to move forward, an act of faith is essential, for skepticism cannot light the way ahead. Perhaps a new rule is in order: *Beware of skeptics bearing answers!* Or to borrow from the poet Rumi: Following a skeptic toward a fulfilled life is like "sitting on a donkey, and asking the donkey where to go."[8]

CHAPTER 12

No Escape—From an Act of Faith

I have several close relationships, people I trust, but when I share my secrets with them, my fears, my longings, I cannot be sure they will treat what I say with respect. I cannot be sure they won't betray my trust in a way that causes great pain. To share deeply I must trust, even though I cannot know whether those I think are my friends will laugh behind my back or make fun of me to others. I must have faith in some people in spite of the dangers, if I am to have close relationships.

I can trust unconsciously, naively—which is a passive act of faith—or I can consider carefully and make an active decision about the friends in whom I will place my trust. But I cannot be certain my trust will be honored. I can use my reason as a tool in evaluating the situation, but no matter how rational I am about it, to share intimately with another requires an act of faith in that person's good intentions and judgment both now and in the future.

Relationships are central to human life. Equally central are decisions about how to live, how to spend one's time, and the values and meanings around which to organize. As we make these decisions, we will never know all the relevant information. Further, our rational minds are not capable of holding all the information we actually have in balanced proportion at the moment a decision is being made. The only way forward is to make acts of faith, either passive or active, and proceed as best

we can. We can change our acts of faith as time goes on, but we cannot escape from making them.

The way we humans acquire information and the beliefs we use to organize that information make acts of faith unavoidable. We are encultured to believe certain things; this is our personal starting point, and that starting point becomes an unconscious act of faith. To recognize this reality, it is only necessary to notice that people in different cultures start with different beliefs. Even within cultures there are many differences, sometimes striking, because of the differences between families and the different groups to which families belong. Therefore, as each of us begins life, what we see and understand is quite different from what those in other cultures, and even in other families, see and understand. Regardless of the chance nature of what we were given, however, as we began life we had to put a certain amount of faith in what we had been taught in order to function.

As life begins, a new human being is bombarded with information—facts, ideas, impressions, and opinions. From this cornucopia each of us had to select some information and some ideas, and ignore or reject much else, for our minds could not take in and use all of it. Furthermore, many of the ideas and opinions we encountered were in conflict with others. So how did we make our decisions about what to store? To a great extent, we did so on the basis of our enculturation, using the acts of faith we had been taught. Next, the information, ideas, impressions, and opinions that we did let in had to be organized into patterns that made sense to us. How did we do that? Again, mostly by using the belief systems we had been given.

As life went along and we began to make decisions for ourselves, another issue arose: as decisions are made, some factors are front and center in our minds while others are in the background. The problem is, there is no way to keep the most important factors relating to a particular decision in the foreground when making a decision. We don't have control of our minds in that way; some thoughts come in, others don't. Moreover, when a decision is being made, a lot of the time there is no way to know which factors *are the most important*, for our knowledge is incomplete at each moment, and the mood we are in brings some factors to the fore while diminishing others. (A person in a fearful state will make a very different decision from someone in a confident state.) Needless to say, this process cannot be entirely rational, for we do not know all the facts and we do not know (in any rational way) how much weight to give each fact and factor. Valuing one thing over another is always a subjective process: Do you prefer chocolate or vanilla, security or excitement, love or power?

> **Thought Experiment: How Do You Organize the Information in Your Mind?**
>
> The content of your mind is organized into categories, patterns, and associations. There are countless connections between different pieces of data—thoughts, ideas, feelings, and impressions. How did these associations and connections happen? Are you aware of having done it consciously? Are you consciously doing it now?

It can come as quite a shock to realize that this massive process of organizing all the things in your mind happened mostly at the unconscious level, and that it was largely conditioned by your upbringing, by what you were taught to focus on and pay attention to at an early age. But it can also be very empowering to realize that you can gradually become more conscious and make more conscious choices. Yet even this does not remove the necessity for acts of faith, for to decide to become more conscious involves an assumption or belief that doing so will be worthwhile. Making this choice, however, has a powerful consequence: It shifts a person from a passively assumed belief system to a more consciously chosen one.

Free Will?

Skeptico: Maybe I don't really have any choice about what I believe.

Wisdom Seeker: In your early years, you didn't have much choice, but the fact that so many people have changed beliefs through the centuries suggests we are not sentenced to stay irrevocably embedded in what we were taught.

Skeptico: Well, maybe all those changes of belief were predetermined and it just looks like people had a choice.

Wisdom Seeker: Choosing to believe you have no choice is a choice you can make. Most people throughout history, however, have chosen to believe they could make choices and have acted as if that were true. You can create a story that says all those people really couldn't make choices, that everything they did was predetermined, but to believe that story requires a major act of faith. Further, it goes against the teachings of most figures human civilizations have considered wise. Not only that, but it goes against a basic instinct we humans feel: Most of us feel that when a major decision comes along (whom to marry, which job to take, which school to attend, where to live), we have a choice. In light of the wisdom teachings of human history and this deep instinct most people feel, the great majority of human beings through the ages have chosen to believe they could make choices. You can choose that view too, Skeptico. No one has sentenced you to believe you have no freedom to choose, so you are free to organize around the belief that you can make choices (and you are also free to believe you cannot). In choosing the affirmative, however, you will be aligning with the great majority of humanity, as well as with the major wisdom traditions of history.

These wisdom traditions are important, for most everyone who has ever lived has been raised within beliefs that originated with them; most of us were taught to have faith in some version of what the great wisdom teachers had to say. (This is true even for those who were not raised within a religious environment, for the values and meanings of the world's cultures have their roots in one or more of these wisdom traditions.)

The point is, we each start within a cultural value and meaning tradition. As we mature, we can reject that tradition, but doing so requires an act of faith, for when starting down such a path, it is impossible to know whether the instructions we were given were right or not. Nor can we know whether we will be able to improve upon what we were taught, so we can only proceed with an act of faith that we will be able to find a better path than the one accepted by those who taught us.

Looking at the lives of real people who made the decision to seek a different path, often they began their journeys motivated by a spirit of rebellion or youthful arrogance. Both of these, of course, are unconscious acts of faith, so an act of faith is always necessary to break away from one's cultural tradition. Those who break away from a tradition and choose a more secular path, such as materialism, are also making an act of faith, either conscious or unconscious. If they then raise their children to believe in materialism, those parents have given their children the faith system of materialism as the starting point for their lives. Needless to say, those encultured to believe in materialism cannot, when they are young, evaluate its truth or falsity any better than those brought up in other faith systems.

Skeptico: But that is not the case with those who adopt materialism after having been brought up in a different worldview.

Wisdom Seeker: That's true, but those who choose materialism as a worldview after having been encultured into another view are making an act of faith that materialism is better. There is no proof that it is an accurate or better understanding of the world. Materialism is based on a set of assumptions that must be accepted or rejected by an act of faith, just like every other belief system.

In short, we all start life embedded in unconscious acts of faith, and we either stay within them or we choose to make others in a different direction. To escape all acts of faith would require that we: (a) know all the information about each topic we consider important, (b) know precisely how much value to give each piece of information in relation to every other piece of information, (c) know with certainty the ultimate goals of our lives, and (d) have perfect vision about which actions have the best chance of carrying us to those ultimate goals. No human being has more than a tiny fraction of this knowledge, so we are forced to make many acts of faith—either consciously, or by following our unconscious habits of mind.

It's All Relative!

Skeptico: Maybe all these acts of faith don't make any difference. Maybe everything is relative and the only point to life is to get as much of the good stuff as we can.

Wisdom Seeker: You can make that your act of faith. You can choose to believe that all values were created by humans for self-serving reasons and that there is no ultimate meaning to life. Of course, under such a view, the values I make up are just as good as the ones you make up (or anyone else makes up), which inevitably leads to organizing our interactions around power alone. Michel Foucault, an influential figure in modern thought, asserted just this in *The Order of Things.*[1] In his view, each culture as well as each period of history has its own truth, and no set of truths should take precedence over any other. For Foucault, this even included the truths of science.

To adopt Foucault's view, however, requires an act of faith, for there are many other possibilities for understanding the world, and there is no proof that his view is correct. Further, looking at his view through his own lens, the conclusion would have to be that he adopted his ideas to serve his self-interest, for his key assertion is that nothing but self-interest and a desire for power motivates anyone. So, if his view is correct, Foucault himself was motivated by self-interest and a desire for personal power, and nothing else. That being the case, why would you want to base your important beliefs on his ideas?

Skeptico: I see advantages to looking at life that way. For instance, I would be less likely to be taken in by false ideas.

Wisdom Seeker: Not necessarily. What if Foucault's ideas are false and you are being taken in by them? The main problem with moral relativism (Foucault's stance) is that it means you have no basis except power or appeal to self-interest upon which to ask others to limit their urges and whims. In such a world, nothing—including cold-blooded murder, rape, slavery, or genocide—is really wrong, for there are no universal values with which these things conflict. In such a world, there are no lasting values that people can jointly refer to in organizing their communities, so those with enough power can do whatever they want and enforce whatever view they like.

This is, of course, the extreme to which moral relativism leads, though its conclusions are seldom stated so starkly. Moral relativism had an upsurge in intellectual circles in the twentieth century, but as far as I can tell moral relativism always leads to nihilism, to a rejection of any common ground for moral action as well as the belief that nothing but fulfilling one's own desires is worthwhile.

Foucault did not want to acknowledge that this was where his ideas led, and to his personal credit he often challenged oppression and unfairness when he saw it. This has been the case with a number of people who thought of themselves as relativists. To their credit, they have held up to public view the many ways those in power have taken advantage of the powerless, rallying victims of abuse and unfairness to stand up for their rights. There is a great irony here, however, for in doing this they have appealed to values beyond power, such as fairness and equality. But these are values that lie beyond the moral relativism they champion.

Like Foucault, moral relativists tend to shy away from the clear implications of their own position, letting transcendent values seep in—whichever ones they happen to like. Many do not wish to find themselves in the dark pit of nihilism, so they assert that society should be organized around the values they personally prefer. Some even carry the irony a step further and assert that everyone should adopt their views as universal values, in essence asserting that every point of view is relative except their own. They are saying, basically, that although all views are relative, their views are not actually relative, but are really superior to other views, and thus should have a privileged position. But choosing relativism as a belief system ties thinking relativists in knots, forcing them to say that their views are superior while asserting that no position is superior to any other. By taking this stance, every attempt to justify their position pulls the knot tighter—like those old Chinese finger traps that bind ever more tightly the harder one struggles to get free.

It's also important to note that relativism, like every belief system, is saturated with universal ideas. It is shot through with beliefs and ideas arising from Judaic, Christian, Greek, and Celtic belief systems, as well as Roman law. Relativists can argue that these systems of thought (which dramatically affected their formative years) did not arise from a universal ground, but they cannot deny that those who gave us these belief systems felt that their views arose from universal ideas. Relativists, therefore, if they wish to deny a universal ground, are choosing to believe that all the great minds of world history were wrong about the source of their ideas.

Since Judaism and Christianity are religions, there is no need to demonstrate that their principles and values have, from the beginning, been attributed to a universal ground. That Greek beliefs and values were understood in the same way might not be as obvious, but the central theme of Socrates and Plato was that there is a transcendent World of Ideas. Aristotle broke from his predecessors on many things, but he retained an emphasis on the existence of a Final Cause toward which human life moves. Prior to all three, as Peter Kingsley has pointed out, the major pre-Socratic philosophers were all spiritual teachers as well as philosophers.[2] In fact, it is difficult to find a major Greek figure of any importance who did not posit a transcendent source for the beliefs and values governing human life.

As for the Celts, the Arthurian stories sung by the troubadours in the twelfth to fifteenth centuries were mostly Celtic in origin and had a powerful influence in creating several central currents in Western culture (romantic love, the significance of individual feelings and actions, and the importance of protecting the weak and defenseless).

Needless to say, all these were attributed to a transcendent ground by the early Celts and by the storytellers of Medieval Europe.

Equally influential is Roman law, which has been used for centuries to govern a major part of the world. First established during the Roman Empire, it has been adapted and used by much of the world since the empire fell. Developed by Greek philosophers and then refined by great Roman lawmakers such as Cicero, Gnaeus Flavius, and Salvius Iulianus, Roman law is based on the idea that universal rights and values exist and that it is important for leaders and citizens alike to do what is "right." In other words, there exists a universal law that applies to everyone, no matter the country of origin, and each person can sense this law and know what is right. (The Romans were certainly not perfect in implementing this idea, but this does not change the fact that it was an ideal that underpinned Roman law.)

This way of understanding is a primary source for the idea of justice in the Western world, and is perhaps the greatest gift of Roman culture to modernity. For over two thousand years, these ideas have been embedded in the democracies of the world and are still part of the education of anyone growing up in much of the world, relativists included. (Legal systems in other parts of the world are different, but all major systems, such as those in India and China, are based on the idea that universal values exist.)

The crucial point: The language of relativists, even their way of thinking, is undergirded by universal ideas that have been in place for a very long time. From many sources, universal ideas and values have "seeped into" and even created the relativists' thinking and positions. And, to emphasize again, those who first articulated these formative ideas centuries ago believed these ideas arose from a transcendent domain, and the great majority of human beings throughout history have believed this to be the case.

In other words, Jewish, Christian, Greek, and Celtic streams of thought, along with Roman law, form the underlying framework within which all Western points of view have come into being— including relativism. Those who adopt a relativistic view, then, do so after having been enculturated into concepts about fairness, equality, freedom, democracy, human rights, and free speech that arose from a mingling of all these formative streams. Since, therefore, all of these streams maintain that some beliefs and values are grounded in a transcendent realm, relativism itself grows from soil created and nourished by a belief in universal values. This becomes obvious when you recognize that Foucault and the other relativists have given a great deal of importance to one or more of these values in their statements and writings. It seems to me they have done so, in spite of the conflict with their theories, because they had been enculturated into these views and still held them at a somewhat unconscious level. Relativism is thus problematic because it is self-contradictory, denies its own roots, and asserts that the wisest people in history, as well as the majority of people who have ever lived, were deluded.

Skeptico: I guess I was indoctrinated pretty well; I have a hard time letting go of thinking that all beliefs are relative.

Wisdom Seeker: Interesting. If you hold that "all beliefs are relative," you must *not* believe that all beliefs are relative. Since *all* means *all*, you are taking a universal and not a relative stand. I fear you are trying to have it both ways, Skeptico—wanting to believe that your truth is universal while asserting that everyone else's truth must be seen as relative. At a deeper level, though, think about what you are choosing. Since there are other ways of viewing the world, if you choose a relativist point of view, what kind of world are you choosing?

Thought Experiment: What Kind of World Will You Choose?

There is no proof that relativism is true, but there is also no proof that universal values and meanings exist. In the absence of proof, we each have a choice about the kind of world we will organize our lives around. What will you choose? What is the likely outcome of choosing one versus the other?

As I wrestle with this question, I think of William James and his comment in *The Will to Believe*: "Believe that life is worth living, and your belief will help create the fact."[3] In terms of our values and meanings, we are affected by the culture we live in and by the people around us, but we also have some choice regarding the beliefs we will embrace and organize around. In this open space, wisdom seems to suggest that believing I have the power to affect the course of my life, that I can choose to align with that which seems worthwhile, leads to the most fulfilling life possible. Choosing to believe that everything is relative does not offer that result.

No Escape

Relativists do make an important point, though: Many of the beliefs, rules, and laws of human history seem to have arisen from specific locales, and often they have served the self-interests of those in power. But seeing this does not mean we must assume such is the case with **all** beliefs, rules, and laws. It is as likely, and perhaps more so, that some local beliefs were inspired by something larger; that they grew out of connection to a universal ground of values and meanings. The strongest evidence for this view is that values and meanings very similar to each other have arisen in different ages and divergent cultures all over the world, as if stemming from a universal source.

Heinrich Zimmer, one of Joseph Campbell's mentors, made a strong argument for this point of view, saying that even beliefs that seem to have arisen locally often had a universal source, even though they might be expressed in the images and ideas of a specific locale. The local coloring, he said, was necessary to communicate with the people in a particular place, but underlying universals were the source of these seemingly local ideas and beliefs.[4] There is no way to prove this, of course, but his view is supported by the wisdom teachings of every culture.

Skeptico: You are being very assertive about the existence of universal values and meanings. Isn't that belief just an act of faith on your part?

Wisdom Seeker: Good point! Yes it is. Each of us must choose what we will believe, and believing that is one of my choices. The only thing I insist upon is that there is no proof for any other point of view, so I am free to make that choice, for it seems to me to lead in the direction of well-being and fulfillment.

Further, just because there is no proof does not suggest a lack of good reasons to believe that some values and meanings are universal. For one thing, all the wisdom figures who promulgated the organizing ideas we humans have lived within for thousands of years believed that some of their ideas came from a universal ground. You can choose to disbelieve that any of these wisdom figures knew what they were talking about, but doing so is an act of faith, without much evidence to support it.

Thinking about this in a slightly different way, economist E. F. Schumacher (quoted in Chapters 4 and 8) argues in *A Guide for the Perplexed* that almost all philosophical, religious, and cultural systems through history have included an understanding and acceptance of the "great chain of being."[5] In the many variations of this theme, it is assumed that some ideas are stronger than others, that some values are more valuable than others, and that there is a hierarchy of values and meanings that exists beyond local conditions and beyond individual opinions. The ultimate existence of this great chain cannot be proven—but it is at least as likely to be true as any other point of view.

Schumacher goes on to describe the danger of ignoring the *great chain* and allowing "science for manipulation" to become too powerful. In such a case, "Faith, instead of being taken as a guide leading the intellect to an understanding of the higher levels," is misinterpreted "as opposing and rejecting the intellect." When this happens, those valuing the intellect begin to reject faith, which is exactly what has happened with some intellectuals today. Unfortunately for them, as Schumacher feared, "all roads to recovery," to finding true meaning in life, "are barred."[6]

Skeptico: You are winning me over. Give me a short version of what you are saying so I can try to hold on to it.

Wisdom Seeker: Every point of view is embedded in and dependent upon assumptions. These assumptions are accepted through either a conscious or an unconscious act of faith. Every point of view starts from these acts of faith and goes on to build its edifice of knowledge on that foundation. Relativism denies the existence of a universal ground but does so by assuming the existence of a universal ground that suits its purposes. Ultimately, every point of view, even relativism, rests on acts of faith as well as on a long human history of belief in the existence of a universal ground of values and meanings. The belief systems of Asia, Africa, India, and earlier tribal peoples are different from the western traditions, but all are based on the assumption that transcendent values exist. And for the record, the originator of modern relativity theory in physics, Albert Einstein, did not think it suggested that values, morals, or meanings were relative.

About Those Mistakes

Skeptico: I just recognized a big problem with what you are saying! If I can't be sure about anything and have to make all these acts of faith, I will probably make a lot of mistakes.

Wisdom Seeker: Yes, any of your acts of faith might be mistaken, and you will make mistakes. Because of this, some people refuse to choose, refuse to move in any direction. But to wait for certainty is a choice involving the act of faith that to wait is best. It might be, but it also might freeze your life, for, as Voltaire said, "Doubt is not a pleasant condition, but certainty is an absurd one."[7] In fact, waiting too long for certainty can be as big a mistake as acting too quickly; it can lead to a dark and stagnant eddy of the stream of life with no hope of emergence until the fear of mistakes is overcome. Or to switch metaphors, there is a chance that any car will crash, so if you want to avoid all danger, you will never ride in a car until you are certain it will not crash.

Skeptico: But I would never be able to get in a car again!

Wisdom Seeker: Just so. If you wish to move along on life's journey, you must climb aboard in spite of the risk. This is true of taking a job, entering a relationship, playing a sport, investing money, joining a group of any kind, or pursuing spiritual development.

The Buddha, as was true of Confucius, Lao Tzu, Jesus, and many other wisdom teachers, was well aware of the necessity for both trying to know as much as possible and also moving ahead on the basis of acts of faith. In fact, the Buddha emphasized that there are usually two extremes with regard to most things, thus he suggested following the "middle way." One aspect of that middle way for him involved the relationship between faith and wisdom. He valued wisdom but he also saw its limitations: "Wisdom without faith can be righteous or anxious." The other extreme presented a danger as well: "Faith without wisdom is only blind faith." Thus the Buddha recognized the necessity of stepping into life with faith, but understood that faith had to be tempered with wisdom, or one might travel a long way in the wrong direction.

Fallible human beings are in charge of all the existing wisdom traditions. If we wish to learn from them, that fallibility can be a problem. Yet it need not be the problem it at first seems. If we simply make the best decisions we can, step into life, and do our work with diligence and a good heart, we will gain the potential rewards—even in an imperfect world. As novelist Charles Williams put it: "Until devotion is given to a thing which must prove false in the end, the thing that is true in the end cannot enter,"[8] which I take to mean that if we commit ourselves to the best way forward we can find, and give it our all, the system does not have to be perfect for us to achieve the highest goals. A famous Zen master said, "A Zen master's life is just one continuous mistake. The purpose of life is to learn from those mistakes."

Thought Experiment: The Possibility of a Wrong Choice

If you wish to keep moving forward in the stream of life, what is the best way to deal with fears of making a wrong choice? What is the best response you can think of when such fears arise?

The nature of human life is that we start with very little knowledge, and we are then enculturated to believe many things by teachers who also have limited knowledge. Yet in this world of partial knowledge we must develop a point of view at an early age in order to function. As we struggle to find our way and make sense of life, we must adapt to the uncertainties as best we can and make the best acts of faith we can muster. In doing this, the best advice I know is: (a) choose the path that seems best to you right now; (b) put your faith, consciously, in that path; (c) do your work diligently; and (d) as you grow and develop, stay open to course corrections, big and small, that arise from increasing wisdom and consciousness.

Remember also that everyone around you is in the same boat, struggling to stay afloat. Everyone is trying to set a worthwhile course in an unknown and often turbulent sea. Realizing this, Henry Haskin's advice becomes especially poignant: "Treat the other man's faith gently; it is all he has to believe with. His mind was created for his own thoughts, not yours or mine."[9]

CHAPTER 13

FAITH AND THE WISDOM TRADITIONS

I have spent forty-five years exploring the world's wisdom traditions, each of which offers guidance for finding meaning, fulfillment, and happiness, as well as ways to live into a whole and complete life. I have gained much from each tradition I have encountered. For a tradition to have a significant impact on one's life, however, it is necessary to move beyond concepts and put into practice some portion of its guidance for living.

Further, to gain real value from any of the wisdom traditions, faith is essential: You must have faith that those who are conveying the teachings are relatively sincere; that they are telling the truth as they know it; that they are not charlatans, delusional, or egomaniacal. You must have faith that the fulfillments offered are worthwhile. (If you haven't yet experienced the fulfillments for yourself, you cannot know that they are real. You can only place your faith in those who report that they are real and attainable.) And you have to have faith that the fulfillments are possible for you. (Even if you believe others have gained great benefit, how can you know at the beginning that you will achieve any benefits?)

Many Different Traditions

We humans have developed many different wisdom traditions in our history, from the shamanic practices of early peoples to the major religions active in the world today. Some groups have kept their teachings secret while others have aggressively promoted their views; some traditions have demanded strict adherence to an orthodoxy while others have allowed a great deal of leeway in what a member could believe. One thing they have all had in common, though, is growing in the soil of the past. Even the greatest spiritual figures, those who had a tremendous impact on history, did not start from a blank slate. Rather, all developed their messages from ideas that came before: Jesus frequently referenced the Jewish tradition, the Buddha used many ideas and practices from Hinduism, Confucius constantly pointed back to Chinese ancestral traditions, and Mohammed used many concepts and ideas from Judaism and Christianity.

The point is this: Since even the greatest wisdom figures did not invent traditions out of thin air, it seems unlikely that any of us will do so today. In fact, for any one of us, by ourselves, to answer all the questions life brings concerning the best way to a fulfilled life would be just as impossible as someone building a rocket without studying what others in the past had to say about building rockets. For any journey toward meaning and fulfillment, in order to discover what is truly important and the most fulfilling way to live, the existing wisdom traditions are the best tools available.

This does not mean that everything presented by the traditions is wise. Times change, the needs of a particular culture shift, and every tradition has allowed unhealthy principles and practices to creep in. Yet the traditions are what we have to work with. In learning how best to live—as with learning anything—we must start with the current state of knowledge and proceed from there. For those who wish to understand physics and make a contribution in that field, the first step is to study what has come before. The same is true with learning how to live: The journey begins with understanding what others have discovered and left for us to work with. Therefore, the way to a fulfilled life always begins with one or more of the wisdom traditions of history. This does, however, present a dilemma that each of us must face: Which tradition (or traditions) will we use for guidance, and which particular teaching (or teacher) will we rely upon?

This dilemma is unavoidable because the various traditions are quite different from each other and there are great differences within each tradition. This means that if we wish to use the guidance of the wisdom traditions to grow and develop, we must choose specific teachings around which to organize our efforts. In my journey, I have found it possible, over time, to incorporate the ideas and practices from several of the traditions into a coherent whole. The danger of this approach, however, is putting together a plan that appeals to the ego and leaves weaknesses in place. If one falls into this trap, important strengths are left undeveloped, strengths that would have emerged through the challenge of following a teacher or teaching.

The alternatives to this approach are to adopt the teachings of an existing system or to choose one specific teacher and follow that teacher's prescriptions and proscriptions as fully as possible. Both approaches can be valuable in the search for meaning, fulfillment, and happiness, and many seekers throughout history have chosen these paths. The danger, though, is of choosing a system or a teacher that, years later, you discover was unhelpful or even unhealthy—for at the beginning of our journeys we seldom know enough to select wisely.

Skeptico: I will follow the teaching or teacher I feel most drawn to.

Wisdom Seeker: That's one approach, but how do you know if your impulse toward one or another system or teacher is a healthy one? In my experience, I can look back and see that I have been powerfully drawn to a number of things (a relationship, a job, a cause) that did not turn out very well—yet my sense at the time was that following that impulse was exactly what would make me happy or fulfilled. How, then, does one know that the path you feel drawn to will not turn out badly?

Skeptico: By analyzing my mistakes and making a rational decision about which path to follow!

Wisdom Seeker: Very good Skeptico; that is exactly right. As we proceed, we can learn from past mistakes and refine our ability to make good judgments through rational analysis. Yet you will never know enough to make a fully rational decision about the way to a fulfilled life. In fact, as I have tried to demonstrate, reason cannot tell you what is most valuable or what the meaning of your life might be. Reason can help you live by the values you have chosen and can help you pursue what you feel is most meaningful, but reason does not provide the answers to key questions. At the most fundamental level, reason cannot tell you what you should do with your time until you have answered several important questions about what is most meaningful to you. Answers to central questions must come from deep inside and must include your emotions and intuitions, which are not subject to reason's control. As David Hume argued, motivations are controlled by emotions much more than we usually think, which means that when we are considering what to do, often the expectation of praise, the hope for pleasure, the fear of making a mistake, or a concern about being blamed count for more than reason.

Thought Experiment: Can Reason Control Your Emotions and Intuitions?

Looking back over your life, have you always been able to control your feelings with reason? Have you been able to stop longings or sexual desires you did not want to have from coming up by being rational about them? Have you been able to stop the desire for food, praise, a job, or a reward that your reason told you wasn't good for you? Have you ever stopped an intuition from arising that did not fit with the way your reason saw the situation?

We can refrain from acting on desires or intuitions, but we cannot stop them from coming up. And when they arise, we have to deal with them in some way, either by following them or struggling to resist them. Reason can work with our emotions, desires, intuitions, and longings, but it does not control them—which means that reason cannot, by itself, select the path you will follow. David Hume went even further, arguing that reason is used mostly to get what we want, to fulfill our base desires. Reason is "the slave of the passions," said he. I would not go quite so far, but it does seem clear that those who frequently try to use reason to override emotions and longings end up very frustrated—and frequently at war with themselves. All this means that reason by itself is *not* the best way to select a path to a fulfilling life.

Skeptico: So what is the best way?

Wisdom Seeker: Be open to all the possibilities, get in touch with your longings and emotions, ask your intuition for guidance, and consider everything with your rational mind. Then, holding and honoring all these currents, make the best decision you can—when it feels like the time for decision has come. Next, having made a decision, place your faith in what you have chosen. (Faith is essential here, for you cannot know for sure that what you have chosen is right.) Now, proceed with determination and discipline. Finally, after following your chosen path for a decent period of time, reevaluate; go through the process again.

Faith in the Buddhist Tradition

Faith is essential in pursuing any path that might lead to a fulfilling life, and it is especially important if one is to use the tools of a wisdom tradition to achieve that end. Although this is true for all the traditions, because Buddhism has placed such a strong emphasis on working out answers for oneself, it is a good tradition in which to examine what is essential and what can be left aside in relation to faith.

The central role of faith in Buddhism starts with the fact that most Buddhists through history have been enculturated into the tradition and then continued on with it through passive acts of faith; they have relied on their upbringing in a way similar to those in every other tradition. The ultimate goal of Buddhism is to go beyond faith into a profound knowing, to experience a liberation that makes faith unnecessary. Most Buddhists through the centuries, however, have not reached this stage; most have had to rely on faith to stay on the path.

By working diligently, though, some Buddhists have gradually made their faith more conscious. But this did not remove faith's necessity, just shifted it toward being more conscious. Ultimately, growing awareness has led a small number over the centuries to report that they have become fully awakened. In this state, faith is no longer necessary; they are awake and know they are awake. But each of them had to rely on faith for a long time before arriving at this liberation.

Besides those enculturated into Buddhism, there are a few people in each generation who make a conscious choice to adopt it as their way. (This is, of course, true of each of the wisdom traditions.) To make such a choice, however, always involves several acts of faith. The first is the assumption that the values and understandings one has been organizing around are not leading to the fulfillment one had hoped to achieve. In other words, to adopt Buddhism means to question the values and goals you have been living within and to place your faith in the possibility that you might be able to "wake up" to that which is more real and true by following a Buddhist path. (To adopt any new way of thinking involves a similar decision.) The Buddha himself made an act of faith of this kind, and as a consequence left his home and family—even left what many thought to be a perfect situation as heir to a throne—to wander in the wilderness of spiritual seeking for many years. (Was his analysis of what is most important correct?)

A person might feel drawn to Buddhism or feel a certain intuition that what the Buddha said was true, but there is no way to know for sure at the beginning of the journey whether the Buddha's analysis was correct, so an act of faith that greater fulfillment might be found is necessary before one can begin. It is the same with every other wisdom tradition: One might hear an inspiring talk or read a motivating book and feel a certain resonance, but such a feeling could be a whim or a passing fancy (like wanting to run away to join the circus). At various points in our lives, various possibilities present themselves, and whether we pursue them always involves an act of faith. In the case of Buddhism, the act of faith revolves around a decision (either conscious or unconscious) about whether the Buddha's analysis has a decent chance of being correct as well as whether his remedy for life's problems might work for us. It is the same with anything we might do. To start on any path that offers value, whether it be signing up for a self-help course, taking a yoga lesson, hiring a therapist, or participating in a spiritual tradition, the starting point is an act of faith that such an action might lead to a more fulfilling or rewarding life.

Thought Experiment: How Would You Know?

If someone you knew left his wife, young son, and a great inheritance to wander in the forest or live in the desert, how would you decide whether or not it was a good decision? What advice would you give a friend who was thinking about going to the desert to join a strict monastic community? How would you know whether that friend was lost in illusion, or was about to become the next enlightened being? If you felt such a calling yourself, how would you know if it was valid?

The key point: For any path you might choose, until you have reached the final fulfillment the exemplars of that tradition describe, there is no way to know for sure whether your choice was a good one. Until fulfillment comes, you can only proceed on acts of faith. Focusing on Buddhism again, anyone choosing a Buddhist path needs to make the following acts of faith: (1) that the Buddha found a meaningful answer to life's most important questions; (2) that the Buddha's answers apply to others and not just to himself; (3) that his answers are still relevant in the world of today; (4) that the path he outlined, the precepts and practices he laid down, might work for you; (5) that, among the many versions of Buddhism on offer, the one you are choosing is authentic and effective, and (6) that the teacher you are choosing is not deluded or a charlatan. There is no way a beginner on a Buddhist path can know whether these things are true—thus the necessity for acts of faith.

A few contemporary Buddhist writers (such as Stephen Batchelor in *Buddhism Without Beliefs*) have argued that Buddhism doesn't require faith, that one can simply try it and see if it works. But there is a dramatic problem with this approach: To gain the rewards the Buddha promised takes a long time. It took the Buddha himself six years of total and complete dedication, during which time he gave up everything else that most people consider important. Those who decide to simply "try it" are unlikely to have the commitment necessary to gain the rewards achieved by the Buddha through his total determination and sacrifice over those six difficult years.

Another problem: Since there are many schools of Buddhism and many teachers within each school, there is not sufficient time to try more than a few, so the only way to select a particular branch and a particular teacher to "try" is by a provisional act of faith. Without such a decision, those who are just "trying" some version will have no reason to stick with their choice when difficult times come; it will seem easier to try something else. The fact is, many people have "tried" Buddhism for long stretches of time (some for a lifetime) without gaining the rewards the Buddha suggested were possible. Some have eventually concluded that they gained few or no rewards at all. How, then, can a beginner know that, even after a great deal of time and effort, the hoped-for rewards will come?

Still another problem with thinking you can "try" Buddhism to see if it works: If you could try it for a short time and get "better" quickly, trying it might be worthwhile. Or, if you experienced steady improvement all along the way, trying it could be a valid approach. The teachings of Buddhism, however, do not suggest these outcomes are likely; on the contrary, the teachings suggest that it takes years before you feel better in any sustained way. Moreover, on a Buddhist path there must be a radical shift in one's understanding concerning what "feeling better" means. Those who try to feel better using the criteria of their old lives will miss the whole point of Buddhism. How, then, can the wish to "feel better" be used as the basis for evaluating whether to stay on the path through hard times?

Simply put, if the criterion by which one is to judge whether to stay on any wisdom path is feeling better in the short run, every authentic path will be abandoned when the going gets tough, for there will be no motivation to do the difficult work of letting go of old ideas and attachments. Letting go of what we have been clinging to is always painful, and any path that involves real growth will cause the seeker to feel worse at times. As Annie Lamott put it, "Most of the things I have let go of have claw marks in them." For confirmation of this universal pattern, simply read the lives of the world's great saints and sages, most of whom had difficult periods as they pursued their journeys. In most traditions, the teachings make clear that following the designated path will often make one feel worse, sometimes for a significant period of time, before feeling better manifests. There are many stories in every tradition of those who underwent privation, struggle, doubt, and suffering in their journeys. This is certainly the case within Buddhism, where stories abound of those who suffered greatly from such things as leaving family and loved ones, severe physical privations, harsh criticism by teachers, sexual abstinence, dramatically restricted diets, and episodes of fear, anger, and anxiety.

In sum, since Buddhism involves letting go of attachments before one can reap the rewards, there will be difficult and painful times caused by the need to let go of things that were once desired. Before the reward, if it comes at all, difficulties are almost guaranteed. The Buddha himself did not just try an experiment of leaving his former life; he left for good. And he certainly did not find immediate reward or experience steady reinforcement for his choice at each stage of his journey. Rather, his story includes much suffering. (It is said he starved himself to the point he could put his hand on his stomach and feel his backbone.) He also had many doubts through the years regarding whether the practices he was following were the right ones.

Skeptico: If he had such a difficult time, why would anyone follow him?
Wisdom Seeker: As with all the wisdom traditions, because the promised rewards are great. Edward Conze lists some of the phrases that those who have traveled the Buddhist path use to describe the end goal, *nirvana*. "It is power, bliss and happiness, the secure refuge ... the place of unassailable safety; ... the real Truth and the supreme Reality; ... it is the *Good*, the supreme goal and the one and only consummation of our life, ... the eternal, hidden and incomprehensible Peace."[1]

These are dramatic fruits, but until one has fully experienced them oneself, it is essential to make acts of faith in order to stay on the path. The same is true for every wisdom tradition. Many Hindus have taken on severe and painful practices and many followers of Islam have done the same. The path that Jesus followed was filled with trials and difficulties, and many of his followers have undergone a great deal of suffering to follow his way. The letters and diaries of Mother Teresa, one of the most revered Christians of the twentieth century, reveal years of great suffering. She wrote to her confessor: "Please pray specially for me that I may not spoil His work and that Our Lord may show Himself—for there is such terrible darkness within me, as if everything was dead. It has been like this more or less from the time I started 'the work'."[2]

The clear conclusion to be drawn from the teachings of the world's wisdom traditions, then, is that feeling better in the short run is **not** the measure of success, as is made vivid in the lives of the Buddha and Jesus. To emphasize again, after six long years of intense striving, the Buddha was not happy and did not feel better. In fact, he was so frustrated he vowed to die if the prize he sought continued to elude him. And it was only with this choice, of being willing to die to achieve his aim, that he finally broke through to the "liberation" he was seeking. Only then did he receive confirmation that awakening was possible; only then was he able to move beyond faith into knowing that the way he had followed was successful. As for Jesus, the suffering of his last days on earth is a central part of his story, and the fulfillment Christianity offers is not focused on feeling good in the moment, but on a longer-term reward.

Skeptico: Why are some people able to persevere during difficult times?

Wisdom Seeker: It varies, but Jesus had incredible faith that he was following the will of his heavenly Father, and the Buddha had extraordinary faith that it was possible to awaken. They both had tremendous faith in the path they had chosen—as have many of their followers.

I Want to Feel Good Now!

Skeptico: But what if my goal is to feel good now?

Wisdom Seeker: Well, first you have to recognize that pursuing such a goal involves an act of faith that following it will make you feel good now. That, however, is by no means guaranteed. Viktor Frankl makes a strong argument in *Man's Search for Ultimate Meaning* that pursuing the goal of immediate happiness doesn't work, that happiness only arises as a by-product of doing what is meaningful. A danger, then, in doing what you *think* will make you feel good now is that doing so may not produce the result for which you hope. For instance, I have often done things that were supposed to be "fun" that turned out to be boring or depressing. And, when I have managed to have fun for a while, actions taken during that time have often made my life more problematic and brought unhappiness later on. This has not always been the case, of course, but there is always that danger. All the wisdom traditions have in fact suggested that frequently pursuing momentary pleasure is a sure way to unhappiness. William James captured the point in a wonderful quip, saying that if we based our decisions strictly on feeling good in the short term, "drunkenness would be the supremely valid human experience."[3] What this means is that if we make feeling good right now our central aim, there is no guarantee we will actually feel good now, and we might well be diminishing the chances of reaching the fulfillments the wisdom figures of history have suggested are possible.

The world's main wisdom traditions don't rule out the possibility of good feelings arising in the process of pursuing what is truly worthwhile, but they all suggest that discipline, effort, and letting go of short-term ego desires—at least part of the time—are crucial in

achieving the goals they offer. They uniformly say that determination, practice, and perseverance are necessary components in dealing with difficult times, and that following short-term urges in an
attempt to feel good now will only lead to a disappointing life.

Skeptico: But how do I know they are right?

Wisdom Seeker: You don't. But neither do you know that trying to "feel
good" right now is a worthwhile strategy for either the short-run or the
long. The only option you have is to make an act of faith in one direction
or another. If you choose to follow one of the wisdom traditions, you will
do so because of a belief that the results offered might be achievable and
that those results will be worth the effort—if they can be achieved.

Whatever goal you decide to pursue, though, whether it be feeling
good now, long-term fulfillment, or any other—you will immediately be
faced with another decision: What actions are likely to lead to the goal?
This decision is seldom easy, for there are many possible approaches to
acquire almost anything you desire. Do you want to improve yourself,
experience the divine, find a good relationship, feel better now, or overcome your internal barriers to success? Whatever the goal, suggestions
cascade from TV shows, friends, magazines, and the internet: start exercising, engage a therapist, eat a better diet, listen to music, tell your troubles to a friend, work harder, go hiking, take up a sport, find a hobby, take
vitamins, change jobs, have better sex, take mood-altering drugs (legal or
illegal), sing, do yoga, meditate daily, pray.

The possibilities are almost endless, and all are advocated by
various authorities (self-appointed as well as credentialed). Any one
of them might work for you. You cannot, however, pursue them all
simultaneously, so you must make a guess as to which will work best.
You can ask others for advice, but since your goals might be different
from theirs, even something that worked for another might not work
in your case. Further, no one has tried all the possibilities, so no one
is in a position to compare all the options. The only thing others can
profitably say is that a specific approach did or did not work in pursuing their goals. Advocates of each approach might exclaim, "Try my
way and see if it works," but the next person to whom you speak will

likely suggest another approach, and a third person another, so all you can do is make an act of faith about what might work for you.

The problem compounds even further, for most of us have several goals, and the actions that are likely to fulfill one often interfere with attempts to fulfill others. For instance, I want to feel good now, but I also want to believe my life has meaning. I want to eat delicious food, but I don't want to gain weight. I want a committed, long-term relationship, but I sometimes want a romantic fling. I want spiritual fulfillment, but I don't want to fulfill the demands of a spiritual discipline. No wonder it is so hard to commit to a path and then stay on it.

Skeptico: You are making me depressed. What do I do?

Wisdom Seeker: All of the wisdom traditions suggest that you choose the goals they have defined as important, and each offers a path to achieve those goals.

Skeptico: But if I choose one of their paths, am I committing to becoming a saint like Mother Teresa[m] or an enlightened being like the Buddha?

Wisdom Seeker: No, you are just pursuing the possibility that by choosing and sticking to a path you will make progress toward a worthwhile result. In doing this, you do not have to believe that you will achieve the dramatic results that the saints and sages of history exemplified. Your goals can be much more modest, such as "being more loving," "feeling closer to God," "being more at peace," or "being present in the moment." You do not even have to feel certain that positive results will follow (you cannot know this anyway, for certainty is seldom a realistic belief). But you do need to make an act of faith that the path you are choosing has a decent chance of carrying you toward a better result than the course you are on now.

Skeptico: If I am going to commit to a path, I want a powerful mystical experience to make it clear what I am to do. Come to think of it, what I really want is an instant connection to God, or instant enlightenment. Do you believe in instant enlightenment?

---

[m] Although not yet officially a "saint" in the Catholic Church, Mother Teresa is considered the greatest saint of the modern era by millions.

Wisdom Seeker: To believe or disbelieve in instant enlightenment doesn't seem worth deciding about. When enlightenment or immersion in the Divine occurs, it happens in an instant. Or perhaps it would be better to say it happens out of time—as we normally experience time. If you are in an out-of-time state, there is no need to think about the question or to make any choices about what to do next; both take care of themselves. For those who wish to have such experiences but are not in one right now, the relevant question is: What can I do that might lead to such an experience? An equally important question for those who have experienced an enlightened moment or a profound connection to the Divine but did not remain there permanently: What might bring me back into the fullness of the glimpse I experienced?

Skeptico: I keep hearing people say, "I don't have to go anywhere or do anything. I just have to live in the present moment."

Wisdom Seeker: Here's the thing: If you are not now fully in the experience of being in the present moment, telling yourself or having someone tell you that you "should" be there does little good. It's like someone telling you that you should be in love when you are not. You might want to be in love, but if you are not, you cannot force yourself to be. You can be open to the possibility; you can pay attention to those who seem to be in love and try to discern how they accomplished it; you can even do things that might make it more likely; but you cannot force it to happen.

It's the same with the idea that we don't have to go anywhere or do anything. If you feel completely fulfilled in this moment, what they say is true. But what if you don't feel that way right now? When I don't feel completely fulfilled, I can't make myself feel fulfilled. I can tell myself intellectually that I should feel it, but that does not create a feeling of fulfillment; in fact, it usually makes me feel worse, because I berate myself for not feeling the way I "should" feel. The only useful approach is to accept the truth of what you actually feel—especially if that truth is that you do not feel fulfilled in the present moment. For me, accepting where I really am has the advantage of letting me consider how I might move more skillfully toward what I seek; it allows me to set goals that might be more beneficial.

Skeptico: But isn't striving toward a goal a problem?

Wisdom Seeker: All the wisdom figures I know strived mightily, often for long periods of time. In addition to the Buddha's six-year ordeal, just read the lives of Christian saints, Sufi mystics, or Hindu sannyasins. If and when they reached their goals, the striving often ceased and they *knew* that the path they had taken had worked. (Or perhaps, at that final moment, they let go of striving and opened into the fulfillment they sought.) In either case, once a profound sense of fulfillment came, faith was no longer necessary; it was replaced by a deep knowing. Until that time, striving and faith were essential for them to begin, as well as to stay on their paths.

Skeptico: You keep saying that faith is necessary on all paths. I thought the Buddha said that aspirants on his path should vigorously test the truth of his teachings for themselves.

Wisdom Seeker: Shortly before he died, as a last attempt to aid his close followers, the Buddha asked if anyone had any questions concerning "the Buddha, or the Dhamma, or the Sangha, or the Path, or the Practice."[4] By this question he was emphasizing that these were the things they could rely on after he passed away. He also specifically said that his followers should turn to each other for help and support. As a result of these messages, one of the main practices in Buddhism for twenty-five centuries has been to "take refuge," to look for support in the Buddha, the Dharma (the teachings the Buddha had given), and the Sangha (the community of followers).

Another quotation, frequently said to be among the Buddha's last words, "Work out your salvation with diligence,"[5] is often taken as an individualistic message. But this phrase was put into the Buddha's mouth by Paul Carus in his book, *The Gospel of Buddha.* (Published in 1894, it was the first widely read book on Buddhism in the western world.) Carus wanted to link Buddhism to Christianity, so he echoed the words of St. Paul in Philippians 2:12: "Work out your own salvation." Compounding the problem, the phrase, "Do not depend on others," is often attached to Carus' words and quoted as the very last words of the dying Buddha. This phrase, however, has no source in ancient Buddhist literature. "Do not depend on others" comes from a book published in 1961 that included an interview with a modern Zen teacher who was trying to recount from memory the English meaning Carus had given to the Buddha's words.[6]

Still, the Buddha did wish for his followers to realize that their ultimate freedom was in their own hands, rather than his. Most of the quotes supporting this idea, however, were given to his close disciples. These instructions, therefore, were for people who had followed him for a long time and who, hopefully, were close to their own realization. To his closest followers, the Buddha was conveying that they would have to take the final steps for themselves, especially since he would no longer be around to guide them. But during his life, he placed great importance on followers accepting his authority and guidance. In the *Kitagiri sutta*, he sternly instructed his followers to have faith in his teachings and follow his instructions. The proper attitude for a student, he said, was to take the view: "The Teacher is the Lord, a disciple am I; the Lord knows, I do not know."[7] Significantly, this was the kind of faith he expected even from Ananda, his long-term disciple—a person who had followed his guidance and done his bidding for forty years.

Ultimately, there is no conflict between the necessity for faith in Buddhism and the necessity of working things out for oneself. Clarity arises when the timing as well as the audience to whom the Buddha was speaking is understood. During the forty years he was present to teach his followers, the Buddha expected them to accept his teachings and follow his instructions. He would reason with and give arguments to potential followers, but those who joined his sangha were governed by specific rules concerning how to act and even how to think. (One of the main points of the Eightfold Path—the heart of his teaching—concerns how to mold one's thinking to the Buddha's understanding of the world.) Beginners, or even those far along on the path, were not instructed to work out their own views for themselves; rather, the instruction was that they should work very hard to adopt the way of thinking the Buddha was offering—until they were ready to take the final step for themselves.

The Buddha almost certainly did believe that each person would have to take this final step for himself, but there is no indication he believed this was possible until seekers had first put their faith in his teaching and closely followed the instructions he had given. This is why guidance from Buddhist teachers has usually been considered essential for aspirants (often strict guidance, for long stretches of time)—until an individual is ready to take the last step into freedom and awakening for herself.

Skeptico: Are you saying that whatever path I choose, I must wait until I have reached the fulfillment it offers before I can move beyond the need for faith?

Wisdom Seeker: Yes. Going through life, we make many choices that seem to work for a while, but do not work out in the long run (romances, jobs, friendships, entertainments). Looking back, some seem to have been harmful. This is unavoidable, and not even a cause for concern, for this is how we grow and learn. But it does mean that in following the guidance of a wisdom tradition, until we reach the final fulfillment it suggests is possible, we cannot know that we are on the right path. Before that final confirmation, we will only continue through conscious or unconscious acts of faith. Every tradition offers an end result that seems worthwhile to its advocates, but whether you personally can achieve those results will only be discovered by proceeding on faith.

Thought Experiment: How Would You Know?

To follow a wisdom tradition without an act of faith (either conscious or unconscious) would be to say: "I don't feel there is anything worthwhile here, but I will commit to this path and make sacrifices for it anyway." Is it likely you would do this? Most importantly, would you make a determined effort to follow a path that you felt this way about?

To emphasize again: Even if you believe that the point of view and practices you have adopted have worked for others, you cannot know whether they will work for you. On any path, until you have reached the ultimate stage it offers, you cannot avoid acts of faith. People are different, and what works for one might not work for another, so to follow a path requires an act of faith that there is something valuable to be gained and that a particular approach might deliver its fruits in your life. For instance, at any moment, how can you know that a completely different course of action wouldn't be more suited to your nature or more in touch with what is really true?

Skeptico: So I don't have to be certain a wisdom tradition is true or certain that it will fulfill my goals before I make a decision to follow it?

Wisdom Seeker: That's right. But to pursue any organizing point of view, including the adoption of materialism as a worldview or taking up a career in science, you must make an act of faith that what you are choosing has a decent chance of carrying you toward fulfillment of your goals. Otherwise, you wouldn't choose it. Further, to follow any path, you need to assume that it is based on sound information and that most practitioners in the past were basically honest. In these and other ways, as you choose how you will organize your life, you will inevitably make several acts of faith.

Skeptico: Is making such a choice a once-and-for-all thing?

Wisdom Seeker: Not at all. Whatever you choose at one point you can reevaluate at another. Many people change their paths from time to time in dramatic as well as subtle ways, and it is fairly common to make several significant changes during a lifetime. To change, however, requires an act of faith, either in a positive or a negative direction. (Positive: I believe there is a better path to take. Negative: The current path is not going to work, so I must try something different. Both these are assumptions; acts of faith.)

Skeptico: I don't fully understand what you mean by a negative act of faith.

Wisdom Seeker: At any moment, whatever your chosen course of action, you might be on the verge of a breakthrough that will provide complete and lasting fulfillment. There is no way to know where you are in relation to a breakthrough into complete fulfillment before the breakthrough comes. The only reason, then, that you ever make a change (no matter how rough the going) is because of a negative act of faith. You change course because of an assumption that your current path is not working or is not a good fit for you anymore. In making that decision, you cannot know whether it is true or not; you cannot know that the course you were following wouldn't have begun to fulfill its promise tomorrow, or in the next moment. Thus, to change course is to make a negative act of faith about the possibilities of that course for the future. In fact, to decide not to pursue a possibility that presents itself is to make a negative assumption about that possibility, as compared to whatever you choose instead. Such a decision might be a wise one, but it involves a negative act of faith about the new possibility.

Skeptico: If faith is always required, what about those dramatic experiences I have read about, those times when someone seemed to know for certain that he or she was on the right path?

Wisdom Seeker: In every spiritual tradition there are accounts of those who say they have reached union with the Divine, experienced permanent awakening, or come to know God beyond any doubt. For these few, if their accounts are to be believed, the journey is over; they no longer need faith. The number of those who have arrived at this point, however, is quite small. Much more frequent is the report of those who have a powerful experience and feel that everything has been confirmed, followed by (sometimes very soon thereafter) new questions and fresh doubts.

In the Christian tradition, I mentioned the letters of Mother Teresa, which are filled with the anguish and doubt she experienced for many years after the powerful mystical experience that set her on her life course. In Evelyn Underhill's *Mysticism,* there are dozens of accounts of the painful struggles undergone by Christian saints *after* they had experienced a deep connection to God. In Islam, the struggles that come after an experience of union are vividly conveyed in the poetry of Rumi. In a more modern account, Irina Tweedie documents in *Chasm of Fire* a years-long journey filled with grief and despair, but which in the end brings a final breakthrough into a deep sense of knowing.

In Hinduism there are countless stories through the centuries of the struggles of sannyasins, and in modern times there is the stirring account given by Gopi Krishna concerning his years-long struggle *after* his first realization of the Divine. And of course there are countless stories of the struggles and pain experienced by those on a Buddhist path, one of the most dramatic being the ordeal of Milarepa, a great Tibetan master. Milarepa was instructed by his teacher to carry out tasks that involved almost unimaginable hardship over a long period of time. Often he wanted to quit, sometimes decided he would quit, but each time he overcame his doubts and made a fresh commitment to continue. Then, after many years of trials and tribulations and after receiving his master's final instructions, Milarepa spent several more years living in a remote cave, eating little, undergoing what most of us would consider severe deprivation—until he felt he had fully mastered the teachings. Only then, after all those years and incredible hardship, did he finally achieve the certainty he sought.

Skeptico: Why are you telling me all these stories about how hard it is?

Wisdom Seeker: Simply to convey that in every wisdom tradition even those who are believed to have reached the greatest fulfillment had to make many acts of faith along the way to stay the course. Even those who ultimately came to a place of certainty were carried along on acts of faith until final fulfillment came.

Skeptico: Was it worth it to them?

Wisdom Seeker: For most of those who come down to us as exemplars, the answer is a resounding "Yes!" Most of them convey a feeling of having reached the fulfillment they sought and that their lives ended up feeling worthwhile.

Technologies of the Sacred

Skeptico: After some of the things we have talked about, I have been puzzling about the role of intuition. Sounds like you are saying faith replaces intuition.

Wisdom Seeker: Not at all. I have found that having an intuition about a particular path is a good way to begin orienting my life. It is impossible, however, to follow each and every intuition that comes up; there have been so many that I have frequently had to choose between conflicting ones. In looking back, I can see that some of my intuitions were good while others were frivolous; some arose from a small desire that did not take into account several parts of my life that were important. It was hard, however, to know this at the time. Consequently, when I have an intuition, I am forced to decide whether to take it as authentic or to conclude it is a fantasy. With each I must decide whether it is important or trivial.

Skeptico: How do you decide?

Wisdom Seeker: You can probably guess. Various factors come into play, but in the end, after having an intuition and carefully reasoning about it, I cannot know for sure what to do, so an act of faith is necessary. Then, there is choosing the best way to proceed, for the best way to reach a destination is seldom given in the choice of destinations. (There are often many paths leading to a sought-after goal.) Therefore, deciding on a path involves another act of faith. Next, when moments come in which the sense of why one is traveling weakens or departs entirely, you have to decide whether to continue, and still another act of faith is involved, either in the affirmative (I will continue even though I do not feel the reasons now), or in the negative (I no longer feel the intuition about where I was going, so I will change course).

In the broad picture of our lives, there is one final act of faith that no one can avoid: accepting or rejecting the common message of the wisdom traditions that there is "something greater" to which we need to find a relationship before our lives come to an end. Ken Wilber frames the issue succinctly:

Are the mystics and sages insane? Because they all tell variations on the same story, don't they? The story of awakening one morning and discovering you are one with the All, in a timeless, and eternal, and infinite fashion.

Yes, maybe they are crazy, these divine fools. Maybe they are mumbling idiots in the face of the Abyss.

But then, I wonder. Maybe the evolutionary sequence really is from matter to body to mind to soul to spirit, each transcending and including, each with a greater depth and greater consciousness and wider embrace. And in the highest reaches of evolution, maybe, just maybe, an individual's consciousness does indeed touch infinity—a total embrace of the entire Kosmos—a Kosmic consciousness that is Spirit awakened to its own true nature.

It's at least possible. And tell me: is that story, sung by mystics and sages the world over, any crazier than the … materialism story, which is that the entire sequence is a tale told by an idiot, full of sound and fury, signifying absolutely nothing? Listen very carefully: just which of those two stories actually sounds totally insane?[8]

In deciding how we will live, each of us is forced to choose what we will organize around, and there are no ultimate proofs to resolve the important questions. Proofs only work for those who have bought into the beginning assumptions (the arguments of the Medieval theologians were exquisite for those who accepted their starting assumptions). Those who want to rely on facts sound the battle cry, "Seeing is believing," but they are answered by the centuries-old rejoinder, "Believing is seeing." When we look at the world, we do so within a set of assumptions that include the expectations, definitions, and categories that determine what we will be able to "see." In the end, each of us must make an act of faith, either conscious or unconscious, concerning how we will understand the world and what constitutes a fulfilled and meaningful life.

Seen in this light, the world's wisdom traditions are sophisticated technologies developed to provide guidance for making life's most important decisions and to help us implement the decisions we make. They offer guidance to help us move toward fulfillment, meaning, and happiness. The price of admission to any system, however, is a provisional act of faith—making the assumption that a particular system will help us fulfill our lives. But making this act of faith in the modern world can be difficult, for the imperfections of each system have been thoroughly documented.

Having the imperfections of the wisdom traditions pointed out so clearly has increased the desire by a lot of people for science to answer the important questions, but science was not designed for that purpose. The only honest scientific response to questions about how to live or what to live for is: "I don't know." Materialists rush into this "don't know" gap with the assertion that whatever science cannot speak about does not exist. But the mission of science has always been to study and understand the material world, so science is not equipped to provide answers concerning love, values, meanings, artistic creations, or the realm of being to which the wisdom traditions point.

Skeptico: What about reason? Is it useless in dealing with these things as well?

Wisdom Seeker: Certainly not. Reason is crucial in dealing with the important issues of our lives. One of its vital roles is helping us sort through the answers we are finding. (There are far too many charlatans afoot to be less than vigilant in examining the answers being offered in the marketplace of ideas.) In fact, all the wisdom traditions have included the use of reason and, like science, all have developed ways of verifying or rejecting the experiences reported and suggestions offered by practitioners in their traditions. Mavericks in both science and the wisdom traditions have claimed many outrageous and unhelpful things, so both fields have developed ways of sorting the authentic from the inauthentic. Healthy wisdom traditions are as concerned about separating genuine teachers and experiences from the deluded and nefarious as good scientists are concerned about separating valid information from the insubstantial and incorrect. As Ken Wilber put it:

> These spiritual endeavors … are purely scientific in any meaningful sense of the word, and the systematic presentations of these endeavors follow precisely those of … science.[9]

Neither science nor the wisdom traditions are perfect in this process, but both are relatively successful. The wisdom traditions do part company with the sciences concerned with worldly things in this way, however: They suggest, according to Wilber, "that there exist higher domains of awareness, embrace, love, identity, reality, self, and truth." He eloquently continues:

> The claims about these higher domains are a conclusion based on hundreds of years of experimental introspection and communal verification. False claims are rejected on the basis of consensual evidence, and further evidence is used to adjust and fine-tune the experimental conclusions.[10]

In other words, the existence and experience of these higher realms is verified in the same way as discoveries in any field of science.
Skeptico: That's pretty heady stuff, but what does it have to do with me?
Wisdom Seeker: The challenge we each face is choosing where we will place our faith in light of the fact that: (a) there is no proof for any organizing point of view; (b) science cannot tell us how to live or what to live for; (c) reason is involved in each and every path known to humankind but reason cannot provide final answers, and (d) within the wisdom traditions there are dozens of answers and dozens of suggested ways to implement those answers, but when we are making our choices, we cannot know which are right and which are wrong for us.

In this open space, each of us is free to choose, and this choosing is one of the central tasks of life. So, Skeptico, what all this means for you is that, along with the rest of us, you must choose where you will place your acts of faith.

CHAPTER 14

THE GOLDEN MEAN

I like clear answers. Perhaps this stems from having Puritans in my ancestry (among many other strains), or maybe it is just part of human nature. This urge for clarity has had its benefits, including a bent for math and science. Opposing this urge has been a growing realization that human understanding seldom involves certitude, which has led to a determined effort to accept reality as it is without trying to convince myself (and others) that I can see beyond the muddy waters that usually limit my perspective.

Giving up the desire for certainty has been a struggle, though, which I have not fully won. Nevertheless, progress has been made, and I have a better understanding of a line by F. Scott Fitzgerald: "The test of a first rate intelligence is the ability to hold two opposed ideas in the mind at the same time."[1] Many wise folks have understood this point intuitively, as exemplified by physicist Niels Bohr's insight (quoted earlier): "Profound truths ... [can be] recognized by the fact that the opposite is also a profound truth."[2] Understanding this has not quenched my thirst for certainty, but it has helped me become more accepting of the fact that certainty is frequently not possible.

One consequence of this is an increased ability to live fully in the absence of certainty, and another is see that the assumptions I bring to any situation have a great deal to do with what I perceive. When I am able to shift my point of view, what I see changes, sometimes dramatically. For instance, I can be quite upset with someone's actions, but then choose to shift my perspective to see their difficulties, and my anger or hurt will be replaced by sympathy and compassion.

The Ancient Promise of the Middle Way

Skeptico: Do your upset feelings disappear?

Wisdom Seeker: No, but other thoughts and feelings create a broader framework, and although the initial feelings might still be present, I am more likely to take wise actions from that broader perspective.

Skeptico: Does the existence of so many different ways to view every situation mean there is no true perspective?

Wisdom Seeker: There is no way to know for sure, but my sense is that there is a level of wisdom at which the contradictions are resolved and harmony emerges from what had seemed to be disharmonious and confusing. Some of the wisest beings who have ever lived have suggested this to be the case, although they have also warned that discovering this level of wisdom is not easily achieved.

To arrive at this place, these wisdom figures counsel that it is necessary to refuse quick and easy answers and to free ourselves from facile certainties. They also advise that we must avoid extreme positions and seek the middle way. In ancient Greece, taking this middle way was considered a great virtue, known as the *Golden Mean*. Socrates taught that a man must "know how to choose the mean and avoid the extremes on either side." This, he declared, would lead to beauty, harmony, and a profound experience of the good. The result? "This is the way of happiness."[3] Even before Socrates, Heraclitus had said that when opposing currents can be brought together, there "arises the fairest harmony."[4] His view was that, beneath the appearance of tension between opposing points of view, "what conflicts with itself agrees with itself: there is a *harmonia* of opposite tensions."[5] At its core, then, for Heraclitus, the goal of life was to find one's way to this harmony. Earlier still, in story form, Homer recounted the journey of Odysseus, who was advised to find the middle way between Scylla and Charybdis if he was to have safe path between these two great dangers on either side of the passageway he had to take. Following the lead of these earlier figures, Aristotle also adopted the Golden Mean, seeing it as the rational and virtuous path between the excesses to which we mortals easily fall prey.

In ancient China, a different version of the Golden Mean held a central place. Life was seen as filled with opposites, but each extreme contained the seed of the other, symbolized by the yin/yang image. In this symbol, still used to this day, there is a point of light in the center of the dark side and a point of dark in the center of the light side, suggesting that opposites are contained within each other—which means that they are not as separate as they might at first appear. A major statement of this idea is given in *The Doctrine of the Mean*, in which Confucius describes the proper balance between the extremes and gives instruction on how to walk this middle way, as well as why this is the best approach to discovering a fulfilled and harmonious life.

In a different part of Asia, the Buddha lived his early life in luxury—completely sheltered from the problems of the world—but then he went to the other extreme and spent many years practicing severe austerities. During those years, he renounced what most of us consider the basic necessities: shelter, possessions, even sufficient food to maintain his health. Eventually, however, he rejected both extremes (ease of life and excessive asceticism) and declared that his was the Middle Way, the way between the extremes.

In the Christian tradition, the parables and sayings of Jesus frequently suggest that we avoid the extremes. For instance, he taught that: (1) We should stand up for what is right, symbolized by throwing the moneychangers out of the temple. But we should also, at times, accept the anger and violence of others without fighting back: "But I tell you, do not resist an evil person. If anyone slaps you on the right cheek, turn to them the other cheek also."[6] (2) We should sometimes speak out concerning the wrongs we see (Jesus frequently criticized the actions of the Sadducees and Pharisees), yet we should also forgive our enemies: "I say unto you, Love your enemies, bless them that curse you, do good to them that hate you, and pray for them which despitefully use you, and persecute you."[7] (3) We should not slavishly follow the rules of society, but at times we *should* follow them. (Jesus frequently broke societal rules, such as when he talked to the Samaritan woman at the well, interacted with criminals and outcasts, and told his followers to harvest what they needed for sustenance—even if it meant breaking the rules of the Sabbath.) On the opposite side, he said it was proper at times to follow society's laws, affirmed with these words: "Render unto Caesar the things that are Caesar's, and unto God the things that are God's."[8] (4) We should neither hoard our talents and possessions nor should we waste them, as taught by the parable of the talents. (5) We should not condemn others—Jesus told the crowd who brought the adulteress before him: "He that is without sin among you, let him first cast a stone at her."[9] Yet we should also stand up for right conduct: After her accusers had departed, Jesus said to her, "Go, and sin no more."[10] In these and many other sayings Jesus continually conveyed a fine sense of the need to find the right balance between extreme positions.

Of course, Jesus was drawing upon his Jewish tradition, which from early times valued balance and harmony. In its mystical and Kabalistic branches, balance and harmony have always been emphasized, and these in turn have had a powerful impact on many other streams of Western thought. In the Kabala, the world is pictured symbolically as the *Tree of Life*, with the two outer sides of the tree containing different energies, but with a reconciling middle channel between them. This is similar in several ways to the Hindu image of the Kundalini, which also has two outer channels of different energies that are reconciled by a middle channel.

Many other examples of the middle way could be given, including some from modern times. Carl Jung, for instance, spent years thinking about the necessity of working with the opposites within ourselves, as well as in the world we encounter. In his system, the key to health and well-being is to strengthen the areas that are weak, thus bringing the whole system into greater balance and harmony. Similarly, the Enneagram, another model of the human psyche, holds that we each have numerous and sometimes oppositional currents within. In this system, finding a proper balance between the different currents is one of the keys to a fulfilled life.

Getting Out of Balance—and Finding It Again

The fact that so many wisdom teachings have emphasized finding balance suggests that we humans are frequently out of balance. No wonder. In our early years, we are each presented with a limited point of view, for a child can only be given a tiny fraction of the accumulated knowledge and wisdom of humanity. Even during a whole lifetime an adult only encounters a small part of that wisdom, and can only assimilate a small fraction of what is encountered. Add to this the fact that some of what is absorbed and assimilated is inaccurate and/or unhealthy, and the seeds of imbalance have been sown. In consequence, part of life's challenge is to discover the things that have been absorbed that are wrong and to add some of the correct things that are needed. For an individual to acquire maturity, then, requires: (a) filling in the gaps, (b) correcting incorrect assumptions, and (c) developing a more wholistic perspective.

Human communities, like individuals, can also be in disharmony and imbalance. At various times in human history, various groups of people (both large and small) have found a way to live together with a high degree of balance and harmony, sometimes for long stretches of time. Yet it is also easy to find communities throughout history in which chaos and disharmony reigned. Following periods of disharmony, though, stability usually returns through the emergence of a new set of leaders or through adoption of a more balanced set of ideas by the existing leadership. (Unfortunately, the disharmony sometimes lasts for a long time with much suffering in the interim.)

An example of a recovery from disharmony occurred in ancient Athens, at a time when the underpinnings of life and thought were called into question by a series of defeats in the Peloponnesian Wars (413 to 404 BC). Athens before and during this period was a trade center and a mixing ground for many different peoples, a place where different cultural ideas mingled and clashed. The Peloponnesian Wars brought to the fore many extreme positions held by the people of Athens, each clamoring for attention. Into this turmoil stepped Socrates, Plato, and Aristotle, who grounded their teachings in the Golden Mean and First Principles (basic principles that exist beyond our ability to explain why they exist, but which we can grasp in a flash of insight or deep knowing). These ideas gradually became the basis for stability in Athens, then in Greece, and gradually in an ever-expanding radius that encompassed Europe. These ideas are still significantly influencing the world today.

The history of China tells a similar story. Around twenty-five hundred years ago there was a time of great disharmony, but out of that turmoil stepped Confucius, Lao Tzu,[n] and others who articulated principles with an emphasis on balance and harmony, grounded in the Tao. Gradually these ideas were accepted by a large percentage of the people of Asia, and this in turn led to several long periods of stability and prosperity in different countries there.

Another dramatic example comes from a time of turbulence in the fledgling colonies of North America in the late 1700's. Into this breech, with extremist positions swirling all around, a remarkable group of leaders came together who recognized the importance of moderation as the basis for the country they envisioned. Their names ring down through U.S. history like tolling bells: George Washington, Thomas Jefferson, Benjamin Franklin, Alexander Hamilton, John Adams, John Jay, and James Madison. With their guidance, the United States was founded on principles of restrained government, a balance of powers, freedom tempered by responsibility, broad political representation, and equality. These ideas were not implemented perfectly, of course: African-Americans, Native Americans, and women were not treated equally. But a major step was taken and a new kind of governmental balance was established.

---

[n] The works attributed to Lao Tzu probably originated with several wisdom figures.

Other examples include the long stretches of time in which parts of India were stable and peaceful and times when various Islamic countries had internal peace and stability, as well as an admirable tolerance for people of other faiths. Although history often pays less attention to these stable periods than to those in which there is turmoil, in every culture and geographic region of the Earth there have been long stretches of time when, instead of chaos and strife, moderation and balance reigned. All this brings to the fore a startling realization: There are so many forces that lead humans toward strife, such as competition over land, sex, power, money, status, and more. This being the case, there must also be strong forces at work that lead toward moderation, harmony, and balance, otherwise the long, peaceful periods in history would never have occurred; peace would not have been able to prevail over the forces of disruption.

Approaching this from a different angle, various researchers have shown that all biological and ecological systems have a strong, inherent force that tries to return the system to balance when it has been disrupted. Think of the body's continuing attempts to heal itself and how ecological systems devastated by fire or flood quickly begin to recover. Recent research has shown this force toward healing and balance to be true for the oceans, and even for the various systems that govern the Earth. The harm done to any system can be too great to overcome, but there is a strong force in all systems to heal, to restore balance, to recover harmony. Not only is it present in the human body, but in the human psyche as well: Many, many people have overcome deep, almost unimaginable emotional wounds and gone on to complete and full lives.

The Extremes

Skeptico: If there is a force toward balance and harmony, why do extreme positions attract so many followers?

Wisdom Seeker: Like me, many people want certainty, and extreme positions offer that. They say, in essence: "Our position is right and if you will join us, you can be certain you have the right answers too." In addition, it is much easier to generate passion (righteousness, fervor, anger) around extreme views. These emotions are appealing; they make us feel alive and confident and suggest that all the problems of the world are caused by someone else, rather than by our own actions and beliefs. The assumption, often unconscious, of those holding extreme views is: "If only other people would see things my way, the world would be so much better!" For all these reasons, a significant number of people are drawn to the extremes, and a lot of political and cultural debates ride on the passion and intensity of the extremists— while the voices of moderation are drowned out and pushed aside. The poet W. B. Yeats captured it well:

> The best lack all conviction, while the worst
> Are full of passionate intensity.[11]

Sometimes fueling the movement toward the extremes are youthful, rebellious energies. When young people begin to sense the shallowness and errors in the "certainties" they were given when growing up, they go to the extreme on the other end of the spectrum.

Skeptico: Are you saying that anyone who feels his convictions strongly is wrong?

Wisdom Seeker: Not at all, just those who feel certain their views are right and insist that all those who believe differently are wrong. Since there is no way to know for sure whether our ideas are right, we can only arrive at core beliefs through acts of faith, and to be adamant that others should accept our acts of faith—to believe that everyone should accept what we think is true—leads to a dangerous extreme.

Skeptico: What's wrong with having strong views if you believe you are right?

Wisdom Seeker: Those who think they have the one and only truth are stuck; they cannot grow and change. Life is about maturing and growing, but if you think you have found "The Truth" at sixteen, or twenty, or thirty, or fifty, it is hard to grow and mature. If you think you have "The Truth," you will defend your views against all other possibilities, even those that might help you become a more complete and healthy person. When encased in this kind of rigid position, the tendency is to become increasingly harsh with others, and even to become harsh with the doubts that arise within oneself. The consequence is that one becomes less rather than more conscious as one gets older. People organized in this way increasingly defend their beliefs whenever they encounter anyone with a different view. They cut themselves off from exchange with other human beings (except the small circle of those who agree with them). And, needless to say, having many different self-righteous groups in a crowded world (all of which think they have "The Truth") is a prescription for conflict and violence.

The Middle Way Versus the Extremes

Skeptico: What is the best way to respond to the assertions of those who think they have "The Truth"?

Wisdom Seeker: When confronted by those holding extreme views of any kind, there are three basic approaches: join them, oppose them, or try to find the middle way. The difficulty with trying to follow the middle way, though, is that extremists will try to frame the issues in such a way as to force you to choose—groups who oppose each other fiercely frequently have this in common. Thus, although most people have a natural inclination toward the Golden Mean, it is hard for them to maintain that position when confronted by the passion and certainty of those who are committed to extremist views. (If you are open to considering the views of others, or to the possibility that you might be wrong, you will have a hard time in arguments with extremists unless you have great confidence in yourself.)

Another valuable thing to remember when confronted by extremists is that there are many different extremist groups in the world, with each representing only a very small fraction of humanity (with some of the fiercest battles occurring between groups that outsiders consider similar to each other). That so many differing groups, each representing only a small minority of humanity, can be persuaded that they and only they are right, and that everyone else is wrong, is an amazing commentary on the human condition. Part of belonging to an extremist camp, however, is to be continually reinforced by those in your camp, with everyone saying you are *obviously right* when you repeat the party line. (When hearing those with an extreme view assert that most people agree with them, I think of how their arguments would sound to a villager in India, or China, or even to someone in a different cultural area of the United States.)

Skeptico: Sometimes I feel drawn to extreme views myself.

Wisdom Seeker: So do I, but I mostly try to overcome that feeling. When it starts to arise, I try to remember the value of humility, of accepting that I do not know everything; then I can listen more openly to those who have different views. This does not mean giving up my own beliefs, but simply listening sincerely to others and considering thoughtfully what they have to say. In doing this, I feel a movement toward wisdom, understanding—and toward living the Golden Mean.

As mentioned before, most of us have a tendency in this direction; few people are *all that certain* that they have *all the answers*. At the same time, many of us share some beliefs with one or more of the extremist camps. But in thoughtful moments, we also recognize that extreme views cannot capture the whole truth. Most of us sense that those with other points of view also see a piece of the larger pattern, and by interacting with them, we will learn things that we have not yet understood. Ultimately, by accepting: (a) that our current views are not complete and final; (b) that it is possible to grow and mature as life goes along, and (c) that wisdom can increase as we get older, we begin to follow the middle way (whether conscious of it or not). In a sense, simply recognizing the incompleteness of the answers to life's important questions given by all extremist camps is the beginning of a journey toward the Golden Mean.

Skeptico: For someone who wants certainty, you are making an awfully strong case against it.

Wisdom Seeker: Although I want certainty, I also have an instinct toward moderation and have come to believe that the only way to true wisdom is to sink my roots into the soil of the Golden Mean. The path to true wisdom—and perhaps even to a feeling of certainty—runs through the land of moderation. Without the reconciling effect of moderation we are stuck in the views of our early enculturations and indoctrinations and can never gain true wisdom.

Skeptico: I can see the dangers of extreme religious positions, but you seem to be saying that those who challenge religious views are a problem as well.

Wisdom Seeker: Yes, they provide a perfect example of the need for the Middle Way. To point out the problems in religions is valuable, but to jump to the extreme of rejecting all the good they have accomplished in human history is also a mistake. Those who make an act of faith that all religions are bad throw out the accumulated wisdom of human history concerning how we can live with each other in an enriching way, as well as how we can have fulfilling lives. When the accumulated wisdom of our history is thrown away, what is left to guide our lives? Only a meager set of personal opinions held by those who have made this grand rejection. What happens next is that each of the rejecters makes up his or her own set of rules to live by, insisting that everyone else should go along with that point of view. But the rejecters do not even agree with each other, and they have found no way of getting broad agreement from others except by force.

The stark dilemma: To say that the wisdom traditions that have guided human beings for millennia have never tapped into a current containing universal values and meanings is to deny that universal currents exist. But if there is no possibility of finding "something greater" than our ego selves around which to organize our lives, the resulting worldview is one in which shared values do not exist either. Then, raw power is the only arbiter of disputes and the possibility of finding inherent meaning in life slips away. Could it be that the rise in the number of people holding such views is one reason that depression and despair are endemic in the modern world?

> **Thought Experiment: Why Bother?**
>
> If you believe there is no meaning to life, if you think the whole shebang is, in Shakespeare's phrase, "sound and fury, signifying nothing," why would you bother to tell the truth, make any effort to improve yourself, help another person, or try to make the world a better place? Wouldn't the pull of the strictly personal goals of money, power, and pleasure catch you and hold you fast?

Skeptico: Would it be all that bad to try to fulfill my personal ambitions for money, power, and pleasure?

Wisdom Seeker: No, but the wisest people through the ages have insisted that if we act only to get those base desires met, we will not find happiness or fulfillment. Most people today (as has been true through human history) have a sense that some values actually do exist beyond self-interest and that there is some meaning to life that is larger than personal ego drives. Today, as has always been the case, most people believe that there is some organizing principle beyond the purely material to which we are called to find the right relationship, whether it be named the Great Spirit, the Tao, God, Buddha-nature, Consciousness, Ayin, the World of Forms, Brahman, the Great Way, Allah, or That which gives direction to evolution.

Skeptico: But isn't the existence of "something greater" at odds with science?

Wisdom Seeker: Skeptico, think about our earlier conversations. Today's science requires a belief in "something greater," requires the belief that the world has an underlying order and that there are discoverable laws governing that order. Both these beliefs are based on the view that there is an underlying pattern and harmony governing the material world. Otherwise, there would be no laws or principles for science to discover and share.

The underlying order has always been a mystery to us, and there are many different ways to try to understand it. But we have had a longing for that understanding since humanity first came to be. This longing is one of the primary reasons the wisdom traditions developed: Humans recognized early on that many choices are required for living, and if we could understand the larger pattern we could make better choices. Consequently, the wisdom traditions developed guidance for the best ways to relate to the larger pattern and for how to bring ourselves into harmony with it.

As for science, one of the reasons it was born was to study the details of the pattern in the material world: If we could understand it, we would be able to make better decisions about how to live in this material world. From its very beginnings, then, science has accepted that there is something beyond the material world, and nothing in science has ever questioned that a pattern exists. In fact, I defy you to find one scientific theory that questions the existence of "something greater."

Of course, science has rightly questioned specific theories about the material world offered by Established Religions, but that is a totally different thing from questioning the existence of a larger pattern. There are certainly those who make an act of faith that nothing beyond the material realm exists, and some of them assert that their views are scientific, but there are no scientific theories that say such a thing. And those who created modern science have almost always shown a personal interest in finding a connection to that "something greater" for themselves.

To pursue such a path in the modern world, however, it is necessary to reject extremism of all kinds and to remember the lessons of history concerning the value of the Middle Way, the Golden Mean. This requires humility and open-mindedness, as opposed to the certainty that one has all the answers in hand. Fending off the allure of extreme views is not easy, but the rewards, suggested by some of the wisest beings who have ever lived, are great.

CHAPTER 15

Summing Up

"I have always thought that feeling empty and losing touch with the meaning of life are in essence only a challenge to seek new things to fill one's life, a new meaning for one's existence. Isn't it the moment of most profound doubt that gives birth to new certainties? Perhaps hopelessness is the very soil that nourishes human hope; perhaps one could never find sense in life without first experiencing its absurdity."[1] — Vaclav Havel

Moving Forward

Finding the path to a fulfilled life is not easy. It requires making hard decisions about what is important and how to live, often with limited information. It requires many acts of faith and involves inevitable mistakes. After the mistakes, moving forward requires finding ways to grow and learn from the mistakes instead of being defeated or overcome by them. All this demands a difficult honesty with oneself in confronting fears, anxieties, expectations, and desires; it requires the courage to face one's own inadequacies and shortcomings as well as those of one's community.

The goal of each human life is to live into the fullest potential that life has to offer. To accomplish this aim, the world's wisdom traditions offer guidance, but selecting among them is a daunting task, for there are errors embedded in every tradition. Not only that, but there are—parading as wisdom in the bazaar of ideas—many simplistic answers on offer. And there are many charlatans trying to make a buck from our longings. In traversing this minefield, it is crucial to be cautious but also crucial to push ahead with determination and courage, to avoid as many pitfalls as possible without becoming fixated on the dangers. As in baseball, those who concentrate too hard on *not* striking out often strike out. The trick is to learn to wait for the right pitch (the right action to take), without waiting too long. It is essential to take a swing at a pitch every now and then; even if you miss, you will learn something. There are many stories of those who became involved with a flawed system or flawed teacher but ended up making progress on their journeys. The trick is to commit to a path while staying attuned to the inner voice that recognizes when something is wrong or when it is time for a course correction.

While it is relatively easy to stay too long or be too quick to change, getting a feel for when it is right to change course is one of the most difficult skills to learn. It doesn't work to frequently change careers, relationships, where you live, or the wisdom tradition on which you are focused. And it doesn't work just to pick the things you like from various traditions, for each system has an integrity that must be respected: The technologies of the sacred cannot be adapted to suit the whims of an unskilled seeker. The danger of letting whims or ego desires drive the journey is proclaimed by all the traditions, along with the insistence that such a path does not bring fulfillment but frustration and thwarted longings. All the traditions advise that we must *not* choose values and meanings that we "like the best," or even those that make us "feel good" in the moment.

Rather, their collective wisdom is that we must mold ourselves to something larger than ourselves. For a fulfilling life, to paraphrase William James, we must bring ourselves into harmony with the unseen order of things.[2] Or as Henry Miller put it: "The world is not to be put in order; the world is in order. It is for us to put ourselves in unison with this order."[3] To accomplish this, commitment, diligence, and determination are necessary; continuing progress requires molding ourselves to the path we have chosen rather than changing paths to suit our whims and desires. This is the only way to break free from the small self and to move into harmony with the larger pattern.

Yet, paradoxically, even though the traditions can help, each of us must ultimately find our own way through the labyrinth. We can do this by sticking with the system of our youth, joining another system, or putting together a path of our own. Whichever route we take, though, we must develop a conscious relationship to it rather than following it blindly—this is how we make it our own. And at some point, there will come a moment when further movement will require an individual, creative response to the unique dilemma our specific life presents.

Riding the Waves

Skeptico: I haven't fully given up my skepticism; I still have an urge to live without making any acts of faith.

Wisdom Seeker: I can see that you haven't fully grasped that a skeptical position is an act faith, just like any other place you might stand. Skepticism has great value in sorting through the various answers available about how to live, but it does not remove the necessity for acts of faith. As Josh Billings said, without faith you couldn't even "eat hash with any safety."[4] Without faith you would have to grow and prepare all your own food, avoid all methods of transportation, give up all close relationships, make no decisions about what is important, and relinquish all values.

Skeptico: Why is that?

Wisdom Seeker: Because anyone you trust might betray that trust, every transportation system has accidents, food is occasionally poisoned, and there are potential problems with every meaning and value system you might adopt. In the face of all this uncertainty, some people become paranoid, but paranoia is itself an act of faith—usually unconscious: A paranoid person sees the world in a way that is not proven but only imagined. Even extreme measures of avoidance do not overcome the necessity for acts of faith; rather, avoidance is motivated by negative acts of faith, such as assuming that no one is trustworthy or that the meanings and values given by the wisdom traditions are not needed for guidance.

Imagine someone from a rain forest tribe who had never before come into contact with the world you live in. If you were introducing that person to your world, wouldn't you have to reassure him constantly that things you took for granted were safe? Your enculturation embedded many assumptions in your psyche, and they have become the unconscious acts of faith within which you live. Or imagine finding yourself joining a rain forest tribe and trying to fit in. Wouldn't you have to be continually instructed about the actions that were safe and those that had to be avoided? You would have to place a good deal of faith in the people who were guiding you, or you would be filled with anxiety a lot of the time.

Thought Experiment: What Are Your Acts of Faith?

You are, at this very moment, living within several beliefs concerning what is important in your life. You might hold them consciously, or they might be unconscious to you, but they are determining where you are placing your time and attention. Take a moment and see if you can formulate your main beliefs, your main acts of faith.

As a second step, consider if you would like to shift or change any of your beliefs or acts of faith in any way.

Ultimately, there is no way to avoid acts of faith. You can change the ones you were given in youth, and you can adapt and change the ones you are living within now, but you must have a framework within which to live. In this unavoidable situation, there is one thing you have a great deal of power to affect, however: You can make your acts of faith more conscious. By doing so, and by aligning your beliefs with the goals, values, and meanings that seem most important, you will gain wisdom; perhaps you will even find your way to a full and complete experience of the possibilities this life has to offer.

The more conscious your acts of faith become, the less you are caught by them and the easier it is to grow and change. If you can take them seriously but hold them lightly, a space is opened for skepticism to play its needed role, as well as for reason and intuition to make their valuable contributions to your life. (Skepticism to help in discovering errors, reason in sorting through possibilities, and intuition in providing insights at significant moments.) In fact, if you pay careful attention to your intuitions, you will sometimes hear an internal whisper (or perhaps a shout) saying, "This is an unusual time: Pay Attention!"

Learning to pay attention to this inner voice is crucial in all areas of life, not just in deciding on important goals and values. In the realm of health and safety, there are countless reports of people who avoided accidents or other problems (or seized opportunities) because they "had a sense" that something important was happening or was about to happen.[5] And several studies of successful business persons have shown that many business leaders operate from intuition. Professor John Mihalasky and Douglas Dean conducted a ten-year research project at Newark College of Engineering that documented in detail how business leaders who relied heavily on intuition tended to be the most successful.[6]

In sum, whatever you are doing in life, as you make your decisions and attempt to move toward fulfillment, do not forget that you are riding on the waves of your assumptions, your acts of faith.

Top Ten Reasons There Is No Conflict

Skeptico: You believe there is no inherent conflict between science and religion or science and spirituality. Can you boil down the main reasons for me?

Wisdom Seeker: Here are my top ten:

1. The vast majority of those who created and carried forward the scientific project in every culture throughout history have been people

who were involved in the religious and spiritual issues of their time and place. A number broke from the orthodoxies of their day, but almost none abandoned religion or spirituality in general. Instead, the ones who were rebels explored alternative approaches to religion and spirituality for themselves. The number of scientists throughout history who were not interested in these questions is a tiny fraction.

2. Almost all the mathematicians, philosophers, and scientists (natural philosophers) who created the scientific revolution in the sixteenth and seventeenth centuries, the names we have heard since childhood—Descartes, Leibnitz, Spinoza, Newton, Galileo, Copernicus, Kepler, Francis Bacon, and Blasé Pascal—all had a deep interest in religious and spiritual issues.

3. The great thinkers who created modern physics (such as Albert Einstein, Niels Bohr, Max Planck, Erwin Schrödinger, Werner Heisenberg, Wolfgang Pauli, and Arthur Eddington) explored spiritual questions and adopted a spiritual perspective of one form or another. None saw a conflict between science and their spiritual interests.

4. Through much of history, religious organizations have been key supporters of the scientific endeavor. Further, today's science was given birth within the core assumptions of western religious thought, and it was nurtured and supported by the educational systems of Medieval Europe, institutions created and maintained by religious establishments.

5. Many key figures in the advancement of science were monks or priests, including Copernicus, Roger Bacon, Gregor Mendel (who laid the mathematical foundation for genetics), Georges Lemaître (who first proposed the Big Bang theory of the origin of the Universe), and Pierre Gassendi (who helped to formulate what we now think of as the scientific outlook). Many others, although not taking official vows, were deeply religious, such as Louis Pasteur, Michael Faraday (whose work on electricity and magnetism helped to create the modern world), Robert Boyle (whose name is

immortalized in "Boyle's Law" and who wrote important works in chemistry), James Clerk Maxwell (his equations for electromagnetism are still considered one of the greatest achievements in physics), and William Thomson Kelvin (who helped lay the foundation for modern physics).

6. Many scientists today have a spiritual interest, and a significant number belong to one of the many active religious traditions. Crucially, through history the scientific works of those with spiritual interests have been as important and valuable as those with none. Further, by looking at their scientific work, you cannot tell the two groups apart. Where, then, is the conflict?

7. Science is a method for understanding how the material world works. As such, it has no way to deal with values, with deciding what is meaningful, with providing guidance on how to live, or helping us know what to live for. Nor can science help us determine what we will experience as beautiful or inspiring, and it certainly cannot help us decide who we will love or how to become a loving person. All these things, however, are central to human life; religions have, through the centuries, helped us find ways to approach these crucial issues. Of course, religious and spiritual thought is not very helpful in learning how to manipulate the material world, which is also critical to human existence, and at which science excels. It seems clear, therefore, that these two great endeavors are complementary pillars of human life.

8. There is no such thing as a single scientific view on anything. Scientists have many different views and what science knows is constantly changing. There are scientists on every side of every major issue in the world today. Equally, there is no single religious view on any issue; religious people are found on every side of every issue. No conflict breaks down into a battle between scientists and those with a religious or spiritual perspective. Just one example: Among those who perpetuate the "battle" myth, it is common to assert that Christians reject scientific claims if they seem to conflict with the Christian Bible. This is true for some Christian denominations, but

not for most. In fact, the mainstream view of the largest Christian denomination, the Roman Catholic Church, is: When something is clearly demonstrated to be true by science, Biblical interpretation must be brought into alignment with that knowledge.[7] This has been the case for almost two thousand years, from Augustine to Aquinas, from powerful Cardinals during Galileo's time right down to the late Pope John Paul II.

9. When considering any conflict, it is valuable to understand who seems to gain by perpetuating the idea of a battle. Today, the battle idea is perpetuated by two competing faith systems, religious fundamentalists and materialists, both of whom are trying to rally their troops and gain adherents through this strategy.

10. No culture in history has provided fulfilling lives for its people by assuming that science and the spiritual dimension are in conflict. Since human history began, the wisdom traditions (the spiritual and religious systems of human thought and belief) have been the doorway to meaning, purpose, and shared values. They have provided paths to inner peace, compassion, and joy. All have proclaimed the supreme importance of love and have offered ways to cultivate it. None of the traditions have done these things perfectly, but they have tried. At the same time, science, by its very definition, is not equipped to accomplish any of these objectives, so the wisest path is to assume that science, religion, and the spiritual dimension are each important and complimentary aspects of a fulfilled human life. Each of us gets to make a choice about what we will believe. To choose to believe that science is in conflict with the wisdom traditions—when there are no models for how this view has ever led to a functional society or to healthy lives—does not seem a wise act of faith.

On the other hand, adopting the view that there is no conflict doesn't mean ignoring the failures or unhealthy actions of the religious traditions. On the contrary, to acknowledge the importance of religions will serve as an incentive to correct their abuses and provide strong motivation to restore faltering traditions to greater health. Embracing the value of religions will also prompt new and exciting ways of thinking about the higher dimensions of reality, ways that will perhaps be more informed by and compatible with modern science. This is exactly what a number of scientists and mathematicians have been doing in recent decades, such as Alfred North Whitehead, David Bohm, Gerhard Etrl (who won the Nobel Prize for Chemistry in 2007), William D. Phillips (who won the Nobel Prize in Physics in 1997), Richard Smalley (Nobel Laureate in Chemistry), Eugene Wigner (recipient of the 1963 Nobel Prize in Physics), Bernard d'Espagnat, Roger W. Sperry, William Tiller, Pierre Teilhard de Chardin, Elisabet Sahtouris, Marilyn Schlitz, Bernard Haisch, Stan Grof, Wilder Penfield, Ervin Laszlo, and many others. The creative and inspiring efforts of these folks have made it clear that the relationship between the religious, spiritual, and scientific is a rich and fruitful territory for exploration.

Needless to say, the ideas of all these great minds go in many different directions, but all have in common the view that we should not limit ourselves to the assumptions of materialism, or physicalism, or naturalism—the view that all that exists is material stuff and/or purposeless energy.

The ideas of each of those mentioned above would be worth exploring, but I will mention only two here. First, Wilder Penfield, one of the great brain researchers of the 20th century, concluded that the ability to make judgments and to exercise one's will are not in the brain; rather, these higher functions are somehow "transcendent" to the brain and not reducible to physiology. In other words, the mind is not limited to the brain. Although Penfield was not a religious person, he concluded after a lifetime of investigation of the human mental process that the mind might even survive the death of the brain. How this could be was not clear to him, but his best sense was that the mind might be able to establish an energetic connection to something larger than itself that lasted beyond the brain's death.

Similar in some ways is the thought of William Tiller, professor emeritus of Materials Science and Engineering at Stanford University.

In his *Psychoenergetic Science: A Second Copernican-Scale Revolution*, he sees each human as having three distinct levels. The first level, the personal self, is similar to the materialist view, but he concludes that there is definitely more to a human being, much more. Using mathematical formulas, he presents a scientific/mathematical explanation for the existence of the two higher levels (which have a lot in common with the views of various spiritual traditions).

I can't speak to the neurobiology of Penfield's ideas or the mathematics of Tiller's model, but I can say with certainty that a large number of scientists through the centuries, continuing right down to the present day, have found no conflict between the existence of higher levels of being and science. Many, in fact, have sought to experience these levels for themselves, have even considered them to be the most important aspects of human life. My favorite example comes from Albert Einstein in a quote used earlier but worth emphasizing again:

> Humanity has every reason to place the proclaimers of high moral standards and values above the discoverers of objective truth. What humanity owes to personalities like Buddha, Moses, and Jesus stands for me higher than all the achievements of the inquiring and constructive mind.

In other words, the greatest scientist of the modern world is saying that spiritual leaders have had a greater importance in human history than all of science's discoveries of "objective" knowledge. (One does not have to fully accept Einstein's conclusion in order to realize that doing science at the highest level in no way conflicts with religion.)

The Message from Artists

Circling back to the role of art in the human journey, it is worthwhile to note again that art has been a central part of every religious tradition and most forms of artistic expression arose as religious practices. Art and spirituality have been deeply entwined in every human culture we know, and the most common motivation for artistic expression through history has been for spiritual purposes. Further, religion and spirituality have been important in the lives of many great artists, and this is still the case in modern times. For instance, many of the pioneers of modern art had significant spiritual interests, including Kandinsky, Mondrian, Arp, Duchamps, Malevich, Newman, Pollack, Miro, and Rothko.[8] The same is true for many of the great writers and poets of the nineteenth and twentieth centuries, including Leo Tolstoy, Fyodor Dostoyevsky, Hermann Hesse, Victor Hugo, T. S. Eliot, W.B. Yeats, Rainer Maria Rilke, J. R. R. Tolkien, Emily Dickinson, Doris Lessing, Walker Percy, e. e. cummings, Jack Kerouac, Maya Angelou, C. S. Lewis, Jane Austen, Aldous Huxley, Elie Wiesel, Helen Keller, Gerard Manley Hopkins, Graham Greene, Somerset Maugham, J.K. Rowling, Flannery O'Connor, Dorothy Sayers, Robert Pirsig, and many more. As with scientists, the nature of the spiritual interests of these folks ranged all over the place, but all had an interest in exploring the mysterious realm that I have called "something greater."

Faith in Two Directions

To live fully requires faith in two directions: in yourself and in the field in which you have chosen to organize your thoughts and perceptions. To make a contribution in any field requires this dual faith—in yourself and in the field in which you have chosen to participate. For instance, to engage in science requires faith that the information that has been passed down is relatively sound, that most practitioners in the past have tried to be honest, and that science is doing something worthwhile. In the same way, acts of faith are necessary if one is to be an artist—faith that art is a worthwhile endeavor and faith in the value of one's own visions and productions. As Julia Cameron, bestselling author on the creative process, captured it:

As artists, we must cultivate faith. We must learn to see beyond appearances. We must trust that there is something larger and more benevolent than the apparent odds stacked against us. For the sake of sheer survival, we artists must learn to have deep and abiding belief in our own work and its worthiness, despite the world's apparent acceptance or rejection.[9]

In other words, an artist must be able to sustain the belief that he or she is doing worthwhile work even if the world provides little or no reinforcement for that belief. Vincent van Gogh is a good example of this kind of faith, for he believed in the worthiness of his work despite the world's continual rejection. Many pioneering scientists have had to persist in the same way, suffering the world's rejection for years. Most of us are not in a situation as extreme as that of Van Gogh or Copernicus, but a certain amount of faith is essential for any undertaking in life, whether it be in art, science, a religious tradition, or following an individual spiritual path. This faith can be unconscious faith—simply assuming one's beliefs about oneself and the world are true. Or it can be a more conscious faith, developed over time through significant effort.

Unconscious faith can lead to success, but its problem is that it can as easily lead to harm, for the individual as well as the community. The reason: If a person blindly follows the unconscious beliefs into which he has been encultured, he might end up as a terrorist, a hit man in a Mafia family, a torturer in a Nazi prison camp, or a rapist of children. If you do not get outside the system you were taught, there is no way you can evaluate whether its views are healthy or destructive of your well-being and that of others. Thus, in order to make it likely that your efforts will be valuable in the larger scheme of things, the key is to move toward conscious faith. Those who have become conscious of who they are and what they are about are more likely to do things that are healthy and harmonious. Some dramatic examples of conscious faith are Jesus, the Buddha, Mother Teresa, Abraham Lincoln, Mahatma Gandhi, Rosa Parks, Nelson Mandela, Martin Luther King, and Florence Nightingale.

Skeptico: Did they have faith that they would succeed?

Wisdom Seeker: No. Perhaps a few did, but many of them did not have faith that they would succeed in the short run. Nor did they view success according to normal standards. They all, however, had faith that what they were doing was worth doing, that the goal toward which they were aiming was worthwhile, and that taking the next step they could envision was worth taking.

What About My Doubts?

Skeptico: I have a lot of doubts. What do I do about them?

Wisdom Seeker: Almost all the great exemplars of history had doubts. Those people who *do not* have doubts but keep on taking actions that affect others are scary, for they are most likely deluded. To develop conscious faith is to choose to act toward what seems right and good even though you have doubts; it is to pursue your best sense of direction in spite of doubts. By making the effort to become conscious, you minimize the possible harm you will do and improve your chances of living into the highest possibilities your life has to offer. This is active faith—to consciously choose the direction in which you will act, and then to act decisively in that direction.

> ### Thought Experiment: On What Basis Will You Organize Your Life?
>
> In the broadest sense, there are four alternatives for organizing your life:
>
> 1. Follow the conditioning you were given in your early years and accept that system's values and meanings.
> 2. Choose another system and follow its guidance.
> 3. Organize around materialism and its end result, nihilism, choosing to believe there is no meaning to life and no path to a higher fulfillment that can be found.
> 4. Work to become conscious, and from whatever consciousness you can achieve, choose what seems best and right and good.
>
> Which of these four options will you choose?

No matter which you choose (or if you alternate between them), you will inevitably make acts of faith. The Bhagavad-Gita, the most widely read Indian spiritual text, declares: "A man consists of the faith that is in him. Whatever his faith is, he is."[10]—suggesting that faith determines our very identity. It does so because every significant action we take involves an act of faith, as does every refusal to act when a possibility arises. Whatever we choose to do—follow a wisdom tradition; pursue a scientific career; take up an artistic endeavor; adopt skepticism, fundamentalism, or materialism as an organizing position—whatever we do requires a conscious or unconscious act of faith before engagement can begin. Furthermore, at each step along the way we must reaffirm or change our acts of faith; we must constantly decide whether to continue on, change course, or turn back. Through these decisions, we gradually create who we are becoming.

Skeptico: But aren't there dangers in making acts of faith?

Wisdom Seeker: Absolutely. One great danger, about which we have been warned over and over by the wisest sages, is to believe that we have "The Truth" before having sufficient wisdom to be able to recognize what truth is. Thinking you know what is true prematurely leads to arrogance, conflict with others, and blindness to the opportunity of finding greater wisdom as you mature. Perhaps this is why Buddhists advise the practice of "Don't Know Mind" and why an influential but anonymous Christian mystic said that the only way to understand God is as a "Cloud of Unknowing." In the modern era, this message has been reinforced repeatedly by quantum mechanics, which keeps pointing out how little we really know about even the material world. Rumi said that thinking you know the truth too early "brings a curse" (as when a rooster crows long before dawn and has to be silenced); however, if you have become fully conscious, seeing the deepest truth about yourself and life brings a great blessing.

Skeptico: So how do I proceed?

Wisdom Seeker: Let go of thinking you know the answers and continually seek a deeper knowing. By doing this (and applying courage, discipline, and hard work) the wisdom traditions say a door will be opened, a door into a complete and fulfilling life. Be warned, however: You will eventually come to a place where the only way through involves surrender; a release of the demands of the small self in favor of organizing around something greater than your personal desires. As Victor Frankl put it, a person then

> ... knows that he is actualizing himself precisely to the extent to which he is forgetting himself, and he is forgetting himself by giving himself, be it through serving a cause higher than himself, or loving a person other than himself. Truly, self-transcendence is the essence of human existence.[11]

Then, finally, according to those who have made this journey before, you will come to a point where you "Know," and "Know You Know." Descriptions of this experience include words like freedom, union, bliss, being merged with the Divine, and certainty of salvation. At this point, you know with a crystal clear certainty that what you are experiencing is real and true.

Skeptico: What is the difference between "knowing you know" and thinking you have "The Truth?"

Wisdom Seeker: Very good question Skeptico! My sense is that those who think they have "The Truth" tend to be judgmental, critical of other points of view, and have a need to persuade others that they are right (hoping deep down that they will feel more secure). On the other hand, those who are centered in a place of deep knowing tend to be open to what others have to say, have a quiet confidence that involves no need to convince others, and are characterized by being kind and considerate. They will share what they know, but only with those who ask and are interested.

The final irony is that to reach this place of freedom, the trail usually runs through the land of limitation: Only by committing ourselves to a specific path (which is a limitation, a temporary imprisonment) will we be able to escape from the bondage of our egos. As Edmund Burke captured it: "It is ordained in the eternal constitution of things that men of intemperate minds cannot be free. Their passions forge their fetters."[12] Or as D.H. Lawrence put it, "Men are not free when they are doing just what they like. ... [they] are only free when they are doing what the deepest self likes. And there is getting down to the deepest self! It takes some diving."[13] In the end, our true self finds freedom by limiting the ego's claims of supremacy. This might sound daunting, but in spite of great difficulties a goodly number who have gone before us have found their way through to a fulfilled life. You can too.

What to Do Before You Are Certain

Skeptico: How can I be certain of what you are saying?
Wisdom Seeker: Everyone wants certainty, but few reach it, so you must learn to live and act in its absence. Until certainty comes (if it ever does), work to become conscious about the acts of faith you are making; proceed with confidence in the direction you are choosing (even though you know you might be mistaken); then be willing to change course as you learn and grow.

No matter whether you start with certainty or uncertainty, great difficulties will arise. A major difficulty for those who were not given fixed and firm beliefs when young is finding a healthy place to live and learn that can be shared with a community of others. The opposite difficulty arises for those enculturated into rigid systems: They must eventually break out of their indoctrinations and explore the mystery of existence for themselves—if they are to become complete and whole.

An image: Learn to ride the waves of your assumptions, your acts of faith, like a champion surfer who waits with poised anticipation until a good wave comes along. When it does, give that promising ride your complete attention, adapting subtly and swiftly to the moving force beneath you. Gradually, as you become more conscious of what you are doing, you will feel how the wave is actually but the tip of a vast ocean, and you will begin to sense how it is possible to attune with the ocean itself. Continuing the metaphor, it is likely that all the world's wisdom traditions are surface manifestations of one deep Source, and that life's supreme task is to learn to move in harmony with That. Abraham Maslow stated succinctly why it is necessary to align with the "Ocean" or "Source" in which we swim:

> Without the transcendent and the transpersonal we get sick, violent, and nihilistic, or else hopeless and apathetic. We need something "bigger than we are" to be awed by and to commit ourselves to. [14]

Isn't this the reason we humans always seem to be reaching for something we do not understand? The American painter Albert P. Ryder, with a somewhat whimsical image, captures where those of us on this journey spend a certain amount of time:

> Have you ever seen an inchworm crawl up a leaf or a twig, and then, clinging to the very end, revolve in the air, feeling for something, to reach something? That's like me. I am trying to find something out there beyond the place on which I have footing. [15]

Poised there, on the end of our branch, each of us must make the best decisions we can as we reach toward a relationship with the unfathomable mystery in which we exist. At the same time, we must try to maintain a healthy relationship with the branch on which we stand—the people and purposes of our current human lives.

Skeptico: Why can't I make up my own values and meanings? That is more my style.

Wisdom Seeker: There are two major problems with making up your own values and meanings. First, anything your thinking mind makes up is unlikely to touch the deepest parts of yourself and thus will not move you in a full and profound way. You cannot think your way to the deepest level; you can't decide by thinking whom you will love or the words and images that will stir your emotions; you cannot decide at the ego level the values and meanings to which your whole being will give assent. For those things, you must open to a deep intuition. As Dag Hammarskjöld, the second Secretary-General of the United Nations, said of his experience of his opening:

> I don't know Who—or what—put the question. I don't know when it was put. I don't even remember answering. But at some moment I did answer Yes to Someone—or Something—and from that hour I was certain that existence is meaningful and that, therefore, my life, in self-surrender, had a goal.[16]

The second reason it doesn't work to make up your own meanings and values is that if you do, you will not be able to participate with others in what you hold dear. If everyone simply makes up their own meanings and values, the crucial need for community is thwarted and a shared journey with others is impossible. At various points along the way, we each need encouragement and support, but how can we support each other if there is no common ground between us? The fact is, however, that thousands of different societies have found a shared ground of values and meanings on which large numbers of people have lived together in harmony and understanding for long stretches of time. The specific ways in which different peoples have understood this shared ground have varied, but the very fact *that* almost all societal groups have believed in its existence and have referred to it in organizing their lives together suggests that there is something transcendent to the individual that is available to provide guidance for human life.

The fact that we cannot make up our own values and meanings, however, does not preclude freedom of choice. You, Skeptico, have the freedom to choose the way you will understand the sea in which you swim. You have the freedom to choose how you will pursue a relationship to the pattern in which you exist.

Further, if you learn to ride the waves of the ocean of existence with skill and grace, you might eventually come to a point where you will be able to offer worthwhile suggestions to others on how to surf the waves of existence. Perhaps, through a deep engagement with art, science, religion, or spirituality—or some combination of all four— you will be able to correct some of the mistakes that have crept into the wisdom traditions through the centuries. You might even find yourself contributing to the accumulated wisdom of humanity by leaving behind an insight or understanding that is of significant service to those who come after you on this journey of life. Who knows, Skeptico? Maybe you will be one of those with the capacity to spark creative innovations that help many others on their way toward meaningful and fulfilling lives.

And as for you, Dear Reader,

May you experience the Harmony that connects art, science, religion, and spirituality.

May your acts of faith be guided by Wisdom.

May Truth lead you to a fulfilled and meaningful life.

And may you find, hidden in the mystery,

the supreme treasures of Love, Beauty, Peace, and Joy.

ENDNOTES AND REFERENCES

When two or three citations from a source occur in close proximity to one another in this book, that source will only be listed once—with the last reference in the sequence.

Introduction
[1] Ralph Waldo Emerson, "Divinity School Address," Divinity College, Cambridge, United Kingdom, July 15, 1838.
[2] Albert Einstein, *Out of My Later Years* (Totowa, New Jersey: Littlefield, Adams and Company, 1967), 16. (First published in 1937 in an essay entitled "Moral Decay.")

Chapter 1: The Way of Art
[1] William Blake, David V. Erdman, Harold Bloom, and William Golding, *The Complete Poetry and Prose of William Blake* (New York: Anchor Books/ Random House, Inc., 1988), 273.
[2] William Blake, *The Complete Poetry and Prose of William Blake* (Berkeley, California: University of California Press, 2008), 146.
[3] Maurice Tuchman, *The Spiritual in Art: Abstract Painting, 1890-1985* (New York: Abbeville Press, 1999).
[4] Dawn Perlmutter and Debra Koppman, *Essays on Reclaiming the Spiritual in Art: Contemporary Cross-Cultural Perspectives* (New York: State University of New York Press, 2010).
[5] Sarah O'brien Twohig, *The Spiritual in Twentieth Century Art Lecture Series* (London, United Kingdom: Tate Britain, 1999).
[6] Mark Roskill, ed., *The Letters Of Vincent van Gogh* (Cambridge, United Kingdom: Cambridge University Press/Touchstone, 2008).
[7] Vincent van Gogh, "Letter to Wilhelmina van Gogh written in Summer/ Fall 1887," trans. and ed. Robert Harrison, Paris, France, Summer/Fall 1887, no. W01.
[8] Willis Harman and Howard Rheingold, *Higher Creativity: Liberating the Unconscious for Breakthrough Insights* (New York: Tarcher/Penguin, 1984), 47.
[9] P. E. Vernon, *Creativity: Selected Readings* (New York: Penguin Books, 1970). Quoted by Mozart to publisher Friedrich Rochlitz, *Allgemeine Musikalische Zeitung*, vol. 17 (New York: Konrad, 1815), 561–566. Some researchers consider the letter inauthentic, but Mozart's first biographer, in collaboration

with Mozart's wife, gave an account of how Mozart composed that has a similar flavor. See Franz Niemtschek, Leben des K. K. Kapellmeisters Wolfgang Gottlieb Mozart, nach Originalquellen beschrieben (Prague, In Der Herrlischen Buchhandlung, 1798), 54–55.

[10] Harman and Rheingold, *Higher Creativity: Liberating the Unconscious for Breakthrough Insights*, 24.

[11] Paul Klee, *The Diaries of Paul Klee 1898-1918* (Berkeley, California: University of California Press, 1964), no. 1104, Jan/Feb. 1918.

[12] Paul Klee, *On Modern Art* (London, United Kingdom: Faber & Faber, 1966).

[13] Johann Wolfgang von Goethe, quoted in Jay Alfred, *Brains and Realities* (Victoria, British Columbia, Canada: Trafford Publishing, 2006), 22.

[14] Harman and Rheingold, *Higher Creativity: Liberating the Unconscious for Breakthrough Insights*, 31-32.

[15] Robert Gittings, *John Keats* (London, United Kingdom: Heinemann, 1968), 297.

[16] John Keats, *The Keats Circle*, vol. I, ed. Hyder Rollins (Boston, Massachusetts: Harvard University Press, 1965), 128-129.

[17] Peter Ilyich Tchaikovsky, *The Life & Letters of Peter Ilyich Tchaikovsky* (New York: Haskell House Publishers, 1905), 274.

[18] Harman and Rheingold, *Higher Creativity: Liberating the Unconscious for Breakthrough Insights*, 23.

[19] Harman and Rheingold, *Higher Creativity: Liberating the Unconscious for Breakthrough Insights*, 46.

[20] Harman and Rheingold, *Higher Creativity: Liberating the Unconscious for Breakthrough Insights*, 46.

[21] Rudyard Kipling, *Rudyard Kipling: Something of Myself and Other Autobiographical Writings* (Cambridge, United Kingdom: Cambridge University Press, 1991), 123.

[22] Harman and Rheingold, *Higher Creativity: Liberating the Unconscious for Breakthrough Insights*, 38.

[23] Samuel Taylor Coleridge, *The Collected Works of Samuel Taylor Coleridge* (Princeton, New Jersey: Princeton University Press, 2001), 511.

[24] Arthur Abell, *Talks with the Great Composers* (Garmisch-Partenkirchen, Germany: G. E. Schroeder-Verlag, 1964), 19-21.

[25] Percy Bysshe Shelley, *A Defence of Poetry and Other Essays* (Whitefish, Montana: Kessinger Publishing, 2010), 43.

[26] Christine Cox, "From Mozart to Mysticism, Art as a Spiritual Path," *Quest Magazine*, Spring 1992, 67.

[27] Vincent van Gogh, "Letter to Wilhelmina van Gogh," trans. Mrs. Johanna van Gogh-Bonger, ed. Robert Harrison, Arles, France, August 1888, no. W08.

[28] Vincent van Gogh, "Letter to Wilhelmina van Gogh," trans. and ed. Robert Harrison, Summer/Fall 1887, no. W01.

[29] Naomi Margolis Maurer, *The Pursuit of Spiritual Wisdom: The Thought and Art of Vincent Van Gogh and Paul Gauguin* (Cranbury, New Jersey: Associated University Presses, 1998), 100.

Chapter 2: The Message in Art

[1] Joseph Campbell, *The Inner Reaches of Outer Space: Metaphor as Myth and as Religion* (New York: Alfred Van Der Mark Editions, 1986), 131-132.

[2] Johann Wolfgang von Goethe, *Sprüche in Prosa,* quoted in Sir Edmund William Gosse, *Books on the Table* (New York: C. Scribner's Sons, 1921), 324.

[3] Thomas Carlyle, *The Collected Works of Thomas Carlyle,* vol. 6 (London, United Kingdom: Chapman and Hall, 1871), Sartor Resartus III, 137.

[4] Sigmund Freud, from a caption on a wall of the Freud Museum in Vienna widely attributed to him.

[5] Frithjof Schuon, *Splendor of the Times,* trans. James S. Cutsinger (Albany, New York: State University of New York Press, 2013), 67.

[6] Plato, *The Republic,* trans. H. D. P. Lee (London, United Kingdom: Penguin Group, 2007), 403.

[7] Helen Vendler, *The Odes of John Keats* (Cambridge, Massachusetts: Harvard University Press, 1983), 134.

[8] Christine Cox, "From Mozart to Mysticism, Art as a Spiritual Path," *Quest Magazine,* Spring 1992, 66.

[9] Paul Brunton, quoted in Christine Cox, "From Mozart to Mysticism, Art as a Spiritual Path," *Quest Magazine,* Spring 1992, 68.

[10] *Notebooks & Ideas of Paul Brunton* available from the Paul Brunton Philosophic Foundation, 4936 NYS, Route 414, Burdett, New York, 14818.

[11] Joseph Campbell, *The Inner Reaches of Outer Space: Metaphor as Myth and as Religion,* 122.

[12] Joseph Campbell, *The Inner Reaches of Outer Space: Metaphor as Myth and as Religion,* 126.

[13] William Blake and Sir Geoffrey Keynes, *The Marriage of Heaven and Hell* (Santa Cruz, California: Trianon Press, 1960), 197.

[14] William Shakespeare, *Shakespeare's Work, Midsummer Night's Dream,* vol. XIII (New York: Harper and Brothers, 1884).

[15] Friedrich Wilhelm Nietzsche, *The Will to Power,* par. 853, quoted in Alan Schrift, *Nietzsche and the Question of Interpretation* (London, United Kingdom: Routledge Publishing, 2014), 50.

[16] Joseph Campbell, *The Inner Reaches of Outer Space: Metaphor as Myth and as Religion,* 123.

[17] James Joyce, *A Portrait of the Artist as a Young Man* (New York: Viking Press/Viking Compass Edition, 1970), 213.

[18] James Joyce, *A Portrait of the Artist as a Young Man*, 204.

[19] T. S. Eliot, *Four Quartets* (New York: Harcourt, Brace and World, Inc., 1971), line 100, 17.

[20] William Shakespeare, *Hamlet*, ed. Charlton Hinman (New York: W. W. Norton and Company, 1996), Act II, Scene 2.

[21] Paul Newham, *The Singing Cure* (Boston, Massachusetts: Shambhala, 1994), 13.

[22] Mahatma K. Gandhi quoted in Eknath Easwaran, *Passage Meditation: Bringing the Deep Wisdom into Daily Life* (Tomales, California: The Blue Mountain Center of Meditation/Nilgiri Press, 2008), 70.

[23] Vilayat Inayat Khan, *The Music of Life* (New Lebanon, New York: Omega Publications, 1998), quoted in Don G. Campbell, *The Roar of Silence: Healing Powers of Breath, Tone & Music* (Wheaton, Illinois: The Theosophical Publishing House, 2014), 75.

[24] Michio Kaku, "Reading the Mind of God," *International Subtle Energies & Energy Medicine Journal*, vol. 17, no. 1 (2006), 49.

[25] Brian Eno, "Singing: The Key To A Long Life," *NPR Weekend Edition*, Nov. 23, 2008.

[26] Carl Jung, quoted in D. T. Suzuki's, *Introduction to Zen Buddhism* (New York: Grove Press, 1964), xxviii.

[27] Henry David Thoreau, *Walden* (New York: A Signet Classic/New American Library, 1960), 65.

[28] Johann Wolfgang von Goethe, 'Gedichte' in *Goethes Werke* (1948, 1952), Vol. 1, 367, quoted in Max Jammer, *Einstein and Religion* (2002), 79.

Chapter 3: In Good Company

[1] Henry David Thoreau, *Walden* (New York: A Signet Classic/New American Library, 1960), 66.

[2] Huston Smith, "Hinduism and Buddhism," *Bill Moyers: Wisdom of Faith*, video transcription, Part 1 (1996).

[3] Albert Einstein interviewed by George Sylvester Viereck, "What Life Means to Einstein," *Saturday Evening Post*, October 26, 1929, 113.

[4] Albert Einstein, "What Life Means to Einstein," 117.

[5] Albert Einstein, "On Science and Religion," *Nature* (1940), 146: 605-607.

[6] Philip Franck, *Einstein, His Life and Times* (New York: Alfred A. Knopf (1947), 284.

[7] Albert Einstein, *Living Philosophies* (New York: Simon and Schuster, 1931), 7.

[8] Albert Einstein, September 1937 statement, quoted in Helen Dukas and Banesh Hoffmann, eds., *Albert Einstein, the Human Side: New Glimpses from His Archives* (New Jersey: Princeton University Press, 1981), 70.

[9] Ken Wilbur, *The Eye of the Spirit: An Integral Vision for a World Gone Slightly Mad* (Boston, Massachusetts: Shambhala Publications, 2001), 6.

[10] Carl G. Jung, "Psychotherapists or the Clergy," *The Collected Works of C. G. Jung*, vol. 11 (New Jersey: Princeton University Press, 1975), 330-331.

Chapter 4: The Way of Science

[1] Albert Einstein, *Out of My Later Years* (Totowa, New Jersey: Littlefield, Adams and Company, 1967), 16. (First published in 1937 in an essay entitled "Moral Decay").

[2] Proverbs 8:30 (King James Version of the Bible).

[3] Georg Feuerstein, Subhash Kak and David Frawley, *In Search of the Cradle of Civilization* (Wheaton, Illinois: Quest Books, 2001), 63.

[4] Albert Einstein, *The World as I See It* (New York: Philosophical Library, 1949), 24-28.

[5] Albert Einstein, *The World As I See It*, 21-22.

[6] Peter Russell, *From Science to God: A Physicist's Journey into the Mystery of Consciousness* (Novato, California: New World Library, 2004), 3-4.

[7] Eliane Strosberg, *Art and Science* (New York: Abbeville Press, 2001).

[8] Leonard Shlain, *Art & Physics: Parallel Visions in Space, Time, and Light* (New York: William Morrow/HarperCollins, 1993).

[9] Lynn Gramwell and Neil deGrasse Tyson, *Exploring the Invisible: Art, Science, and the Spiritual* (New Jersey: Princeton University Press, 2005).

[10] Arthur I. Miller, *Einstein, Picasso: Space, Time, and the Beauty That Causes Havoc* (New York: Basic Books, 2002).

[11] Theodore L. Brown, *Making Truth: Metaphor In Science* (Champagne, Illinois: University of Illinois Press, 2008*)*.

[12] Alan Lightman, "The Future of Science ... Is Art," *SEED Magazine*, Jan. 16, 2008, 5.

[13] Niels Bohr, quoted in Werner Heisenberg, *Physics and Beyond: Encounters and Conversations*, trans. Arnold J. Pomerans (New York: Harper Torchbooks/Harper and Row, 1971), 41. The words are not verbatim, but as recalled by Werner Heisenberg in describing his interaction with Bohr in 1920.

[14] Ernst Friedrich Schumacher, *A Guide for the Perplexed* (New York: Harper Colophon Books, 1977), 55.

[15] Ken Wilber, *The Eye of the Spirit* (Boston, Massachusetts: Shambhala, 1997), 2.

[16] Arthur S. Eddington, "Swarthmore Lecture of 1929," *Science and the Unseen World* (New York: Macmillan, 1937), 73.

[17] Eugene Wigner, *Symmetries and Reflections – Scientific Essays* (Bloomington, Indiana: Indiana University Press, 1967), 172.

[18] As demonstrated by a thought experiment called "Wigner's friend," which is Wigner's extension of the Schrödinger's cat thought experiment. Wigner's original remarks about this thought experiment first appeared in his article "Remarks on the Mind-Body Question," quoted in I. J. Good, ed., *The*

Scientist Speculates (London, United Kingdom: Heinemann, 1961) and then reprinted by E. Wigner, *Symmetries and Reflections – Scientific Essays.*

[19] Niels Bohr, quoted in Werner Heisenberg, *Physics and Beyond: Encounters and Conversations*, trans. Arnold J. Pomerans (New York: Harper Torchbooks/Harper and Row, 1971), 114.

[20] Werner Heisenberg, *Physics and Philosophy* (New York: Harper Torchbooks, 1971), 114.

[21] Ken Wilber, *Quantum Questions* (Boston, Massachusetts: Shambhala Books, 1985), 5-6.

[22] Ken Wilber, *Quantum Questions*, 4.

[23] Max Planck, Das Wesen der Materie, "The Nature of Matter," speech in Florence, Italy, 1944, from Archiv zur Geschichte der Max-Planck-Gesellschaft, Abt. Va, Rep. 11 Planck, Nr. 1797.

[24] Arthur S. Eddington, *Science and the Unseen World* (New York: Macmillan, 1937), 73.

[25] Roger Penrose, *The Emperor's New Mind* (Oxford, United Kingdom: Oxford University Press, 1989), 580.

[26] Max Plank, "The Paradox of the Quantum Space and Time, No Moral Progress of Mankind, Beliefs and Phantasies," *The Observer* (January 25, 1931).

Chapter 5: Science versus Religion?

[1] Maurice A. Finocchiaro, *The Galileo Affair: A Documentary History* (Oakland, California: University of California Press, 1989).

[2] An excellent on-line paper by Edoardo Aldo Cerrato, C.O., trans. Fr. Timothy E. Deeter, sums up the current state of understanding: "It is commonly held that Cesare Baronio is the person from whom Galileo directly heard the words just quoted, and he wanted people to know this. If this cannot be proven through documentary evidence, the attribution is nevertheless unanimously accepted and is in complete agreement with the thought of this well-known member of the Oratory." The paper has a good discussion about the many different positions held within the Roman Catholic Church regarding Galileo's ideas. http://www.oratoriosanfilippo.org/galileo-baronio-english.pdf (accessed July 25, 2014).

[3] I am indebted here to Professor Stephen L. Goldman's lectures available at The Great Courses entitled *Science Wars: What Scientists Know and How They Know It*. His lectures confirmed and enriched my understanding of the distinction between the permission given to Galileo to present his ideas as a theory "that worked" versus something that was "the Truth." I highly recommend his lectures with regard to the history of modern science.

[4] Professor Goldman's lectures, quoted above, were also very valuable with the issue concerning Tycho Brahe.

[5] Thomas S. Kuhn, *The Copernican Revolution* (Cambridge, Massachusetts: Harvard University Press, 1957), 191.

[6] Galileo Galilei, *Dialogue Concerning the Two Chief World Systems, Ptolemaic and Copernican,* trans. Stillman Drake, foreword Albert Einstein (Berkeley, California: University of California Press, 1962).

[7] Sir James Frazer, *The Golden Bough* (New York: Touchstone Books, 1996), 825-826.

[8] All the quotes in this paragraph are by Herbert Dingle, *The Scientific Adventure: Essays in the History and Philosophy of Science* (New York: Philosophical Library, 1953), 38-39.

[9] Albert Einstein, *Cosmic Religion: With Other Opinions and Aphorisms* (New York: Covici-Friede, Inc., 1931), 97.

[10] Willis Harman and Howard Rheingold, *Higher Creativity: Liberating the Unconscious for Breakthrough Insights* (New York: Tarcher Penguin Books, 1984), 40.

[11] Arthur Koestler, *The Act of Creation* (London, United Kingdom: Penguin Arkana Publishing, 1990).

[12] Charles Darwin, *The Autobiography of Charles Darwin: From the Life and Letters of Charles Darwin* (Auckland, New Zealand: The Floating Press, 2009), 78.

[13] Arthur J. Deikman, M.D., *The Observing Self: Mysticism and Psychotherapy* (Boston, Massachusetts: Beacon Press, 1983), 18.

[14] Isaac Newton, as quoted in Gale E. Christianson's *Isaac Newton* (Oxford University Press, 2005), 21.

[15] William James, *The Will to Believe and Other Essays in Popular Philosophy* (New York: Longmans, Green and Company, 1912), 16.

Chapter 6: The Battle as Propaganda

[1] John Hedley Brooke, *Science and Religion: Some Historical Perspectives* (Cambridge, United Kingdom: Cambridge University Press, 1991), 1-51.

[2] Alfred North Whitehead, *Science and the Modern World, Lowell Lectures 1925* (New York: The Free Press/Simon & Schuster, 1967), 12.

[3] David Barrett, George Kurian and Todd Johnson, eds., *World Christian Encyclopedia: A Comparative Survey of Churches and Religions in the Modern World* (Oxford, United Kingdom: Oxford University Press, 2001).

[4] Ralph Waldo Emerson, *The Collected Works of Ralph Waldo Emerson,* "Essay II: Self Reliance" (New York: Greystone Press, 1941), 40.

[5] John Maynard Keynes, quoted in Paul Samuelson, "The Keynes Centenary," *The Economist* vol. 287 (1983), 19.

[6] John William Draper, *A History of the Conflict Between Science and Religion* (Charleston, South Carolina: Nabu Press, 2010).

[7] Andrew Dickson White, *History of the Warfare of Science with Theology in Christendom* (Amherst, New York: Prometheus Books, 1993).

[8] Lawrence Principe, Professor of the History of Science and Technology and Professor of Chemistry at Johns Hopkins University, made these comments in lectures available at the Teaching Company entitled *Science and Religion*. I highly recommend them.

[9] David Tacey, *The Spirituality Revolution* (New York: Brunner-Routledge, 2004).

[10] William James, *The Varieties of Religious Experience* (New York: Penguin Books, 1985), 120.

[11] Will Durant, *The Story of Philosophy* (New York: Washington Square Press/Simon and Schuster, 1953), 271.

[12] Isaac Asimov and Jason A. Shulman, *Isaac Asimov's Book of Science and Nature Questions* (New York: Weidenfeld & Nicolson, 1988), 281.

[13] Alfred North Whitehead, quoted in Peter Russell, *From Science to God: A Physicist's Journey into the Mystery of Consciousness* (Novato, California: New World Library, 2010), Intro, x.

[14] Stephen M. Barr, *Modern Physics and Ancient Faith* (Notre Dame, Indiana: University of Notre Dame Press, 2006), 6-7.

Chapter 7: A Brief History of Materialism

[1] Francis Bacon, *Of Atheism* (Whitefish, Montana: Kessinger Publishing, LLC, 2006).

[2] Stephen M. Barr, *Modern Physics and Ancient Faith* (Notre Dame, Indiana: University of Notre Dame, 2003), Chapter 2.

[3] Francois-Marie Arouet (better known as Voltaire), *A Philosophical Dictionary* (London, United Kingdom: W. Dugdale, 1843), ver. 2, sec. 1, 473.

[4] Steven Weinberg, *The First Three Minutes: A Modern View of the Origin of the Universe* (New York: Basic Books, 1977), 154.

[5] Francis Crick, *Astonishing Hypothesis: The Scientific Search for the Soul* (New York: Touchstone Books, 1994), 3.

Chapter 8: Science and Consciousness

[1] Albert Szent-Gyorgyi, quoted in Robert A. Wallace, *Biology: The World of Life* (New York: Harper Collins Publishers, 1990), 45.

[2] Roger W. Sperry, "Changing Priorities," *Annual Review of Neuroscience*, March 1981, vol. 4, 7.

[3] Sir John C. Eccles, *Evolution of the Brain, Creation of the Self* (London, United Kingdom: Routledge Publishing, 1989), 241.

[4] Sir John C. Eccles and Daniel N. Robinson, *The Wonder of Being Human: Our Brain and Our Mind* (New York: Free Press/Collier Macmillan, 1984), 36.

[5] David Chalmers, *The Character of Consciousness* (Oxford, United Kingdom: Oxford University Press, 2010), 6.

[6] "Toward a Science of Consciousness," The Center for Consciousness Studies, University of Arizona. Archives of the conferences: www.consciousness. arizona.edu (accessed June 4, 2014).

[7] Erwin Schrodinger, *My View of the World* (London, United Kingdom: Cambridge University Press, 1964), 31.

[8] George Wald, "Life and Mind in the Universe," *International Journal of Quantum Chemistry; Quantum Biology Symposium* (1984), 1-2.

[9] Christof Koch and R. Clay Reid, "Neuroscience: Observatories of the Mind," *Nature*, 483, March 22, 2012, 397–398.

[10] Arthur Schopenhauer, *The World as Will and Representation*, trans. E. F. J. Payne, vol. 2 (Indian Hills, Colorado: Falcon's Wing Press, 1958), 13.

[11] Gary Marcus, "The Trouble With Brain Science," *New York Times*, July 11, 2014.

[12] Gary Marcus, "The Trouble With Brain Science."

[13] E. F. Schumacher, *A Guide for the Perplexed* (New York: Harper Colophon Books, 1978), 56.

[14] E. F. Schumacher, *A Guide for the Perplexed*, 56-58.

[15] Carl Gustav Jung, *Modern Man in Search of a Soul* (Abington, United Kingdom: Routledge Books, 2001), 234.

[16] Sir James Jeans, *The Mysterious Universe* (Cambridge, United Kingdom: Cambridge University Press, 2009), 139.

[17] Max Planck, *Where is Science Going?*, trans. James Murphy (Oxford, United Kingdom: Ox Bow Press, 1981), epilogue, 217.

[18] Dawna Markova, *The Open Mind: Exploring the Six Patterns of Natural Intelligence* (Newburyport, Massachusetts: Conari Press, 1996), 82.

[19] Alfred North Whitehead, *Science and the Modern World, Lowell Lectures 1925* (New York: Macmillan, 1925), 64-74.

Chapter 9: Science and Spirit in Harmony

[1] Alfred North Whitehead, quoted in Peter Russell, *From Science to God: A Physicist's Journey into the Mystery of Consciousness* (Novato, California: New World Library, 2010), intro, x.

[2] J.H. Tiner, a mathematician at Duke University, discovered these words among the many unexamined papers of Newton. John Hudson Timer, *Isaac Newton: Inventor, Scientist and Teacher* (Fenton, Michigan: Mott Media, 1975), 107.

[3] Issac Newton, *The Principia: The Mathematical Principles of Natural Philosophy* (New York: Snowball Publishing, 2010), 501.

[4] J.E. Force and R.H. Popkin, eds., *Newton and Religion: Context, Nature, and Influence*, International Archives of the History of Ideas (New York: Springer Publishers, 1999). A good source for considering Newton's spiritual thought.

[5] John Chambers, *The Secret Life of Genius* (Rochester, Vermont: Destiny Books, 2009).

[6] John Fauvel, Raymond Flood, Michael Shortland and Robin Wilson, eds., *Let Newton Be!* (New York: Oxford University Press, 1989).

[7] Richard Tarnas, *The Passion of the Western Mind: Understanding the Ideas That Have Shaped Our World View* (New York: Ballentine Books, 1993), 299-300.

[8] Karen Armstrong, *The Battle for God* (New York: Ballentine Books, 2001), 61-61.

[9] Albert Einstein, *Living Philosophies*, ed. Henry Leach (New York: Simon and Schuster, 1931), 6.

[10] Albert Einstein, quoted in Peter Barker and Cecil G. Shugart, *After Einstein: Proceedings of the Einstein Centennial Celebration, March 14-16, 1979* (Memphis, Tennessee: Memphis State University Press, March 1981), 179.

[11] Albert Einstein, statement in September 1937, quoted in *Albert Einstein: The Human Side*, eds. Helen Dukas and Banesh Hoffman (Princeton, New Jersey: Princeton University Press, 1981), 70.

[12] J. Robert Oppenheimer, *Science and the Common Understanding* (Charleston, South Carolina: Nabu Press, 2011), 8-9.

[13] Dean Radin, *The Conscious Universe: The Scientific Truth of Psychic Phenomena* (New York: HarperEdge, 1997), 19.

[14] Tom Huston, "The Genesis Device," *Enlighten Next Magazine*, March-May 2009, 79-80.

[15] Brian Swimme, *The Universe Story: From the Primordial Flowing Forth to the Exozoic Era – A Celebration of the Unfolding of the Cosmos* (New York: HarperOne, 1994).

[16] *Newsweek* Staff, "For Quark Hunters, A Minute Surprise," *Newsweek Magazine*, Feb. 18, 1996.

[17] John Gribbin, *In Search of Schrodinger's Cat: Quantum Physics and Reality* (New York: Bantam Books, 1984), 211.

[18] Philipp Frank, *Einstein: His Life and Times* (Boston, Massachusetts: Da Capo Press, 2002), 272.

[19] Bernard d'Espagnat, interview by Reuters upon receiving the Templeton Prize from The John Templeton Foundation, March 16, 2009.

[20] K. B. Chandra Raj, *Your Sense of Humor: Don't Leave Home Without It* (Bloomington, Indiana: Trafford Publishing, 2012), 261.

[21] Ludwig Wittgenstein, *Tractatus Logico-Philosophicus* (London, United Kingdom: Routledge & Kegan Paul, 1951), 187.

[22] Winston Churchill, *My Early Life 1874-1904* (New York: Touchstone/Simon and Schuster, 1996), 119.

[23] Albert Einstein, *Ideas And Opinions* (New York: Broadway Books/Random Press, 1995), 46.

[24] Charles Darwin in a letter to John Fordyce on May 7, 1879. Darwin Correspondence Project, https://www.darwinproject.ac.uk/letter/entry-12041 (accessed June 18, 2014).

[25] David Loye, *Darwin on Love* (Boston, Massachusetts: Benjamin Franklin Press, 2007).

[26] David Hume, *The Natural History Of Religion*, ed. H.E. Root (Redwood City, California: Stanford University Press, 1957), 9.

[27] Evelyn Underhill, *Mysticism* (Oxford, London: Oneworld Publications, 1911), 370.

[28] Bertrand Russell, *The Autobiography of Bertrand Russell, 1872-1914* (New York: Little, Brown and Company, 1967), 3.

[29] Bertrand Russell, *The Autobiography of Bertrand Russell, 1872-1914*, 3.

[30] Werner Heisenberg, as quoted in Ulrich Hildebrand, "Das Universum - Hinweis auf Gott?" in *Ethos* (die Zeitschrift für die ganze Familie) (1988), no. 10, Oktober, Berneck, Schweiz: Schwengeler Verlag AG.

[31] Werner Heisenberg, *Across the Frontiers* (Woodbridge, Connecticut: Ox Bow Press, 1990), 213.

Chapter 10: On the Wings of Assumptions

[1] Max Plank, *Scientific Autobiography and Other Papers,* trans. Frank Gaynor (New York: Philosophical Library, 1949), 33-34.

[2] Alexander Leaf and John Launois, *Youth in Old Age* (New York: McGraw Hill Book Company, 1975).

[3] Dr. John P. A. Ioannidis, "Why Most Published Research Findings are False," August 30, 2005, Public Library of Science Medicine, www.plosmedicine.org (accessed September 3, 2014).

[4] Marilyn Schlitz, "Why We Can Be Dogmatically Against Things We Know Nothing About," *Spirituality And Health Magazine*, March-April 2014, 40.

[5] William James, *The Will to Believe and Other Essays In Popular Philosophy,* (New York: Longmans, Green and Company, 1912), 54.

[6] William Shakespeare, *Hamlet*, ed. Charlton Hinman (New York: W. W. Norton and Company, 1996), Act I, Scene 5.

[7] William Shakespeare, *Julius Caesar* (Mineola, New York: Dover Publications, 1991), Act II, Scene 2.

[8] This quote is widely attributed to the Talmud, but I have never seen a specific reference. It seems to have first been attributed to the Talmud in a 1961 Anaïs Nin novel, *The Seduction of the Minotaur*, which reads, "Lillian was reminded of the talmudic words: 'We do not see things as they are, we see them as we are.'" I do not know if the idea originated in or was inspired by the Talmud, but the belief is widespread, so I follow that assumption here.

[9] William James, "1896 Presidential Address to the Society for Psychical Research," *Essays in Psychical Research* (Cambridge, Massachusetts: Harvard University Press, 1986), 132.

[10] Mary Midgley, *Can't We Make Moral Judgements?* (New York: St Martins Press/Macmillian, 1991), 162-163.

[11] E. A. Burtt, *The Metaphysical Foundations of Modern Science* (Mineola, New York: Dover Publications, 2003), 228-229.

[12] Henry Louis Mencken, *A Mencken Chrestomathy*, "The Divine Afflatus" (New York: Alfred A. Knopf, 1949), Chapter 25, 443.

[13] Stephen Rozental, ed. *Niels Bohr, His Life and Work as Seen by His Friends and Colleagues* (Amsterdam: North–Holland Publishing Company, 1967), "My Father," 328.

[14] These ideas are also discussed in my book *On Being Human*, at the end of Chapter 8.

Chapter 11: Is Your Faith Conscious or Unconscious?

[1] Francois Marie Arouet de Voltaire, *The Works of Voltaire: A Philosophical Dictionary*, vol. IV (New York: St. Hubert Guild and E. R. Dumont, 1901), 326.

[2] Max Planck, *Where Is Science Going?* (New York: W. W. Norton and Company, 1932), 214.

[3] Alfred North Whitehead, *Science and the Modern World*, Lowell Lectures 1925 (New York: The Free Press/Simon and Schuster, 1967), 13.

[4] Albert Einstein, "Religion and Science," *New York Times Magazine* (Nov. 9, 1930), 1-4.

[5] Albert Einstein, as quoted by Walter Isaacson in *Einstein: His Life and Universe* (New York: Simon and Schuster, 2007), 388.

[6] Sir Leslie Stephen, *An Agnostic's Analogy and Other Essays* (London, United Kingdom: Smith, Elder and Company, 1893).

[7] Rupert Sheldrake, "The Skepticism of Believers," *What Is Enlightenment Magazine*, May-July 2008, Issue 40, 36-37.

[8] Coleman Barks, trans. A. J. Arberry and Nevit Ergin, *Rumi: Bridge to the Soul: Journeys Into the Music and Silence of the Heart* (New York: HarperOne, 2007), "A Bowl Fallen From the Roof," 27.

Chapter 12: No Escape—From an Act of Faith

[1] Michel Foucault, *The Order of Things: An Archeology of the Human Sciences* (New York: Vintage Publishing, 1994).

[2] Peter Kingsley, *Reality* (Point Reyes, California: The Golden Sufi Center, 2004).

[3] William James, *The Will to Believe and Other Essays in Popular Philosophy*, "Is Life Worth Living?" (New York: Longmans, Green and Company, 1912), 62.

[4] Heinrich Robert Zimmer, *Myths and Symbols in Indian Art and Civilization*, ed. Joseph Campbell (Princeton, New Jersey: Princeton University Press; 1972), Book 6.

[5] E. F. Schumacher, *A Guide for the Perplexed* (New York: Harper Colophon, 1978), 15-25.

[6] E. F. Schumacher, *A Guide for the Perplexed*, 56.

[7] Letter to Frederick William, Prince of Prussia, Nov 28, 1770, quoted in S. G. Tallentyre, ed, *Voltaire in His Letters* (New York: G.P. Putnam's Sons, 1919), 232.

[8] Charles Williams, *He Came Down From Heaven and the Forgiveness of Sins* (London, United Kingdom: Faber & Faber, 1950), 25.

[9] Anonymous, *Meditations in Wall Street* (New York: William Morrow and Company, 1940), 66.

Chapter 13: Faith and the Wisdom Traditions

[1] Edward Conze, *Buddhism: Its Essence and Development* (Mineola, New York: Courier Dover Publications, 2003), 40.

[2] Letter written by Mother Teresa to Archbishop Perier, March 18, 1953 as quoted in *Mother Teresa: Come Be My Light: The Private Writings of the Saint of Calcutta*, ed. Brian Kolodiejchuk (New York: Doubleday Religious Publishing, 2007), 149.

[3] William James, *The Varieties of Religious Experience: A Study in Human Nature* (New York: Penguin Books Edition, 1982), 16.

[4] Walpola Rahula, *What the Buddha Taught* (New York: Grove Press, 1974), 137-138.

[5] Paul Carus, *The Gospel of Buddha* (Seattle, Washington: Pacific Publishing Studio, 2011), 120. First published in 1894, this was the first widely read book on Buddhism in the western world.

[6] An interesting discussion of how this phrase came to be so widely attributed to the Buddha: http://www.fakebuddhaquotes.com/work-out-your-own-salvation-do-not-depend-on-others/ (accessed September 3, 2014).

[7] Bhiikhu Bodhi, ed., *Majjhima Nikaya: The Middle Sayings* (Barre, Massachusetts: Wisdom Publications and Barre Center for Buddhist Studies, 1994), Kitagiri Sutta, Sutta 70.

[8] Ken Wilbur, *A Brief History of Everything* (Boston and London: Shambhala, 1996), 42-43.

[9] Ken Wilber, *Sex, Ecology, Spirituality*, 265.

[10] Ken Wilber, *Sex, Ecology, Spirituality* (Boston, Massachusetts: Shambhala, 1995), 265.

Chapter 14: The Golden Mean

[1] Frances Scott Fitzgerald, *The Crack Up* (New York: New Directions, 1993), 69.

[2] Stephen Rozental, ed., *Niels Bohr, His Life and Work as Seen by His Friends and Colleagues* (Amsterdam: North-Holland Publishing Company, 1967), "My Father," 328.

[3] Plato, trans. Benjamin Jowett, *The Republic and Other Works* (New York: Anchor Books/Random House, Inc., 1973), 314.

[4] Heraclitus, *Fragments of Heraclitus*, fragment 34(8), trans. M. R. Wright. http://www.philosophy.gr/presocratics/heraclitus.htm (accessed August 2, 2014).

[5] Heraclitus, *Fragment of Heraclitus*, fragment 49(51).

[6] Matthew 5:29 (New International Version of the Bible).

[7] Matthew 5:44 (King James Version of the Bible).

[8] Mark 12:17 (American Standard Version of the Bible).

[9] John 8:7 (King James version of the Bible).

[10] John 8:11 (King James version of the Bible).

[11] W. B. Yeats, *The Collected Poems of W. B. Yeats* (New York: Scribner, 1996), 187.

Chapter 15: Summing Up

[1] Vaclav Havel, Untitled lecture at The Salzburg Festival, Salzburg, Austria, July 26, 1990. http://www.vaclavhavel.cz/showtrans.php?cat=projevy&val=302_aj_projevy.html&typ=HTML (accessed August 21, 2014).

[2] William James, *The Varieties of Religious Experience: A Study in Human Nature*, Lecture III, "The Reality of the Unseen" (New York: Penguin Books, 1985), 53.

[3] H. Thomas Johnson and Anders Broms, *Profit Beyond Measure: Extraordinary Results through Attention to Work and People* (New York: The Free Press, 2000), 199.

[4] Josh Billings, pen name for Henry William Shaw, *Josh Billings' Allminox with Comic Illustrations* (New York: G. W. Dillingham Company, 1902), sec. Faith.

[5] Larry Dossey, *The Power of Premonitions: How Knowing the Future Can Shape Our Lives* (New York: Dutton/Penguin Books, 2009).

[6] Douglas Dean and John Mihalasky, *Executive EPS: The Proven Links Between "Hunches" and Success—And How Businessmen Employ ESP On A Practical Basis* (Upper Saddle River, New Jersey: Prentice Hall Publishers, 1974).

[7] Lawrence Principe, Professor of the History of Science and Technology and Professor of Chemistry at Johns Hopkins University, makes this point in his series "Science and Religion," available at the Teaching Company. I highly recommend the whole series.

[8] Roger Lipsey, *An Art of Our Own: The Spiritual in Twentieth Century Art* (Boston, Massachusetts: Shambhala Publications, 1997).

[9] Julia Cameron, *Finding Water: The Art of Perseverance* (New York: Tarcher Press, 2009), 106.

[10] Yogi Ramacharaka, *Bhagavad-Gita or The Message Of The Master* (Chicago, Illinois: The Yogi Publication Society, Masonic Temple, 1907), XVII, The Threefold Faith.

[11] Viktor Frankl, *Man's Search For Ultimate Meaning* (New York: Basic Books, 2000), 138.

[12] Edmund Burke, "A Letter From Mr. Burke To A Member Of The National Assembly," *In Answer To Some Objections To His Book On French Affairs* (London, United Kingdom: James Dodsley Booksellers, 1791), 69.

[13] D.H. Lawrence, *Studies in Classic American Literature*, vol. 2 (Cambridge, United Kingdom: Cambridge University Press, 2003), 18.

[14] Abraham Maslow, *Toward a Psychology of Being* (New York: Van Nostrand Reinhold Publisher, 1968), iv.

[15] Albert P. Ryder, "A Poet's Painter," *The Literary Digest*, vol. 54 (April 21, 1917), 1164.

[16] Dag Hammarskjöld, *Markings,* trans. Leif Sjoberg and W.H. Auden (New York: Alfred A. Knopf, 1964), 169.

INDEX

academic committees, 116–17

active faith. *See* conscious faith

Age of Reason, 129–30

alchemy, 178–79

analogies, in art and science, 29–33, 71–73

analysis, of art, 30

Aquinas, Thomas, 27, 124

Arabic numerals, 65

arguments, and changing beliefs, 233–34

Aristotle

    and Golden Mean, 285

    and moral relativism, 248

    and scientific development, 62

Armstrong, Karen, 180, 182–83

art

    analysis of, 30

    in caves, 48–49

    "drifting" and inspiration in, 16–19

    faith in, 307–8

    inspiration and breakthroughs in, 12–16, 98–99

    interaction with science, religion, and spirituality, 41

    meaning in, 49–51

    message in, 21–26

    metaphors and analogies in, 29–33

    motivation for creating, 9–11

    music, 37–40

    power of, 5–6

    and sacred, 7–9, 306–7

    science and, 69–73

    taking advantage of, 34–37

    types of, 26–29

Asimov, Isaac, 121

assumptions

    and acts of faith, 222, 253

    as basis of human life, 200–201

    changes in, 207–9

    correctness of past, 209–12

    and decision-making, 215–18

    and mysteries in science, 188

    problem of, 212–15

    in science, 202–5

    and success in science, 205–7

    in travel, 199–200

Athens, 287–88

Augustine, St., 190–91

Australia, battle between science and religion in, 113

authenticity, 46

Bacon, Francis, 132
balance, and Golden Mean, 287–89
Bali, creative culture of, 36–37
Baronio, Cesare, 88
Batchelor, Stephen, 264
beauty
    and creative culture of Bali,
    36–37
    and meaning in art, 22–24
    in proper art, 28
Beethoven, Ludwig van, 12, 14–15
belief. See also faith
    faith versus, 222–23
    formulating and changing, 300
    James on, 251
    and universal law and ideas,
    251–53
belief systems. See also religion;
spirituality; wisdom traditions
    conversion between, 231–34,
    245
    dialogue between, 232–33
    number of, 230–31
    skepticism of our own, 238
Bellarmino, Roberto, 88
Bhagavad-Gita, 310
Billings, Josh, 299
Blake, William, 7, 13, 25
Bodin, Jean, 90–91
Bohm, David, 72, 173–74
Bohr, Niels
    on art and science, 73
    on consciousness, 78

Einstein and, 106
    inspiration of, 97
    on mysteries in science, 189
    on profound truths, 216, 283
Brahe, Tycho, 89
Brahms, Johannes, 14, 15
brain
    consciousness and, 154–56,
    158, 159–60
    versus mind, 148–50, 305
    study of, 162–63
Brown, Theodore L., 71
Brunton, Paul, 24
Buddha, 66–67, 254, 262–63,
265–67, 271–73, 285
Buddhism, 67, 112, 261–67
Burke, Edmund, 311–12
Burtt, E. A., 214

calling
    determining validity of, 263
    in science and spirituality, 196
Cameron, Julia, 307–8
Campbell, Joseph
    hero's quest described by, 56
    on justification of art, 21, 28
    on meaning in art, 24–25
    on proper and improper art, 26
Carlyle, Thomas, 22
Carus, Paul, 271–72
categories, thinking in, 1–3
causation, versus correlation,
155–56

caves, art in, 48–49
Celts, 248–49
censorship, 29
certainty
  and Golden Mean, 292–93
  living and acting in absence
  of, 312–15
  possibility of, 283
  waiting for, 253
chakras, 66–67
Chalmers, David, 156
change
  capacity for positive, 169
  getting feel for, 298
  in scientific assumptions, 204–
  5, 207–11
chanting, group, 37–38
China
  battle between science and
  religion in, 112–13
  and beginnings of science, 66
  Golden Mean in, 285
  recovers from disharmony, 288
  scientific paradigms of, 206
choice
  fear of making wrong, 253–55
  and free will, 244–46
Christianity
  and beginnings of science,
  64, 65–66, 68
  and conflict between science
  and religion, 303–4
  middle way in, 285–86
  suffering in, 275

Churchill, Winston, 192
climate change, 119
Coleridge, Samuel Taylor, 15
concerts, 39
conditioned reflex, versus memory,
161
conflict, and conscious faith,
227–28
Confucius, 66
conscious faith, 223–30, 308, 309
consciousness. *See also* mind
  disagreements regarding,
  157–60
  materialism and, 78, 79–80,
  143–44
  memory and, 160–62
  modern developments
  regarding, 169–74
  and receiving creative inspiration, 14, 16–19
  theories regarding, 153–57
  understanding, 162–69
contradictions, and conscious
faith, 225
conversion, between belief systems, 231–34, 245
Conze, Edward, 266
Copernicus, 86, 87–88, 180
correlation, versus causation,
155–56
Cox, Christine, 16–17, 24
creativity
  art and science and inspiration of, 69–70

engaging in, 35–37
music and, 37–40
Crick, Francis, 144
culture. *See also* enculturation
and battle of religion versus
science, 117–21
consciousness and problems
in, 163–66
importance of, 58–59
purpose of, 101
"curved spacetime," 33, 96

Dalai Lama, 124, 196
dark energy, 184–85
dark matter, 184–85
Darwin, Charles
inspiration of, 97
and metaphors in science, 33
on science and religion, 193
Da Vinci, Leonardo, 41, 70
Dawkins, Richard, 51
Dean, Douglas, 301
debate, and search for meaning,
57–58
decision-making
assumptions and, 215–18
faith and, 242–43
free will in, 244
reason and, 260, 261
Deikman, Arthur, 97
Deism, 132
Dennett, Daniel, 51, 154, 155
Descartes, Rene, 176–77, 179
Descent of Man, The (Darwin), 193

desires, reason and, 260–61
difficulty, in wisdom traditions,
265–67, 275–76
Dingle, Herbert, 94
*Discourses and Mathematical
Demonstrations Relating to
Two New Sciences* (Galileo),
92
Dominant Established Religion
in Australia during colonial
period, 113
and battle of religion versus
science, 102–3, 107–10
defined, 85
freedom from, in science, 115
Galileo and, 86–93
Newton's disagreements with,
178, 179
Schumacher on, 167
science's relation to, 122
donkey, Nasrudin and, 219
doubt, 253, 309–12
Draper, John William, 106–7
"drifting," and receiving creative
inspiration, 14, 16–19
drugs, and mental well-being, 54
Dunbar, Kevin, 207
Durant, Will, 121

$E=mc^2$, 147
"Each Note" (Rumi), 160
Eccles, John C., 154–55
Eddington, Arthur, 77, 79
Edison, Thomas, 194

Einstein, Albert
art and science and, 50–51, 71
Bohr and, 106
and connection between science and spirituality, 180–81
"curved spacetime," 96
on finding meaning, 51–52
on intuition and inspiration, 96
on matter and existence, 189
on problem solving, 205
on religion, art, and science, 4, 63
on science and religion, 51, 68, 79, 193, 236, 306
on universal law, 253
Eliade, Mircea, 7
Eliot, T. S., 28
Emerson, Ralph Waldo, 2, 105
emotion, reason and, 260
enculturation
in Buddhism, 261–62
faith and, 219–23, 225, 226, 227–28, 242, 245, 300
engineering, following launch of Sputnik, 61–62
Enlightenment, 130–31, 133–34
enlightenment, instant, 269–70
Enneagram, 286–87
Eno, Brian, 39–40
Enquiry Concerning Human Understanding, An (Hume), 141
environmental protection, 119
d'Espagnat, Bernard, 190

Established Religion
defined, 85
Schumacher on, 167
science's relation to, 122–23
ether, and composition of universe, 184–85
Europe, battle between science and religion in, 110
evidence
faith and, 230–34
objective, 98–99
evolution, 118
existentialism, 46
extremes
appeal of, 289–91
and middle way, 285–86, 291–95

facts, and assumptions in science, 202–3, 207
faith. See also belief
active and passive acts of, 219–24
acts of, as unavoidable, 242–43, 300–301
becoming more conscious in, 225–30
belief versus, 222–23
in Buddhism, 261–67, 272
doubt and, 309–12
dual, 307–9
and free will, 244–46
and immediate happiness, 267–76

versus intuition, 277
mistakes in acts of, 253–55
proof and, 230–34
in relationships, 241–42
and relativism, 246–51
skepticism and, 234–39, 299,
   301
versus trust, 224
and universal law and ideas,
   251–53
and wisdom traditions, 257,
   273–76, 279
false findings, 207
"felt sense," 99
first incompleteness theorem, 202
Fitzgerald, F. Scott, 283
Force, J. E., 178
Foucault, Michel, 246–47
Frank, Philipp, 189
Frankl, Viktor, 267, 311
Frazer, James, 92
freedom, 165, 311–12
free will, 244–46
Freud, Sigmund, 22
Fugelsang, Jonathan, 207
fulfillment. *See also* meaning
   in materialistic desires, 294
   search for, 297–99, 311–12
fundamentalist worldview, 111

Galileo, 86–93, 94, 102, 180
Gandhi, Mahatma, 38
Gilgamesh, 48
goals

happiness and, 269
   striving toward, 271
God, belief in, 182–83
Gödel, Kurt, 202
Goethe, Johann Wolfgang von
   on beauty, 22
   creative inspiration of, 13
   on interaction of art, science,
   religion, and spirituality, 41
Golden Mean
   and appeal of extremes,
   289–91
   balance and, 287–89
   versus extremes, 291–95
   societies and wisdom traditions promoting, 284–87
gravity, 95–96, 188
"great chain of being," 252
Greenfeld, Liah, 53
Gribbin, John, 189
Gross, Neil, 182
group chanting, 37–38
guidance, 43

Hammarskjöld, Dag, 314
happiness
   immediate, 267–76
   search for, 11, 294
Harman, Willis, 12
Harris, Sam, 213
Haskin, Henry, 255
Haub, Carl, 221
Havel, Vaclav, 297
healing, 289

Hegel, Georg Wilhelm Friedrich, 145–46

Heisenberg, Werner, 78, 197, 198

Heraclitus, 284

Hinduism, 276

History of the Conflict Between Science and Religion, A (Draper), 106–7

History of the Warfare of Science with Theology in Christendom (White), 107

Hobbes, Thomas, 136–39

Homer, 284–85

Human Brain Project, 162

Hume, David, 141–42, 193–94, 236–37, 260–61

Huxley, Aldous, 143 n. g

Huxley, Thomas, 141

Ibn al-Haytham, 65

imagination, 30, 51

improper art, 26–29

Incas, 67–68

independence, 43–44

India

    battle between science and religion in, 113

    and beginnings of science, 66–67

    recovers from disharmony, 289

individuality, 166

insights. *See* inspiration

inspiration

    "drifting" and receiving creative, 16–19

    practical and spiritual, 175

    and scientific breakthroughs, 95–99, 180

    source of creative, 8–9, 12–16

    and taking advantage of art, 34–36

instant enlightenment, 269–70

interconnectedness, 173–74

intuition

    versus faith, 277

    meaning and, 314

    paying attention to, 301

    reason and, 260–61

Ioannidis, John, 207

Islam

    and beginnings of science, 64–66, 68

    suffering in, 275–76

James, William

    on belief, 251

    on change in scientific paradigm, 208

    on consciousness, 171–72, 173

    on fulfillment, 298

    on immediate happiness, 267

    on objective evidence, 98

    on relationship between spiritual and scientific, 121

    on science as arbiter of truth, 213

Jeans, James, 79, 169
Jesus, 266–67, 285–86
jnana yoga, 66
John Paul II, Pope, 196
Joyce, James, 24, 26–28
Judaism
    and beginnings of science, 63–66, 68
    middle way in, 286
Jung, Carl, 40, 54–55, 167–68, 286

Kabala, 286
Kaku, Michio, 38–39, 186
Kant, Immanuel, 30, 121, 237
Keats, John, 1–2, 13, 23
Kepler, Johannes, 86, 89, 90, 180
Keynes, John Maynard, 105
Khan, Hazrat Inayat, 38
Al-Khwarizmi, 65
Kierkegaard, Søren, 237–38
Kingsley, Pater, 248
Kipling, Rudyard, 14
Klee, Paul, 12–13
Kuhn, Thomas, 90, 98, 204

Lamott, Annie, 265
Laszlo, Ervin, 172–73
Latin America, 67–68
Lawrence, D. H., 312
Leaf, Alexander, 206
Lee, Robert E., 227
Leibniz, Gottfried Wilhelm von, 95

lifespan, 206
Lightman, Alan, 71
love
    Darwin on, 193
    understanding, 159–60
Loye, David, 193
Luther, Martin, 133

Mafia families, 228
manipulation, science for, 74–77, 166–67, 252
Maoism, 112
Maslow, Abraham, 313
materialism
    beginnings of, 128–31
    core assumption of, 143–44
    and freedom of thought, 132–35
    versus fundamentalist worldview, 111
    and problem of assumptions in science, 213
    promissory, 154–55
    Pure Materialism, 135–40
    as religion, 140–51
    versus science, 215
    and science versus philosophy, 75–77
    and spread of religious freedom, 131–32
material world, 78–79, 187
McLean, Don, 19

Meade, Michael, 187
meaning. *See also* fulfillment
    in art, science, religion, philosophy, and psychology, 49–56
    art and, 7, 36
    making up own, 313–14
    measuring, 145–47
    and modern understanding, 168
    others and finding, 56–60
    science and, 77–80, 303
    search for, 1–3, 11, 44–49, 294
medieval theology, 103–4, 235–36
memory, 160–62
Mencken, H. L., 216
mental illness, 52–54
metaphors, in art and science, 29–33, 71–73
metaphysics, 214–15
middle way. *See* Golden Mean
Midgley, Mary, 214
Midsummer Night's Dream, A (Shakespeare), 25
Mihalasky, John, 301
Milarepa, 276
Miller, Arthur I., 71
Miller, Henry, 298
mind. *See also* consciousness
    versus brain, 148–50, 305
    defining, 158–59
    organizing information in, 243
mistakes

    in acts of faith, 253–55
    admitting, 228–29
    learning from, 259–60, 297
moderation. *See* Golden Mean
moral relativism, 246–51, 253
Mother Teresa, 266, 275
Mozart, Wolfgang, 12
M-theory, 38–39, 185–86
Murdock, Maureen, 56
music, 37–40
    consciousness and, 173
    Einstein and, 50
    experience of, 147–48
    powerful experiences with, 127
mysteries, in science, 183–94

Nabokov, Vladimir, 189
Nasrudin, 219
naturalism, 135–36
Nature article, 160–62
negative act of faith, 274–75
negativity, 55–56
neuronal activity, and understanding consciousness, 148–50, 156, 159–60
Newham, Paul, 37
Newton, Isaac
    on analogies in science, 31
    and connection between science and spirituality, 177–80
    motivation of, 30
    and mysteries in science, 188

and scientific breakthroughs, 95–96, 97

Nietzsche, Friedrich, 25–26

"Ode on a Grecian Urn" (Keats), 2

Oppenheimer, Robert, 181

others, in finding meaning, 56–60

pain, in wisdom traditions, 265–67, 275–76

Paleolithic caves, art in, 48–49

paradigms. *See* assumptions

paranoia, 299

Pascal, Blaise, 2

passive faith, 220–24, 226–27

Pasteur, Louis, 204

Penfield, Wilder, 305

Penrose, Roger, 80

perspective, 283–84

philosophy

and battle of religion versus science, 108–9

meaning in, 51–52

science and, 63, 73–77

physicalism, 135–36

physics

connection between music and, 38–39

limits of, 77–79

Picasso, Pablo, 71

Planck, Max

on consciousness, 80

on faith, 235

on new scientific truth, 204–5

on science and religion, 79

on solving mystery of nature, 171

Plato

on beauty, 22–23

criticism of, 28–29

and moral relativism, 248

Pogo, 172

Poincare, Jules Henri, 97

Polanyi, Michael, 94

politics, and battle of religion versus science, 117–21

Popkin, R. H., 178

Popper, Karl, 72, 186

prayer in public schools, 119

present moment, fulfillment in, 270

primitive cultures, 211–12

prioritizing, 46

problem-solving, 175

profane, versus sacred, 8. *See also* improper art

promissory materialism, 154–55

proof, faith and, 230–34, 278

proper art, 26–29

Protestantism

Reformation and, 132–34

Roman Catholic Church and, 106–7, 108, 109

psychology, meaning in, 52–56

Puccini, Giacomo, 14

Pure Materialism, 135–40

Pythagoras, 127, 196–97

quantum mechanics, limits of, 77–78, 210

questions, revisiting core, 56

Radin, Dean, 181–82

reason
  and dealing with spiritual matters, 279–80
  decision-making and, 260, 261
  desires and, 260–61
  faith and, 236
  materialism and, 144–45

rebellion
  and appeal of extremes, 290
  and conscious faith, 225, 226, 229–30
  as part of developmental process, 43–44

reflex, conditioned, versus memory, 161

Reformation, 132–34

relationships
  faith in, 241–42
  skepticism in, 238

relativism, 246–51, 253

religion. *See also* belief systems; Dominant Established Religion; Established Religion; spirituality; wisdom traditions
  art and, 7–8, 306–7
  battle with science as propaganda, 106–10
  challengers of, 293–94
  complexity of science and, 110–15
  conflict between science and, 301–6
  cooperation between science and, 85–93
  cultural and political battles and, 117–21
  defined, 84
  diversity in science and, 104–6
  and foundation of modern science, 101–4
  interaction with art, science, and spirituality, 41
  Jung on, 167–68
  materialism and freedom of, 131–32
  materialism as, 140–51
  meaning in, 49–52
  and mysteries in science, 190–94
  Schumacher on science and, 167
  science and, 65–68, 78–79, 83–85, 176
  science as complement to, 123–25
  science's relation to, 123

Renaissance, 129

Rheingold, Howard, 12

right, being, 228–29, 290–92, 310

Rilke, Rainer Maria, 18

Roman Catholic Church

and battle of religion versus science, 102, 109, 304
and freedom of thought, 132–34
Galileo and, 86–93
Protestantism and, 106–7
Roman law, 249
Roman numerals, 65
Rumi, 160, 239, 310
Russell, Bertrand, 196–97
Russell, Peter, 68–69
Ryder, Albert P., 313

sacred
    and meaning in art, 21–22, 24
    and source of creative inspiration, 7–9, 12–16
sacrifice, in creating art, 9–11, 17–19
Sand, George, 12
Sartre, Jean-Paul, 46
Schopenhauer, Arthur, 162
Schrodinger, Erwin, 157
Schumacher, E. F., 74, 166–67, 252
science
    art and, 69–73
    assumptions and success in, 205–7
    assumptions in, 202–5
    authority and open-mindedness in, 93–95
    battle with religion as propaganda, 106–10
    beginning of, 63–64

complexity of religion and, 110–15
conflict between religion and, 301–6
cooperation between religion and, 85–93
correctness of past paradigms in, 209–12
cultural and political battles and, 117–21
and dealing with spiritual matters, 279–80
and disagreements regarding consciousness, 157–60
diversity in religion and, 104–6
effects of, 62–63
following launch of Sputnik, 61–62
foundation of modern, 101–4
inspiration and breakthroughs in, 95–99
and integrating answers to major questions, 115–17
interaction with art, religion, and spirituality, 41
Laszlo on consciousness and, 172–73
limits of, 77–81
versus materialism, 128–30, 215
materialism and, 134–35
meaning in, 49–52

metaphors and analogies in, 30, 31–32

mysteries in, 183–94

paradigm shifts in, 207–9

philosophy and, 73–77

and problem of assumptions, 212–15

and Pure Materialism, 137, 139–40

purpose of, 295

religion and, 83–85, 167

religion as complement to, 123–25

and search for wisdom, 170

and spiritualism in modern day, 180–83, 196

spirituality and, 175–79, 194–98

and spirituality in fulfilling life, 121–23

and theories on consciousness, 153–57

ubiquity of, 64–69

Whitehead on faith and, 235–36

science for manipulation, 74–77, 166–67, 252

science for wisdom, 75, 76, 77

"Scientific Materialism," 128, 139–40

scientific method, 94, 97

Scientific Revolution, 134

Shakespeare, William, A Midsummer Night's Dream, 25

Shankara, 172

Sheldrake, Rupert, 239

Shlain, Leonard, 70

Simmons, Solon, 182

singing, 37–40

skepticism, 234–39, 299, 301

Skinner, B. F., 129

"sleeping mind," 175

Smith, Huston, 50

Smolin, Lee, 185

social contract, 137–39

social problems, consciousness and, 163–66

Socrates, 2, 183, 248, 284

solar system

and battle of religion versus science, 86–93

Newton on, 177

space race, 61–62

specialization, 212

Sperry, Roger W., 154

Spinoza, Baruch, 132

Spiritual Dimension

defined, 84

science's relation to, 123

spirituality. See also belief systems; religion; wisdom traditions

art and, 306–7

conflict between materialism and, 128

interaction with art, science, and religion, 41

science and, 175–79, 196–98

and science in fulfilling life, 121–23

and science in modern day, 180–83, 196

and scientific breakthroughs, 95–98, 194–95

Sputnik, 61–62

"Starry Night" (Van Gogh), 18–19, 34–35

Stephen, Leslie, 238

Stradonitz, August Kekule von, 96

Strauss, Richard, 13

string theory, 38–39, 185–86

Strosberg, Eliane, 70

sublime, 24, 28

suffering, 54–55, 265–67, 275–76

superstrings, 38–39, 185–86

Susskind, Leonard, 186

Swimme, Brian, 187

Szent-Gyorgyi, Albert, 153

Tanzi, Rudolf, 160

Taosim, 66, 112

Tart, Charles, 191

Tchaikovsky, Peter Ilyich, 13

Teresa, Mother, 266, 275

Tesla, Nikola, 96–97

theories, 72

Thirty Years' War, 90, 136

Thoreau, Henry David, 40, 44

thought, materialism and freedom of, 132–35

Thurber, James, 2

Tiller, William, 305–6

Tomatis, Alfred, 37

"Toward a Science of Consciousness" conference, 157

travel, assumptions in, 199–200

"Trouble With Brain Science, The," 162–63

trust

versus faith, 224

in relationships, 241–42

Tweedie, Irina, 276

unconscious faith, 220–24, 226–27, 308

Underhill, Evelyn, 195

United States

battle between science and religion in, 110–12

Enlightenment thought and creation of, 130

recovers from disharmony, 288

universal law and ideas, 248–49, 251–53

universe, composition of, 184–87

Urban VIII, Pope, 86, 87, 88, 90, 91

value, assigning, to people and things, 46

values, making up own, 313–14

van Gogh, Vincent, 10–11, 17–19, 34–35, 308

Voltaire, 103, 133–34, 219, 253

Wagner, Richard, 13

Wald, George, 158

Weinberg, Stephen, 135–36
White, Andrew Dickson, 107
Whitehead, Alfred North
    on consciousness, 173
    on faith and science, 235–36
    on science and religion, 103, 121–22, 176
Wigner, Eugene, 78
Wilber, Ken
    on branches of psychology with broad views, 54
    on higher domains, 277–78, 280
    on inspiration and scientific breakthroughs, 97
    model for understanding world and ourselves, 150–51
    on quantum theory and modern thought, 210
    on science and spiritualism, 77, 280
Williams, Charles, 254
wisdom
    faith and, 254
    loss of, 167–68
    science for, 75, 76, 77
    search for, 1–2, 63–64, 66–69, 169–70
wisdom traditions. See also belief systems; religion; spirituality
    adopting and following, 259–61
    Buddhism, 261–67
    challengers of, 293–94

    faith and, 273–76
    and finding fulfillment, 270–73, 297–99
    and immediate happiness, 267–69
    influence of past on, 258
    and instant enlightenment, 269–70
    purpose of, 295, 304
    as sophisticated technologies, 277–81
Wittgenstein, Ludwig, 192
wrong, being, 229

Xanadu (Coleridge), 15

Yeats, W. B., 290
yin/yang, 285

Zimmer, Heinrich, 251